24TL

Si

Greenwich Readers

Education & Training for Life

Student Support:
Tutoring, Guidance & Dealing with Disruption

This Reader is one of a series designed to support teachers and trainers in the post-compulsory sector of education. It will be of value to those who are working in colleges of further and higher education, sixth form colleges, adult and community education institutes, training units, and institutions of specific vocational preparation in the health service, the police service and the armed forces. The topics have been selected to represent a wide view of currently important issues and, by providing appropriate material for critical reflection on professional practice, the book will meet the needs of experienced teachers and trainers as well as those in the earlier stages of their careers.

In addition to such general use, the volume is one component of an integrated Certificate in Education/Postgraduate Certificate in Education course offered by the School of Post-Compulsory Education and Training at the University of Greenwich. Further information on this and other programmes of study and related academic services may be obtained from:

School of PCET
University of Greenwich
Maritime Greenwich Campus
Old Royal Naval College
Park Row
London
SE10 9LS

telephone: 020 8331 9230
fax: 020 8331 9235
e-mail: pcet@gre.ac.uk
www.gre.ac.uk

The planned range of titles in this series is as follows:

- Adult Learners, Key Skills & the Post-16 Curriculum
- Equality, Participation & Inclusive Learning
- Flexible Learning & ICT
- Language, Communication & Learning

- Perspectives on Learning
- Planning Teaching & Assessing Learning
- Professionalism, Policies & Values
- Student Support: Tutoring, Guidance & Dealing with Disruption

Enquiries about the current availability of these publications should be addressed to the School Office at the above address.

Tony Lewis
Series Editor

Student Support:
Tutoring, Guidance & Dealing with Disruption

A Reader

Charles Atkinson &
Barbara Chandler

Published in 2001 by Greenwich University Press and prepared for publication by:

Procurement and Business Services Department
University of Greenwich
Woolwich University Campus
Wellington Street
London
SE18 6PF

ISBN 1 86166 176 2

Cover designed by Pete Birkett

Text design and layout by Christine Murray

University of Greenwich, a charity and a company limited by guarantee, registered in England (reg no 986729). Registered Office: Old Royal Naval College, Park Row, Greenwich, London SE10 9LS.

Contents

Part Four – Interpersonal Skills *(Continued)*

Part Five – Preventing Disruptive Behaviour   129

Part Six – Responding to Disruption   161

Acknowledgements

Acknowledgement is made for permission to reproduce the extracts quoted:

Bond M (1982) 'Dare you say no?' *Nursing Mirror* October 13, pp40–42

Bradley J (1987) 'Appendix III' in Further Education Unit *Behaviour and motivation: disruption in further education* Longman/FEU, paras 12–29

British Association for Counselling (1999) *Code of ethics and practice guidelines for those using counselling skills in their work* BAC

d'Ardenne P & Mahtani A (1989) *Transcultural counselling in action* Sage Publications, pp31–43, 61–72

Huxley M (1987) 'Mismatch and disruption' in FEU *Behaviour and motivation: disruption in further education* Longman/FEU, paras 42–62

Lago C & Thompson J (1996) *Race, culture and counselling* Open University Press, pp38–52, 68–69, 78–82

Lambert C (1986) *Secrets of a successful trainer: a simplified guide for survival* John Wiley, pp258–268

McManus M (1995) *Troublesome behaviour in the classroom* 2nd edn Routledge, pp1–4, 8–15, 114–117, 148–153

McPhillimy B (1996) *Controlling your class* John Wiley, pp53–67

Marsh D (1988) *An interpersonal skill: handling conflict* Information Bank Paper no 2481 Further Education Staff College

Miller JC (1982) *Tutoring: the guidance and counselling role of the tutor in vocational preparation* FEU & NICEC, paras 16–59, 60–95, 96–138

Mitchell C, Pride D, Howard L & Pride B (1998) *Ain't misbehavin'* FEDA, paras 4.1–4.29, and Appendices 7, 12, 13

Pederson P (2000) *A handbook for developing multicultural awareness* 3rd edn American Counseling Association, pp91–95

Rogers B (1997) *The language of discipline* Northcote House, pp11–21

Smith C & Laslett R (1993) *Effective classroom management* Croom Helm, pp1–13

Tannen CD (1995) *Talking from 9 to 5* Virago Press, pp114–121, 292–305

Turner C (1983) 'Transactional analysis: the basic concepts' in *Developing interpersonal skills* Further Education Staff College, pp5–26

The School of Post Compulsory Education and Training

The School of PCET, as it is known, has its origin in Garnett College in London, one of three institutions set up by the Ministry of Education in the late 1940s for the initial training of technical college lecturers. After many developments and organisational changes over the past 50 years, its future within the University of Greenwich will be from a campus on the banks of the River Thames in Christopher Wren's former Royal Naval College.

The School's services and students, though, are not only locally based, but nationwide and international. PCET is a leader in distance provision for lecturers, trainers, administrators and other support staff from all sectors of post-school provision, as well as from the public services and voluntary and commercial training organisations. It has associated centres in various parts of the United Kingdom, and there are projects in China, South Africa and Russia, and leadership of research and information networks within the European Union.

We aim, in both our teaching and our research, to relate professional practice to learning theory and current policy issues. This permeates all of the School's programmes – from initial training on Cert Ed/PGCE programmes, through professional development at BA/BSc and Masters levels and the work of our Training and Development Office, to our portfolio of short courses and bespoke in-house provision. There is a thriving group of research students, and the School has been at the forefront of innovation in computer mediated communication. We provide a comprehensive service for further, higher and adult education, helping people to help others learn through life.

Ian McNay
Head of School

Charles Atkinson worked for a number of years in FE colleges before joining the University of Greenwich in 1986, where he is currently Subject Leader for Higher and Professional Education. His teaching interests include classroom management and the handling of disruptive situations which may arise in the education and training of adults.

Barbara Chandler spent ten years as a counsellor and counsellor-trainer, amongst other roles, before entering teaching. During her time in further education she tutored YTS trainees and provided staff development for teachers of pre-vocational studies. She is now a tutor to teachers and trainers in the post-compulsory field at the University of Greenwich, where she also carries out in-house training of academic staff.

Introduction

Over the past twenty years or so the unveiling of successive central government curriculum initiatives for the vocational and pre-vocational education and training of 14–19 year olds has gradually pushed the issue of student support towards the centre of our attention in FE provision. Indeed, the concept of 'support systems' is placed at the hub of the FEU/FEDA representation of the processes of curriculum development, sustaining and being sustained by the cyclical factors of values and needs, design, implementation, and evaluation and review (see FEU, 1987: 57, and other FEU publications). As an earlier working paper commented: 'If the prime purpose of the college is to facilitate student learning then it can be argued that all activities of the college should directly or indirectly be supporting that learning...' (FESC & NICEC, 1984).

In compiling this present volume we have taken the view that while individual teachers are responsible for promoting and facilitating the learning of their students, a full and comprehensive system of support can only be achieved institution-wide by the commitment of senior management, the allocation of adequate resources, and the involvement of all members of course teams. Far too often being in a 'tutorial' role is not a choice: staff are frequently allocated the job according to the imperatives of the timetable and are given little chance to acquire and maintain the necessary skills and knowledge to perform it. It is thus common for tutors to feel inadequate in the early days of carrying out their tutoring role, and it is very helpful to seek support from some trusted colleague, to identify common needs, to establish and attend regular tutors' meetings and to agitate for appropriate staff development.

This Reader is intended for such people, who work with learners to develop their knowledge, skills and awareness of ideas and contexts which are built into effective tutoring and support work. For teachers and trainers in the early stages of their careers in post-compulsory education and training – and for the more experienced too – advice and guidance will be offered on appropriate ways of building professional relationships with students and trainees. Ideas underpinning both the tutorial relationship and the complex interactions in more formal classrooms and training situations are explored. Practical suggestions are put forward in how teachers may use these ideas to help create more effective, purposeful and orderly learning environments for themselves, their students and their organisations.

The practice of 'tutoring' has many meanings, not all of which are our concern here; in adult and continuing education it is commonplace to refer to all teachers as 'tutors' (see, for instance, Rogers, 1989); in higher education those with administrative responsibilities for programme teams are often called course 'tutors'. Chandler's contribution in section 3 of this Reader makes it clear that by 'tutor' we mean a teacher who carries out guidance and counselling activities aimed at the general 'academic', vocational and personal welfare of an individual student or small group of students. We believe firmly that effective work with learners is a matter of both personal and professional commitment, and that such commitment entails an openness to reconsidering ourselves as individuals and a readiness to learn from others' experience.

The literature and research on pastoral and behaviour issues in schools is, naturally, more extensive than we will find in further and higher education, and a number of the extracts were written for teachers and managers working in the compulsory phases of education. In every such case the issues raised are of immediate relevance to the post-16 context. Similarly, two or three contributions are aimed at professional counsellors; here we emphasise our belief that it is vital to distinguish between the boundaries obtaining for those who use counselling skills in their professional lives as 'tutors' and those for people who are labelled 'counsellors'.

Part One deals with this issue directly, identifying the tasks and values which make up the counselling and guidance activities of the tutor. Part Two introduces alternative perspectives on tutoring and the contexts of tutoring, while Part Three addresses the theme of 'difference' by indicating how the communication process which is central to the tutor-student relationship can be affected by individual, social, cultural and other differences between the participants. Part Four scrutinises in more detail the specific skills which need to become part of the portfolio of teacher behaviour – skills which can be learned and practised by all.

The last two Parts address the area of discipline, motivation and disruption in the classroom. Part Five considers institution-wide strategies and individual tactics for avoiding disorderly behaviour, while Part Six re-affirms the importance of a whole-college approach to the treatment of disruption when it occurs.

We intend that the extracts in this Reader will contribute significantly to a tutor's repertoire of skills and the ability to analyse practical, daily tutoring and classroom management, by providing a range of appropriate conceptual frameworks and approaches.

Charles Atkinson & Barbara Chandler

July 2001

References

Further Education Staff College & National Institute for Careers Education and Counselling (1984) *Curriculum-led institutional development* FEU
Further Education Unit (1987) *Relevance, flexibility and competence* FEU
Rogers J (1989) *Adults learning* 3rd edn Open University Press

Part One – The Teacher's Role in Supporting Students

We set the scene in Part One by considering the responsibilities of the teacher or trainer when seen as one who supports students by enabling and facilitating learning rather as one who simply instructs students by delivering a curriculum or by sharing vocational skills.

In the first of several substantial extracts from John Miller's long out of print FEU book *Tutoring*, three issues are identified and explored:

- the significant stages in the total student experience (or 'programme of opportunities', as Miller calls it) when tutorial guidance and counselling support are likely to be of most importance;
- the specific tasks which teachers need to perform when carrying out the tutorial role;
- and the fundamental values which seem to lie behind these tasks.

Miller outlines four stages which learners pass through in their encounters with institutions of formal learning:

- at selection,
- at induction,
- during the experience of learning,
- and at transition.

He explores the significant issues for the student and the different consequences for the supporting tutor at each of these stages, and identifies sixteen specific tasks which the tutor may need to perform, including counselling, teaching and disciplining. Examples are given of two extreme approaches to a teacher's carrying out of these tasks: one which inhibits student learning and personal involvement (Approach A), the other which leads to the enhancement of motivation and commitment to learning (Approach B). These two categories are reminiscent of McGregor's (1960) two types of management style: Theory X (believing that people work as little as possible and have to be coerced) and Theory Y (believing that people have a desire to work, exercise self-direction and control, and take responsibility for their own progress).

It is clear that different sets of personal values lie behind the two approaches, both in learning and in the institutional management which provides the organisational setting for learning. Miller goes on to propose the fundamental values of openness, equality of worth and trust, and to identify and explore those 'core conditions' which inform the work of the tutor: acceptance/respect, appreciation/empathy and authenticity/genuineness.

Such values will also underlie that group of guidance activities which we call 'counselling'. The Code of Ethics which forms the second reading was devised by the British Association for Counselling (since September 2000 the British Association for Counselling and Psychotherapy, BACP) as a checklist for those professionals, like teachers, who use counselling skills in their work, and for their managers and institutions. The BACP document helps us to explore the key ethical issues of respect for persons and confidentiality; it acts as an extension of Miller's statement of values, and will inform our reflections on practice.

In both of the contributions to this Part the contributors are careful to distinguish, as we shall do from time to time throughout the Reader, between those who are trained as and work as counsellors and those who use counselling skills in their professional lives. Miller shows how guidance and counselling skills are part of the tutoring work which his book supports. The BACP extract explicitly identifies the boundaries which BACP believes should contain the use of counselling skills in other professional areas. Miller writes about those values he thinks should underlie tutoring work. The BACP extract offers an ethical framework within which to 'place' our tutorial decisions, such as those about confidentiality, or about working within our skills.

Reference

McGregor D (1960) *The human side of enterprise* New York: McGraw-Hill

1.   Responding to Students' Needs

John Miller

[Editor's note. The paragraph numbering in this extract is from Sections 2, 3 and 4 of the 1982 FEU publication: *Tutoring*.]

Stages of intervention

16.   One way of exploring the tutoring role ... is to consider the stages through which the student is likely to pass in each opportunity – be it specific college courses, course elements, schemes, work experience, placements, or some other – that makes up the student's own ... programme. This section identifies and explores four such stages: *selection*; *induction*; *experience*; and *transition*. Each stage is expanded by identifying the kind of issues that are likely to be presented by the student, the aims for the tutor, the other agents that are likely to be involved, the tasks that require to be performed, and the settings in which they may be carried out... More detailed discussion of the tasks is to be found [later].

1) Selection

17.   Before entry, students are likely to be uncertain about the exact direction they wish to take. Thus, the purpose of the selection stage should be seen to be as much concerned with giving the student a chance to select relevant and appropriate options, as with enabling the college or other agency to select suitable candidates for the opportunities it has on offer.

18.   The kinds of questions that students may well want to ask include:

What are my existing skills?

Which of these do I wish to develop further?

What might I do with such new or developed skills?

In what ways will the opportunity (e.g. the college course) offer me the skills I want?

What will the opportunity demand of me?

What will being a student/trainee at this college/scheme demand of me?

19.   The aims for the tutor at this stage will therefore tend to focus on:

a) helping students to identify their learning needs and develop a learning agenda;

b) assisting students to appreciate the aims, methods and content of the opportunity in which the tutor is involved, and to understand what will be expected of them; and

c) enabling students to understand the potential advantages of attending a college course (e.g. skills learned, social life) and also to understand its potential disadvantages (e.g. travel difficulties, split sites).

20.   Many people may be involved in this process of selection. Links need to be made with the variety of other guidance agents such as careers officers, school guidance staff, house/year tutors, and careers teachers, concerned with helping the students in mapping out the overall balance and direction of their ... experience.

21.   The central tasks at the selection stage are, therefore, those of negotiating and contracting, and of liaising with other agencies involved. The most appropriate approach is likely to be by individual interview...

2) Induction

23.   Once the student has embarked on the opportunity, the issues that are posed tend to move toward those of 'finding one's feet'. This is a task that everyone has experienced in moving, say, from one job to another. The conscious attempt to help students work through it is referred to here as 'induction'.

24.   The kinds of issues presented by the student at this stage are typically those to do with being in a new setting ('Where is everything?', 'Who is everybody?'), but also include expectations ('What do fellow-students and staff expect of me?', 'Is this what I thought it would be like?').

25.   The aims for the tutor are to:

a) assist students to cope with the transition into this fresh opportunity;

b) help students to come to terms with what being on the opportunity entails (following on from the clarification of these demands at the selection stage); and

c) enable students who feel anxious about the decision they have made to confront, explore and work through such anxiety. (This may sometimes involve recognising that a wrong decision has been made and that re-negotiation needs to take place.)

26.   The guidance agents involved in this process will tend to be those internal to the organisation offering the opportunity; in a college, for example, it will involve the tutor and other relevant teachers, and – in cases where the student experiences particular difficulties – the student counsellor or perhaps the careers adviser. If it appears that re-negotiation is needed and that the student should move to a different opportunity, then guidance agents outside the opportunity – those involved in the overall mapping of the student's [programme] – may need to take part.

27.   The tasks required of the tutor at this stage, therefore, will be those of informing, advising, monitoring, counselling, referring, liaising, and re-negotiating. The most appropriate approach is likely to be through a balance of group-work where issues common to all the students can be dealt with, and of individual work where the specific needs of particular students can be met...

3) Experience

29.   Assuming the student has coped with the transition into the opportunity, the next identifiable stage will be that of coping or managing the experience itself. Issues that are likely to be posed at this stage include those of coping with the work ('How

am I doing in each bit of the course?'), of managing the demands of being a student ('Why do I have to go to . . . class?'), and of checking out whether the opportunity itself meets the original contract ('Am I getting what I am "paying" for?').

30.   The aims that the tutoring role might attempt to meet are those of:

a) helping the students to review and reflect on their performance on the course, and where appropriate to identify ways of seeking changes in work habits or behaviour;

b) helping students to face the consequences of their acceptance of the student role and to respond to the demands that, therefore, are legitimately made on them;

c) checking out with students whether their course or opportunity is in accord with the contract agreed originally between the parties involved (student, tutor, employing institution, etc); and

d) keeping a vigilant eye on the student's progress through the course, and ensuring that any blocks to learning are identified and that strategies to remedy such blocks are devised and implemented.

31.   The tutor's role is the prime one here. If the contract is clearly not being met, then there may be a need for discussion with other teachers, supervisors etc, and also with other agencies involved in making the contract (careers officers, for example), the aim of which may be to seek change in the opportunity itself. In addition, individual students may have particular personal difficulties that are affecting their work and that require the services of other guidance agents, such as the college counsellor.

32.   Therefore, the tasks required of the tutor at this stage are likely to consist of assessing, coaching, disciplining, representing, feeding-back, counselling, and referring. The possible approaches include general vigilance to pick up the early signs of particular problems, complemented by group-work to explore issues of general applicability, and work with individuals to explore these issues in greater depth...

4) Transition

34.   The final stage of any opportunity is the one that is most easily described as 'getting ready to leave', and also 'facing what comes next'. Again, this is an experience that every adult will have met in leaving school/college for a job, one job for another, etc. The process is referred to here as 'transition', and the kinds of issues that are likely to be posed by the students at this stage are those of taking stock ('What have I learned?'), uncertainty ('What do I want to do next?'), deciding ('What will I do next?'), and implementing ('How will I go about putting my decision into action?').

35.   The aims appropriate for the tutor here include:

a) helping students to review and reflect on what they have achieved during the opportunity, particularly in terms of skill acquisition, but also more widely in terms of their personal development;

b) assisting students to examine the range of possible options available for the future, and to make tentative choices about the direction of the next step;

c) helping students to explore the possible consequences of not getting exactly what they want; and

d) helping students to take the necessary steps to implement any decisions made.

36.   At this stage it is essential that contact be made with the other agencies that may be involved in implementing the overall balance and sequencing of the student's ... experiences. This will help the needs of the student to be matched more closely to the other opportunities available in the locality, whether inside or outside the college. The tasks for the tutor at this stage are likely to include assessing, evaluating, counselling, referring and refereeing.

37.   Inevitably at this point the main focus of attention will need to be on the individual. While some preparation for transition issues can be met through group-work, each individual student will merit personal attention...

General comments

39.   Describing a student's progression through an opportunity in this way tends to suggest an equality between the stages and a neat progression through them, neither of which may be true. Some students will indeed progress with relative ease through the opportunity because, perhaps, they know exactly where they are going and what comes next. But others may get stuck at a particular stage and may need considerable help to work through the issues that are blocking them.

40.   Over-riding all the aims and tasks identified above for the tutor, the most important are the issues of 'enabling' and of 'vigilance'. The tutor is first and foremost an *enabler* of learning, and to carry out this role must be *vigilant* to the issues that block the student's learning or progression. The tasks outlined briefly above and described in more detail [below] can help the student to overcome these blocks, with guidance skills ... as the vehicles for carrying out the tasks.

Tasks

41.   The preceding section identified a number of stages for the tutoring role, together with a multiplicity of tasks which need to be performed if the aims at each stage are to be met. This section briefly explores each of these tutorial tasks in turn, and also considers the potential conflicts inherent when one person, such as a tutor or workshop supervisor, attempts to perform a range of such tasks with young people.

42.   The tasks are:

Negotiating – identifying the skills and experience of the student, exploring the range of opportunities that are available, and seeking through discussion (involving all the participants) to achieve a 'best fit', having due regard to the inevitable constraints that will be met.

Contracting – identifying clearly the expectations of the student held by the tutor and by the college, helping the student to express his/her own expectations, and committing the tutor and college on the one hand and the student on the other to *realistic* offers and demands for the one to make to/of the other.

Liaising – communicating with other teaching staff, or with others outside the college, who are involved in carrying out the negotiated contract, and dealing directly with any difficulties that may arise.

Informing – offering data, divorced from a personal judgement of its worth.

Advising – making a suggestion based on a personal evaluation or experience.

Monitoring – checking that the contract originally agreed to as a result of the negotiation process is being adhered to by all the participants – student, college course, work placement, etc.

Counselling – exploring the feelings that lie behind the student's experiences of difficulty or distress, or his/her wishes and hopes.

Referring – knowing who is the most appropriate person to help the student deal with a particular issue, and determining *who* should make contact, *when* and *how*.

Assessing – reviewing and recording progress and achievements by using one or more of a variety of measures, including profiles.

Teaching – imparting knowledge, attitudes and skills through structured experiences.

Coaching – assisting students who are having particular difficulties in aspects of their work.

Disciplining – confronting students with the consequences of stepping over the limits set by the rules and regulations of the college and/or other organisation in which they are based.

Representing – speaking for or acting 'on behalf of' a student, perhaps at a course team meeting or a disciplinary hearing.

Feeding-back – informing colleagues and management about issues affecting students that require some form of institutional development or change to resolve.

Evaluating – investigating the effectiveness of the course or other opportunity which the student is experiencing in relation to the agreed contract and stated aims.

Refereeing – preparing reports for the purpose of making statements about the student to relevant other people.

43.   Each of the tasks in this list can be performed in a variety of ways; there is no one correct way of teaching, of assessing, and so on. It seems clear, however, that some approaches are likely to enhance learning and increase self-reliance ... while others are likely to inhibit these processes.

44.   To illustrate this distinction, it may be useful to examine the task of ***disciplining***. Including this alongside, for example, ***counselling*** within the role of one tutor would be seen by some as being unmanageable, on the grounds that the two are too much in conflict. But, while at first glance it may appear to be true that

enforcing rules and exploring feelings are contradictory purposes, on closer examination it becomes clear that it is possible for them to share a consistent underlying approach.

45.   On the one hand, disciplining can be simply seen as the administration of sanctions to those who fail to meet certain standards of behaviour, of work performance, and so on. The danger in this approach to the task of disciplining is that it can lead to the application of automatic sanctions without considering, for example, whether the recipient is aware of the consequences of his/her action – 'make the punishment fit the crime', 'ignorance of the law is no excuse', 'if you allow special considerations you open the door to further abuses'. Such application of automatic sanctions is likely to inhibit the development of a sense of purpose or of enriched motivation, as the student will often experience no sense of involvement, or of responsibility for the consequences of what he/she has done – 'they never told me about that'. It can also distance the student from the tutor – 'silly old . . .' – with the result that the tutor is less likely to be able to help the student deal with other issues that may arise during the course.

46.   An alternative approach to the task of discipline is to see the main function as one of setting, clarifying and maintaining clear ground-rules for the individual within the opportunity for which the tutor has responsibility. These ground-rules will then link to, and form part of, the task of contract-building between tutor and the students.   This approach views the objective as being to establish clear and contracted boundaries within which the student has freedom to act and to take responsibility for his/her actions, including those that infringe or step across the boundaries. Such an approach may use sanctions, but only after discussion to ensure that the student understands why. It is likely to enhance the development of motivation, and to sustain the student's involvement in learning, because the student is treated as an equal, an adult.

Example 1
A student consistently arrives late to college, takes long coffee and lunch breaks, and seems to have scant regard for the comments on these infringements by teachers and placement supervisors. The course tutor is informed, with the clear expectation that disciplining is necessary.

At first contact:
Approach A: *Tutor arranges to be outside the room when a class finishes, and buttonholes the student in the corridor. 'Look, this lateness has got to stop'.*

Approach B: *Tutor makes a point of arranging a time and place where they can meet and discuss the student's persistent late-coming.*

---

47.   In writing, the difference between these two approaches may appear too subtle. Nevertheless, the consequences for the student's attitude to learning may be dramatically different according to which approach is taken.

In Example 1, it is possible, following approach A, that the student will be hostile and resent being 'shown up' in front of others, that the truth behind the situation will not emerge, and that the student's hostility will affect his/her future dealings with the tutor and his/her attitude to the college generally. In approach B, the student is not being pre-judged but is offered privacy in which to discuss what *may* emerge to be a sensitive issue behind the presenting problem of late-coming (e.g. the student is exhausted by working early in the morning and late at night to earn money, as no-one else in the family is able to earn), and time to prepare for such a discussion.

48.   Other tasks for tutoring ... can also be approached in similarly contrasting ways, for example, as follows:

Task: *Negotiating*

> Approach A
> *Going through a pretence that choice exists where what is really happening is that students are being simply slotted into already existing courses within an 'off-the-peg' rather than 'bespoke' model.*
>
> Approach B
> *Being open with the student, explaining that the college has courses already designed which are not perfectly attuned to his/her needs; but also being willing to discuss the possibility that the student will be better served on another opportunity.*

Task: *Advising*

> Approach A
> *A suggestion made to the student offered off the 'top of the head' and based on the promise that 'this is what I would do if I were you' – often ill-considered though well-intentioned, and based on out-of-date or irrelevant information (after all, the student is not the tutor).*
>
> Approach B
> *A suggestion made to the student after careful discussion ensuring that the tutor understands the real issue causing concern to the student, and that both student and tutor can recognise the valid but limited place for knowledge-based suggestions.*

Task: *Contracting*

> Approach A
> *Explaining that the student will be expected to . . . and if they don't they can be assured of the consequences . . . which will be none too pleasant. The over-riding sense is one of vagueness and threat, in terms both of expectations and of consequences.*
>
> *Continued...*

Approach B
Exploring the student's hopes and fears for the course, helping to dispel the myths that may have been built up – that this course leads automatically to a job, etc; stating clearly the expectations the course will have to the student, of attendance, punctuality, speaking up when they do not understand, etc; and also stating clearly what the course will offer.

Task: *Assessing*

Approach A
A 'once-and-for-all' event, usually at the end of a course involving a pass/fail measure. This may be complemented by regular marks given by the teacher/instructor based on judgements which the student has not been invited to discuss or contribute to.

Approach B
A continuous process involving immediate positive and negative feedback on performance, and with opportunities to discuss and to make plans jointly for any remedial action that may be needed.

Task: *Counselling*

Approach A
Telling a student authoritatively how they must be feeling about an issue or dilemma – making assumptions based on supposition in order to short-cut the process, and forcing the student to work at the pace of the tutor.

Approach B
Encouraging a student to explore the issue at his/her own pace and in his/her own way – tentatively checking out the feelings behind the words, accepting the possibility of being wrong, and being able to put aside preconceptions.

Task: *Referring*

Approach A
Informing a student that he/she should 'go and see . . .' because that's the person who deals with their type of problem.

Approach B
Being clear with the student that in order to help with the issue in question more resources are needed; checking out that the student would be happy with the idea of referral, and discussing whether the most appropriate person to seek the help is the student or the tutor.

General comments

49.   Traditionally many of the tasks described briefly above have been performed from an 'inhibiting' stance. Assessment is a good example: only recently has the concept of student involvement in a continuous review process been given real credence in education in general and in further education in particular. Other tasks in the list, such as counselling, have lent themselves more readily to an 'enhancing' approach. It is this that points to the potential conflict for a tutor in, for example, attempting at one point to make a final judgement on a student, while at the next helping the student to work self-directingly through a problem.

50.   The opportunity provided by [many programmes], however, is that [they] encourage each of these tasks to be performed from the standpoint of learning enhancement and increasing self-reliance. The tutor is, therefore, afforded a greater degree of consistency in his/her approach to students.

51.   The tasks described here should not be seen as representing an exhaustive list, nor should it be inferred that each student will require every one of these tasks to be performed for them. The suggestion behind this analysis is that some care needs to be taken to ensure that these tasks are accessible to a student as and when the need arises. While tutors may take a prime responsibility for such accessibility, it is also clear that they will not themselves be able to perform all these tasks for all their students, and that they should not be expected to do so.

Example 2

A student enrols on a college course a few days after the course has started, due to pressure from home to go and do something or get out for good. After a brief discussion, the careers office suggests that a general foundation course may be a relevant opportunity.

The likely result of all this is a state of low commitment to the course: the student has not been involved in real negotiation or contract-building, and may well feel resentment at the family ultimatum which led to enrolment.

Several tasks may need to be performed to help this student overcome this low commitment:

i)   *contracting with the student in order to balance the requirements the course will make of the student with the student's expectations of the course;*

ii)   *liaising with the careers office to check out what level of negotiation was carried out and what general direction in terms of programme was discussed and agreed with the student; and*

iii)   *counselling the student to explore the feelings of resentment that may be expressed as hostility to other students or to adult staff members.*

In Example 2, it may be that the course tutor is in a position to be involved in all the tasks identified. Equally, however, other adult staff members and referral agents, such as the college counsellor, may be involved. It may be, for example, that the student gets on particularly well with one of the teachers, and during an encounter talks to him/her about the 'ultimatum'. Thus, the start of counselling may be with this staff member, with the possibility of subsequent referral elsewhere, if necessary.

52.   The purpose of Example 2 is to reinforce the point that other people are involved in the process and performance of these tasks, and that some attention needs to be paid to the organisation of tutorial work with students so that the communication links between these various people are clear. This does not imply that what a student tells one person offering help should automatically be passed to every other adult who is potentially involved. Rather it means that the teachers, tutors, counsellors, careers advisers, supervisors and others need to be clear about each other's role and perspective, and to understand the framework from which each of them works, and the values each is likely to hold including, for example, those relating to the degree of confidentiality offered. This identifies a major element of a staff development programme in the area of tutorial work.

Values

53.   It has been emphasised that the tasks of tutoring, performed in what has been termed an 'approach B' manner, are more likely to promote a readiness to learn in a self-directed way in the student. If the examples [presented] in the 'A' and 'B' model [above] are analysed, it is clear that there are certain underlying values which are assumed to promote such readiness. Perhaps the fundamental ones are:

i) Openness

The assumption is that people are more likely to accept, cope with and manage their learning opportunities and experiences if the dealings they have with those responsible for the management of the learning environment – that is, teachers, tutors, supervisors, etc – are based on a willingness to share openly the relevant issues. In other words, the student is more likely to show 'readiness to learn' if the tutor has discussed the limitations of the course in terms of its capacity to meet the student's needs, rather than if the tutor has appeared unwilling to accept that the course has any such limitations at all. It is not intended to imply that such openness has no boundaries and that the tutor has to discuss with the student every issue relating to the course. Rather what is implied is the need to *move towards* openness in relationships with students, inviting a reciprocal response from the students themselves.

ii) Equality of worth

The second assumption is that students will be more ready to learn if they feel that their treatment by tutors is one characterised by equality in terms of basic human respect. In other words, while the tutor has expertise in terms of knowledge or skill, it is important to avoid allowing this to develop into an attitude which students will see as being one of 'I know more . . . so I am better than . . .' The antennae of adolescents to adults putting them down in this way are finely tuned and highly sensitive, and many problems in adult/adolescent relationships seem to revolve around this issue.

iii) Trust

Close to openness is the assumption that students will be more able to overcome any blocks to their learning if they are able to trust the tutor. The process whereby one person comes to trust another is complex, but an important factor in the case of student/tutor relationships can be the way in which the tutor handles any information the student offers. It is, therefore, vital for the tutor to consider his or her stance towards the issue of *confidentiality*. Students may well expect that anything said to a tutor will remain absolutely secret: if the tutor is unable to offer such an absolute undertaking, this issue needs to be openly shared, or the delicate building of trust will be seriously impaired.

54. The quality of the relationship between tutor and student is critical if the guidance-related tasks of tutoring are to be efficiently performed. Studies of the helping professions [e.g. Truax & Carkhuff, 1967] have shown that such relationships are at their most effective when certain conditions or qualities on the part of the helper are met.

55. The first condition for an effective relationship is for the helper – in this case, the tutor – to listen attentively to what the student says, to take time to help to clarify what has been said, and not to pre-judge the student (e.g. on the basis of appearance or past experience). This willingness to listen and not judge the student indicates an *acceptance* of the need for the student to explore and a *respect* for the worth of the student's own experience.

56. The second condition for an effective relationship between the tutor and the student is the tutor's willingness to try to *appreciate* how the student thinks and feels about the experience being related, and the tutor's capacity to communicate that appreciation and understanding to the student. Thus, if, for example, a student is talking warmly about his work-experience placement, the tutor needs to recognise the student's feeling of excitement and pride when the supervisor praised the work he has done, and to communicate this awareness to the student: 'I see you felt proud of that . . .' This willingness and ability to check out and reflect the student's thoughts and feelings indicates that the tutor is trying hard to understand the unique world of the student – that is, to *empathise*. It recognises and respects the fact that while two people may share a similar event, they will each experience that event in a unique way, depending on a vast range of factors relating to their own personal histories.

57. The third condition for an effective relationship between the tutor and the student is the tutor's ability to be as natural as possible, within the limits of his/her role. This may become evident, for example, when the tutor is prepared to admit his/her lack of knowledge to the student, rather than to sustain the myth that anyone who offers help to another must necessarily know, or appear to know, all the answers. Such preparedness to disclose something of oneself (in Example 2, a lack of knowledge) indicates a willingness and ability to be *authentic* and *genuine* in the tutoring role, and demonstrates to the student the essential humanness of the tutor.

58.   These core conditions of *acceptance/respect*, *appreciation/empathy* and *authenticity/genuineness* are the elements that will influence whether the helping relationship between a student and a tutor is sound. If they are present, they are likely to pave the way towards effective implementation of the guidance component of the various tutoring tasks identified earlier.

59.   At the same time, it is important to recognise that tutors too are human, and that from time to time tutors may encounter a student they simply dislike, so impairing their ability to be of help. On such an occasion it is important for the tutor to ensure that the student has other people available; it may also be useful for the tutor to explore what it is about the interaction with the student that is 'getting in the way'.

Reference

Truax CB & Carkhuff RR (1967) *Towards effective counselling and psychotherapy* Chicago: Aldine

2. Code of Ethics and Practice Guidelines for those Using Counselling Skills in their Work

British Association for Counselling

A: Introduction

The purpose of this code is to outline the ethical principles involved in the use of counselling skills.

The attached practice guidelines which relate to this code (Section D) are primarily intended for those who are trained in the use of counselling skills within another role. For those working within an explicitly contracted counselling relationship, [BAC's] *Code of Ethics and Practice for Counsellors* applies.

The user of counselling skills will hereafter be known as 'the practitioner' and the recipient of counselling skills will be known as 'the client'. Counselling skills users, their organisations, their managers and their clients should have access to this code.

All BAC members abide by its Equal Opportunities Policy Statement. The full statement can be found at the end of this code.

B: Counselling skills

For the purpose of this code and the practice guidelines, the practitioner respects the client's values, experience, thoughts, feelings and their capacity for self-determination. The practitioner aims to serve the best interests of the client.

Counselling skills are being used:

- when there is intentional use of specific interpersonal skills which reflect the values of counselling;
- when the practitioner's primary role (e.g. nurse, tutor, line manager, social worker, personnel officer, helper) is enhanced without being changed;
- when the client perceives the practitioner as acting within their primary professional or caring role which is not that of being a counsellor.

C: Code of ethics

C.1   Values

- The practitioner's values are those of integrity, impartiality and respect for the client.
- The practitioner works in a non-exploitative way.

C.2   Anti-discriminatory practice

Practitioners must consider and address their own prejudices and how they stereotype others. They must ensure that anti-discriminatory practice is integral to their work when using counselling skills.

C.3   Confidentiality

C.3.1   Practitioners offer the highest possible levels of confidentiality consistent with their primary professional or work role.

C.3.2   Any limits to confidentiality must be made explicit.

C.4   Competence

C. 4.1   Practitioners are responsible for ensuring that they have training in the use of counselling skills and that this training is appropriate and sufficient for the counselling skills work they undertake.

C. 4.2   Practitioners are responsible for working within the limits of their competence.

C. 4.3   Both practitioners and the organisations for which they work have a responsibility for monitoring and developing the practitioner's competence in the use of counselling skills. Non-managerial supervision is recognised as one of the best methods for achieving this.

C.4.4   Both practitioners and their organisations have a responsibility for addressing those aspects of an organisation which impede the ethical use of counselling skills.

C.5   Integration of codes of ethics and practice

Many of those who use counselling skills in their work are also bound by another code of ethics and practice relating to their primary professional or work role. Practitioners therefore have responsibility for managing the integration of this code with any other code and for resolving difficulties or conflicts which may arise. It is important to recognise any way in which the primary role limits the use of counselling skills.

D: Practice guidelines

These guidelines apply the values and ethical principles outlined in this code of ethics for use in practice. Within another role the counselling skills user may help someone to recognise feelings, thoughts and behaviours and, when appropriate, to explore them in greater depth. The guidelines address issues of competence relating to these skills in practice.

D.1   Confidentiality

Confidentiality is crucial to the working relationship. For this reason any limits to the degree of confidentiality offered must be carefully considered. As the use of counselling skills often takes place within a network of overlapping accountabilities, the following clauses need to be understood within the context of the network.

Practitioners must therefore:

D.1.1   have clarified for themselves the extent of confidentiality which is consistent with any other roles they hold whilst using counselling skills;

D.1.2   when appropriate, reach agreement with the client at the outset about the extent of confidentiality;

D.1.3   take great care not to disclose, either inadvertently or under pressure, information given in confidence;

D.1.4   wherever possible, negotiate any change in the agreement with the client;

D.1.5   ensure confidentiality of material relating to the use of counselling skills which is used either for research purposes or in presenting cases for supervision or training.

Practitioners using such material must therefore:

D.1.6   where appropriate, obtain the consent of the client for such use;

D.1.7   effectively disguise the client's identity;

D.1.8   ensure that discussion about such material is respectful and purposeful and is not trivialising.

D.2   Competent practice

Practitioners should consider:

D.2.1   whether it is appropriate to use counselling skills within their other role;

D.2.2   whether their level of training in the use of counselling skills is adequate for the work in each individual instance or setting;

D.2.3   how any other relevant professional codes might affect their use of counselling skills within the work and whether any specific limits to confidentiality arise;

D.2.4   how any emerging areas of potential role conflict could be resolved;

D.2.5   whether the purpose of using counselling skills within a given context is clear to the client;

D.2.6   whether the necessary arrangements have been made with colleagues to ensure that an environment offering safety and privacy can be provided;

D.2.7   the power aspect of relationships within the work and any consequent need to address this;

D.2.8   the significance of their own and the client's social and cultural contexts in the work undertaken;

D.2.9   establishing an appropriate referral network;

and should:

D.2.10   value and facilitate the expression of thoughts and feelings;

D.2.11   acknowledge the client's thoughts and feelings and consider whether further exploration is appropriate or not at that moment;

D.2.12 be aware of their responsibility to resolve conflicts between ethical priorities;

D.2.13 be respectful of the client's world;

D.2.14 ensure non-discriminatory practice in their counselling skills work;

D.2.15 recognise when it is appropriate to refer a client elsewhere;

D.2.16 recognise and work with the client's reaction to the referral process;

D.2.17 wherever possible, make an appropriate closure of any counselling skills work;

D.2.18 consider any responsibilities there may be for follow-up.

D.3   Supervision

Regular and formalised non-managerial supervision for practitioners is widely recognised as good practice and is highly recommended. It should be an adjunct to managerial supervision of the total work.

Supervision offers practitioners a regular opportunity, outside the line-manager system, to discuss and monitor their counselling skills work whilst still maintaining client confidentiality. It is a formal, collaborative process which is primarily concerned with the well-being of the client and secondarily with that of the practitioner.

The supervisor will have knowledge and experience in using counselling skills and will also be familiar with the code of ethics and practice.

Supervision can:

- help practitioners to maintain ethical and professional standards of practice;
- enhance confidence, clarity and competence in the work;
- develop constructive thinking about the effectiveness of the work;
- acknowledge and help to recognise and manage the emotional impact of the work in order to enhance effectiveness and prevent burnout.

Further guidance on the ethics and practice of supervision can be obtained from BAC's *Code of Ethics and Practice for Supervisors.*

D.4   Accountability

Practitioners are accountable for their work to the client, the organisations in which they may practise and their professional bodies.

Practitioners should therefore:

D.4.1   have received adequate basic training;

D.4.2   maintain on-going skills development and relevant learning;

D.4.3   monitor their personal functioning and seek help or withdraw from using counselling skills, temporarily or permanently, if their personal resources become sufficiently depleted to require this;

D.4.4   take all reasonable steps to ensure their own safety;

D.4.5   evaluate their practice, drawing where appropriate on feedback from clients, colleagues and managers;

D.4.6   recognise the impact of their own beliefs and prejudices on the work they do;

D.4.7   monitor their work to ensure that they are not discriminating against or disadvantaging their clients;

D.4.8   exercise caution before engaging in a different type of relationship with those who are or have been clients (e.g. to a business, social, sexual, training, therapeutic or other relationship) and consult with a supervisor or manager whether such a change is appropriate.

Equal Opportunities Policy Statement

The British Association for Counselling (BAC) is committed to promoting equality of opportunity of access and participation for all its members in all of its structures and their workings. BAC has due regard for those groups of people with identifiable characteristics which can lead to visible and invisible barriers thus inhibiting their joining and full participation in BAC. Barriers can include age, colour, creed, culture, disability, education, ethnicity, gender, information, knowledge, mobility, money, nationality, race, religion, sexual orientation, social class and status.

The work of BAC aims to reflect this commitment in all areas including services to members, employer responsibilities, the recruitment of and working with volunteers, setting, assessing, monitoring and evaluating standards and the implementation of the complaints procedures. This is particularly important as BAC is the 'Voice of Counselling' in the wider world.

BAC will promote and encourage commitment to equality of opportunity by its members.

Part Two – Tutoring

In Part Two we explore in a little more detail the contexts of tutoring and what is entailed in accepting or being allocated to the job of being a tutor. Barbara Chandler re-affirms the importance of acknowledging the exact nature of the power differentials within the tutor-student relationship, and gives a warning against allowing any such relationship to become too close. Particular attention is paid to issues associated with the tutoring of students with learning difficulties and/or disabilities.

A 'typology' of tutoring models is presented:

- personal tutor model,
- action planning model,
- learning development model.

This provides a conceptual framework within which Chandler identifies and explores seven categories of tutorial role. These include both pastoral and academic responsibilities.

The essence of tutorial work is that it is carried out with single students or small groups of students, and in the second of the extracts by John Miller, clear distinctions are made between the purposes and management of group work and of individual work. Miller goes on to consider the 'organisational settings' within which guidance activities are carried out. By this he means recognising that tutors need to know at what point an issue is beyond their current skills, knowledge or capabilities and referral needs to be made to other 'guidance agencies' or managers within the institution. Throughout Miller's section specific examples are given of incidents and occasions which illuminate the matters being discussed.

3.   Being a Tutor

Barbara Chandler

Being a tutor is about taking on a particular responsibility for supporting individual students. Whether the curriculum context is a university degree programme, a vocational training scheme, a basic skills course, or preparation for an external examination, it is now widely recognised in further and higher education and training that learners have legitimate needs that cannot all be met within an institution's instructional timetable of classes, workshops and lectures.

This does not mean, however, that it is a tutor's job to fulfil their students' friendship needs. It is always of some concern to me when I hear a teacher declare him/herself to be a learner's 'friend'. As teachers or trainers we are *not* their friends: we have professional responsibilities other than and in addition those we have towards our students, and imperatives which can conflict with those of friendship. Moreover, we do not actually know the student/learner: we may think we do, but the setting in which our knowledge is based is far removed from those which friends inhabit. Inextricably bound up with these factors is that of differential power.

The tutor's power

Whether we like it or not, we are in a more powerful situation than our students. At the very least we are responsible for taking the lead in ensuring safety in the physical space we share. If we are working within an organisation, we are its representatives. For most teachers, this organisation also pays us; and if we are freelance trainers, we have an interest in the relationship between the learners' frequency of attendance and our pay!

We also have greater access to certain kinds of information than the learners. In both formal and informal settings, as teachers, we are likely to have to relate on equal terms with other professionals who can influence aspects of our learners' lives. We are almost always required to record and pass on information about their attendance at classes; in many cases we will be assessors of their work; often we have formal influence over their academic and career progression through the writing of reports and references.

Our interests, therefore, are not the same as those of our students, and we are not free to offer the kinds of affection and loyalty, mutual support, intimacy and spontaneity, which would characterise friendship. Even if we think we are not so powerful, and/or we wish to act democratically in the way we conduct our teaching, we should assume that most learners will perceive us as better informed and more knowledgeable than they are. After all, why are they prepared to have us teach them? And when they ask us for 'tutorial' help, why do they approach us, rather than one of their friends?

Given that we recognise we are not our students' friend, then, we do not have to behave as if we were. Indeed must not, for everyone's sake. The best way to achieve this is to identify our responsibilities and ensure we keep to them.

The tutor's responsibilities

Tutorial duties are frequently allocated to teaching staff by departmental timetablers without any significant discussion, and all too often tutors feel inadequately prepared for taking on the job they have been given. Here is a short list of some of the principal procedural responsibilities:

- making public and keeping tutoring 'hours' when timetabled;

- honouring appointments made . . . except of course in emergencies; and when this happens, being punctilious about notifying students, apologising and explaining; these are matters of courtesy which, sadly, not all traditions of teacher-student relationships adhere to;

- keeping careful records of formal tutorial encounters, together with any 'casual' encounters which might have serious outcomes – a common one is dispute with other learners or teachers, or with the organisation and its rules;

- ensuring reasonable privacy of conversation, not only in personal tutoring exchanges, but also those concerning academic progress;

- working out a proper boundary of 'engagement', ensuring that a proper concern for the welfare of the learner never develops into an inappropriate level of involvement;

- establishing a protective level of personal privacy, consistent with the need for 'openness' in tutorial discussions; so, for example, one should not be sharing details of one's own personal life or relationships, and at all times the tutor's address is their own concern;

- identifying sources of help for tutors within the institution, getting to know the people concerned and working closely with them; team work between tutors and other experts is particularly important within an educational or training enterprise which offers tutoring to students needing additional help.

A note on working with students with learning difficulties and/or disabilities

This may require extra skills and supports and – in some cases – specialised professional expertise. The student with a specific learning difficulty or disability might need access to appropriate expert help, and the personal tutor will have to be able to engage with both student and specialist.

Students with more severe learning difficulties, however, could well have different expectations of a tutor from those of our other students. The tutor will recognise the challenging nature of providing support in such a case, and will work with the student in order to identify individual learning and support needs within the programme of study, as well as being ready to address the sometimes unpredictable issues which arise in tutorials, such as clarity and ease of communication, concerns of family and personal relationships and uncertainty about the future.

And some general survival approaches:

- being clear about the limits of your ability, confidence, individual and group work skills, and your available time;

- trying not to do the job of other guidance agents (especially longer-term counselling);

- learning to be personally assertive, and helping your 'tutees' to be like this when they talk with you;

- being patient and inventive – every interpersonal exchange is unique;

- being prepared to manage, and hopefully resolve, disputes between students, or with other staff members;

- recognising that you may have a disciplinary duty: finding out how the organisation's systems work and your part in them;

- discovering the formal limits of the confidentiality you are able to offer, and adjusting to your own capacity.

Models of tutorial provision

In order to place our discussion of specific tutorial roles within a wider framework, it might be helpful to consider ways of looking slightly more theoretically at the concept of tutorial support. A manual produced by the Further Education Development Agency (FEDA, 1995: 11–20) identifies three different general perspectives, each with its own strengths and weaknesses and underlying values.

The personal tutor model

This is a pastoral/parental 'enrichment' model, primarily concerned with the development of general academic, social and cultural skills and – often – progression on to higher education. It seems to be particularly appropriate for full-time A level students, and is thus more commonly found in school sixth forms and universities than in further education colleges. The key to an effective personal tutorial system lies in the quality and commitment of the individual tutors and the nature of the relationship with their students, though formal evaluation of effectiveness seldom takes place.

The action planning model

Still targeted mainly at full-time students, action planning systems have developed largely because of the recording and tracking requirements of new curriculum developments, especially in vocational education and training. The tutor becomes a manager of students' learning, and works as part of a professional team concerned with the tasks of negotiating the planning of programmes, monitoring and assessing progress, and recording the evidence of individual achievement. This rather instrumental approach to the tutorial and guidance function has the merit of being clearly defined, planned and evaluated institution-wide, though the FEFC inspectorate in its review of GNVQs did comment on 'a belief amongst students and teachers that there is too much emphasis on planning and recording, compared with teaching and learning'

(FEFC, 1994). However, the system is focused on the management of an individual student's learning and on the successful completion of sometimes very complex programmes.

The learning development model

The principal difference between this perspective and the previous one can be seen in the nature of the relationship between tutor and student, which is less that of 'manager and managed' and more that of 'partners in the learning process'. Tutorial provision 'guides and supports students to become more effective and autonomous as learners' (FEDA, 1995: 15–16). Such guidance is made available to all students, part time as well as full time, and the tutors have to be highly skilled and well trained in the requirements imposed by this system. The tutorial process is characterised by negotiation of individual programmes with the learners, co-ordination between the activities of learning and those of guidance and support, and the integration of planning, recording, teaching and learning.

The tutor's roles

The specific roles carried out by a tutor are very much dependent on the environment in which they work. Each context is likely to involve interpreting the word 'tutoring' in local ways, hence we may have many different kinds of tutoring roles and expectations within or across the models presented above. An individual teacher's tutorial roles may vary from programme to programme, or may straddle two or more of the following categories:

- *directing learning (teaching);*
- *planning, and overseeing the completion of plans;*
- *academic supervision;*
- *vocational guidance;*
- *support with personal and social concerns: 'pastoral care';*
- *informal tutoring;*
- *distance tuition.*

Directing learning (teaching)

At its most obvious, the process of working with a learner or small group of learners to help them study their subject or build their skills, is often described as 'tutoring'. I find this an uncomfortable use of the term, since hopefully all but the most formal lectures and the largest classes will contain this kind of supportive activity.

It is characteristic of some disciplines in Higher Education that all sessions where students work on set problems with the teacher circulating in support of them, are labelled 'tutorials'. My own view would be to describe these as 'workshops', and the activity of the teacher as teaching. On that basis, whilst the comment and analysis found in the literature represented in this Reader will be of interest and concern, those who wish to improve such 'tutorials' will find it better to seek sources of advice on effective lesson planning and classroom management.

Planning, and overseeing the completion of plans

In FE, however, we will find that tutors often have the task of helping individual students to plan their learning, based on the rules of their programmes, the students' known abilities and potential, and the capacity of the college to match their needs. This is an example of the 'action planning' approach and involves establishing and reviewing the student's learning contract. In HE institutions which have modular curriculum structures, or degree programmes which carry some degree of student choice (e.g. combined studies), a similar role may be carried out by the personal tutor or, sometimes, the course or programme 'tutor' (i.e. leader).

Academic supervision

This is where the tutor has to help individuals or small groups of learners through preparation of academic work, outside formal classroom time. The same basic rules and principles, such as keeping appointments etc., apply as in as other tutoring, but there are some uniquely important features:

- recognising the limits of one's expertise: it is often essential to make this explicit and refer uncertainties to others for further consultation;

- being familiar with the literature of the subject and its sources, and keeping this up to date;

- being honest about one's own bias in relation to the subject (the preferred 'school of thought') and making reference to alternative disputing sources;

- judging that the boundaries to be negotiated are likely to be those of how much the tutor/supervisor contributes to the learner's enterprise;

- encouraging learner self-reliance: inspection and external review regimes now expect programmes to include the development of key 'learning to learn' skills; tutors should use, and help learners to use, the many available additional sources on study skills relevant to their field and the level of study;

- checking that groups of teachers provide a comparable 'service': extreme differences in levels of support can give rise, quite reasonably, to serious learner discontent, and tutors with cognate responsibilities should meet and discuss common issues;

- noting the difference between guiding the preparation of on-course assessment work and supervising end-of-course synoptic studies:

  Helping in the preparation of on-course seminar papers and essays
  This may occur as part of any academic programme, and some separate one-to-one tutorial time should be set aside. This is usually the explicit part of an implicit contract: it also helps to make clear how much help a learner can expect. Group work on such expectations can help, and can be supported by reference to some of the excellent texts on the management of seminars and the preparation of assignments (e.g. Fairbairn & Winch, 1996; Northedge, 1990).

  Supervision of end-of-course dissertations, projects and theses
  For these there should be some formal exposition of mutual expectations, a published system of supervisor support or supervision: sadly, this is still often not

the case, or the roles are only described in the most general terms. Keeping records is essential, especially of dates of tutorials arranged, action agreements made, and important advice given. Both learners and tutors need the protection of agreed and open processes, and both parties should know what the system is. Once again, there are a number of suitable texts which will provide additional support to students (e.g. Bell, 1999).

Vocational guidance

This may often arise as a component within a formal tutorial system: the organisation may allocate this as part of the role either of the 'course tutor' or of the personal or group tutor.

Specialist knowledge and experience of a particular field or vocation makes tutors the experts here, provided they are up to date with their subject and its current vocational practices. In addition, a tutor should be well informed on such crucial issues as means of applying for further study, and what sorts of selection procedures a particular workplace might use. The capacity to offer vocational guidance in individual or small-group tutorials is of course also dependent on the tutor's knowledge of each student's current skills, potential for development and motivation. Current government policy on 'lifelong learning' includes encouraging the offering of a range of local support services for learners. The tutor needs at least to be aware of the range available or the local contact point for them.

It is common in HE, and increasingly so in FE, for there to be a careers guidance department. Good relationships with them, timetabled introductions to their work, and timely referral are all useful tools. In such a context the tutor has an initiating and 'background' supporting role to play, once a referral has been made. Where workplace liaison is expected – for example in work experience provision – the tutor may find their role extended. All the general rules of good tutoring practice apply here: being predictable, fair and positive, and maintaining records of all agreements. In addition, the tutor must use, and work to improve, the liaison system, build and maintain all the essential contacts the learner needs, and take advantage of the placement to update personal knowledge of the field.

Support with personal and social concerns: 'pastoral care'

This kind of tutorial duty is most commonly seen as a formal general welfare responsibility in work with secondary school students. In sixth form colleges too a tutor may expect, for example, to have contacts with a learner's parents or carers. In programmes for mature students and 'returners to study', there may be a highly developed network of 'home-related' sources of support, with the tutor as the pivotal point of contact. More generally, from time to time learners ask for help in dealing with personal/ interpersonal issues.

Informal tutoring

We can often see tutoring activity taking place, even where other terms are used to describe the relationship between the participants and the 'tutor' carries other responsibilities towards the learner. An obvious case is where a subject teacher of a class of students finds themselves being treated by one of the group as though they were the personal tutor: the student has chosen who to confide in. If there is a system of 'tutors', then the teacher may be able more or less immediately to refer back to this person. But one has to ask why the choice has been made, and attempt at least to begin to help the student face whatever dilemma they present. Almost always this should result in referral to some other person, even if not the designated 'personal tutor'.

In some situations there may be no such thing as a tutorial support system, e.g. private tuition, 'crammer' classes, adult education for leisure, skill-based vocational training. In these instances teachers may quite often find themselves having to carry out an unrecognised tutorial function. It is particularly important in these situations to identify and maintain a record of at least a minimum range of sources of support appropriate for the kinds of difficulty which crop up most frequently.

Distance tuition

This is a growing part of academic (and to some extent vocational) teaching. Typically the learner will have some instructional materials to work with, an assessment regime to conform to, and a separate relationship with the administrators of the providing organisation. The tutor may or may not be a subject expert.

All the same principles of good tutoring apply in this context as in face-to-face work. But distance students often have different characteristics from attending ones, and the very fact of being at a distance makes a considerable difference to the relationship. It is more important, for instance, that the tutor knows how to access, and helps learners independently use, whatever the various parts of the instructional system are and its rules as they affect learners.

A good direct educational provider should have a comparable range of supports available to distance learners as to attenders, but this is not yet widely established, and may have severe limits. Some 'distance' tuition is so delegated to associates that there are few supports either locally or centrally. Vocational distance schemes, seeing the learning as 'pure' training, may make no 'support system' provision at all; others may depend on the backup to learners provided by local mentors or supervisors.

The tutor is likely only to be concerned with the learner's progression through the distance programme. To this end, it is essential to be familiar with the given materials and assessment requirements, and interpret them appropriately for the individual learner. It is even more important than with attenders that consulting hours are adhered to, and changes notified promptly. Tutors seldom 'see' their students, and must rely on 'talking'; so they must try to avoid ambiguity in communication and seek simplicity in explanations and agreements in both telephone talk and the written word, including e-mail.

Just as it is not possible to make assumptions about who the learner is, so it is important to be clear about the nature of the tutorial role. Tutor and learners may have met at some face-to-face study session, but this cannot be taken for granted. So checking out each other's reactions to situations, being open about the 'contract', and adapting to each other's style is very important. The student needs to be confident in the professionalism and expertise of the tutor, and in the knowledge that formative assignments will be marked quickly and the feedback will be comprehensive.

There are some excellent texts on tutoring in distance and open learning (see, for example, Simpson, 2000; Tait, 2001).

References

Bell J (1999) *Doing your research project: a guide for first-time researchers in education and social science* 3rd edn Open University Press

Fairbairn GJ & Winch C (1996) *Reading, writing and reasoning: a guide for students* 2nd edn Society for Research into Higher Education & Open University Press

Further Education Development Agency (1995) *Tutoring for achievement – frameworks* FEDA and Learning Partners

Further Education Funding Council (1994) *General National Vocational Qualifications in the further education sector in England* FEFC

Northedge A (1990) *The good study guide* The Open University

Simpson O (2000) *Supporting students in open and distance learning* Kogan Page

Tait A (2001) *Student support in open and distance learning* RoutledgeFalmer

4. Tutorial Settings

John Miller

[Editor's note. The numbering of paragraphs and illustrative examples in this extract is from Section 6 of the 1982 FEU publication: *Tutoring*.]

96. ... The methods most commonly used by tutors in their work with students are those of *individual* work (the interview setting) and *group*-work (the group setting). This section contains a discussion of those two settings, and attempts to identify approaches that may be useful, additional skills that may be worth exploring, and the dynamics that are particularly noticeable in each setting...

97. In addition, the section will conclude with a discussion of *organisational* settings in which the tutor works with other adults – that is, working *for* rather than *with* the student.

1) Group settings

98. For most tutors this is the most familiar setting in which they meet the students for which they have a tutorial responsibility. Often the group setting, apart from when it is a particular subject class, is used for administrative purposes – giving out notices, arranging the details of visits, etc. Sometimes it is used for little else. The argument of this section is that such limited use of group time, while no doubt useful, does not realise the full potential of the group for meeting successfully some of the tutorial tasks... The group can be a valuable means of helping students to empower themselves and each other to manage the issues related to each stage of their progress...

102. Groups can meet for at least the following purposes:

i) to help individual group members work through personal issues and themes that are relevant to or shared by other group members *(individual-oriented group);*

ii) to help individual group members to work together on a shared and understood group goal *(work group);* and

iii) to help individual group members to understand the processes and dynamics of a group by exploring the way the group itself works *(process group).*

Some groups will aim to focus essentially on one of these categories: a 't-group' will primarily meet to understand group processes (process group); a team on a residential setting may be oriented towards a common goal (work group); a discussion group will encourage each member to arrive at his or her own conclusion about the issues in question (individual-oriented group). The reality, however, is rarely as tidy as this and all three purposes can be evident in a group at any one time. In all groups, the processes or dynamics of the group will affect the way the group tackles the task, and individuals' commitment to that task will affect their involvement and learning.

103.   All three strands, therefore, need to be considered by the tutor in working with a group. Nonetheless, perhaps the most valid and obvious purpose of a group in tutoring ... is that it offers a chance for individual students to work through the issues and themes relating, say, to the stages of *induction* and *experience*, alongside other students who are also working through these stages. Therefore, the *primary focus* of the group is likely to be that of the 'individual-oriented group'.

104.   The tutor's task is to manage and structure the group's work – for example, by the use of a group exercise – so that the students are able to work through some of the key issues and themes identified. A brief description of a first meeting of such a group might help to describe this and also to identify where the other themes, relating to the dynamics of the group, are likely to emerge as significant.

Example 12

A group of twelve students has just arrived on a college course, and the tutor is meeting them as a group for the first time. The tutor recognises that the stage the students are in is that of induction: they need to become oriented to the new world of the college in general and the course in particular. The tutor intuitively predicts that the issues that will be most relevant to the students will include those of 'Who else is here?' and 'Why are they all here?'

Thus, in Example 12, the procedure followed by the group might be as follows:

i) the tutor meets the students and introduces himself to them, including a brief history of his background;

ii) the tutor invites each student to introduce themselves briefly to two other students, at a level at which they feel comfortable – perhaps including what they have done since leaving school;

iii) each group of three students discusses what they hope to get from the course;

iv) the tutor brainstorms these hopes, and identifies themes and issues from what has been said; he also identifies his own hopes for the course and for the tutorial work of which this session is part; and

v) the tutor recognises that while the groups of three now know each other a little better, they may not know the rest of the group, and some form of 'name game' is used.

There are a number of issues woven into this example that are worth unravelling:

105.   Firstly, the tutor identifies that while each student may already have been interviewed individually, they are unlikely to know each other. The setting for all of them is unfamiliar. Therefore, the issue of 'Who else is here?' will inevitably affect the progress of the group. Accordingly, it must be attended to. Having thus used an identifying-theme skill ..., the tutor goes on to use a structuring skill, introducing an exercise that will help the students start talking to each other within a working

setting, rather than informally (e.g. over coffee later) where individual first impressions are less likely to be explored.

106.   Secondly, the tutor suspects that an additional question which will be underlying the work of the group will be 'Why are we all here?' He accordingly sets out in the second stage of the exercise to encourage the students to explore their hopes for the course, thereby identifying some of the answers to that question. He divides the group up to talk in twos and threes because it is essential that *each* student be helped to address the induction stage issues individually. In addition, many students will find it easier to talk in a small group than in the whole group, where one or two people are likely to emerge as the group 'talkers'.

107.   Thirdly, the tutor takes part at appropriate stages of the session, particularly in the introduction and at the 'hopes' stage. This indicates that he is performing a different function from that of a transmitter of knowledge or a trainer of skill; instead, he is involved in the process of the group. As such, failure to disclose something of his own work and expectations will encourage students to avoid such self-disclosure themselves. This sets the beginnings of a contract for what can be discussed inside the group.

108.   Thus, the tutor is using the session in an 'individual-oriented group' way to assist in the individual students' induction, while also paying attention to the dynamics of 'who' and 'why', which are essentially 'process group' issues.

109.   The use of structured approaches in the way described in this example is particularly useful for tutors and can be used within subject classes or in more general tutorial-group settings. From the group's work themes will emerge, and exercises can be constructed to encourage students to explore and possibly resolve them. The themes may include those related to study skills, to skills of working with others, skills of finding a job etc; additional suggestions might come from the group's own other experiences.

Example 13

A tutor is met by one of the students in tears due to the persistent bullying of other students in the group.

What does the tutor do?: support and care for the student being bullied?; use sanctions/punishments against the main culprits?; find a way of changing the aggressive, scapegoating climate that seems to have developed in the group?

---

110.   An example is the issue of bullying presented in Example 13. All too often the first two strategies named in the example (that is, supporting and caring for the student being bullied, and using immediate sanctions against the bullies), highly necessary though they may be, are the only ones adopted. The tutor fails to do anything about the climate, and ends by adopting a threatening posture – 'If you do it again, there'll be trouble' – which tends to become a self-fulfilling prophecy.

111.   It is possible in this example to conceive of ways in which, when the heat of the moment has cooled and when specific remedial action in terms of support and sanctions has been taken, a sensitive tutor might introduce the issues of bullying, aggression, scapegoating, putting another person down etc, into a group tutorial. It is, after all, a problem that relates to the *group;* some of the group members may not have been actively involved in the bullying, but they are sure to be aware of it, and perhaps not a little concerned about the whole thing.   Therefore, a careful introduction, followed by a staged series of exercises exploring the issues of aggression, assertion, passivity, negative emotions, and roles group members play, would all be relevant, not as a subtle way of telling the group off, but as a means of helping students understand more clearly what is going on.

112.   This developmental approach, using incidents in a positive, planned way, is particularly useful in tutoring.   There are many examples of exercises designed to help such an approach, including some from resource materials relating to social and life skills, drama, health education, etc.

113.   With any exercise used in this manner with students, it is vitally important that adequate processing time is allowed. In an earlier FEU document (FEU, 1978) the importance of time to review any experience, in order that learning might be enhanced, was stressed;   in this type of work particularly, such review time is essential, and can often take as long or longer than the exercise itself. In such ways the inherent tension between the needs of individual students on the one hand, and of the group on the other, can be explored, and strategies adopted to make that tension bearable.

114.   *Groupwork issues*
... All tutorial skills are relevant to work with groups of students.   There are, however, additional issues that the tutor as group-worker will need to take account of:

i) Interaction between students
The tutor, as has been made clear in the examples given, needs to pay attention to and be aware of the interaction and relationships between students in the group.

ii) Selection of appropriate vehicle
The tutor, having identified appropriate themes, will need to translate those themes into exercises or other appropriate structures that will assist the individuals in the group to work on them.

iii) Encouraging the participation of the group
Various structures and exercises can be employed which encourage all the group to participate, while allowing the right of members to remain silent if they so wish. The issue of silence in a group may indeed well be an appropriate theme for the group.

iv) Controlling without manipulating
If the tutor works within a value system that encourages openness, then structures and the reasons behind them are likely to be explored. Though the experience may

be controlled, the students are unlikely to feel manipulated. Manipulation seems to be closely associated with lack of trust, and lack of trust may be rooted in a lack of genuineness and authenticity on the part of the tutor.

v) Fostering a constructive and conducive atmosphere
The climate of a group is a mysterious yet influential factor. It again at least initially depends very much on the tutor modelling the desired behaviour. For example, if the tutor is sarcastic, the students are likely to be cruel too.

vi) The physical setting and size
Groups that meet in educational institutions are often under a serious disadvantage, because most of such institutions are physically designed on the assumption that one teacher will be working with 30 or more students. It is important to have space that is reasonably private for the group to work in. If, for instance, the tutor expects group members to use role-play, then to have it working at the back of a publicly-visible hall is to abort the session before it has started. If the group tutorial is considered important, then this fact must be reflected in an appropriate setting where chairs, uncluttered by desks, can be arranged so that students can see each other's faces. Groups of around 12 would appear to be ideal for group tutorial work of this kind: this size encourages participation, and allows the tutor to concentrate on facilitating individuals' learning without being overly concerned with issues of group control.

vii) The management of discussion
In order to consider the issues arising from the structure of the group, a tutor needs to have the ability to understand how to conduct discussion, how to allow students to have their say, and how not to feel obliged to impose his or her own values, beliefs, or opinions on the students. Some tutors consider that they should apply the rules of academic seminars by challenging students and by imposing their own views to encourage students to challenge them in return. But ... the tutor may well be faced with a group of reluctant or resistant students who are not likely to be highly articulate. Thus, to challenge and impose views at an early stage may be seen not as a legitimate part of the 'game', but rather as the patronising behaviour that it all too often is. Another danger for tutors is to fail to recognise the inevitable and important boundaries around their role and to fall into the trap of trying to be 'one of the boys' [sic]. Being a group-worker has important responsibilities, and one of those is to maintain clarity about the relationship between the tutor as manager of learning experiences and the student as learner.

2)   Individual settings

115.   For many tutors, the individual setting is the setting with which they feel most unfamiliar; for others, it is the most common means of accomplishing their tutorial tasks. Often the individual interview is brought about by the tutor's need to see the student to discuss progress, identify issues, and so on. The argument of this section is two-fold:

a) that by paying attention to the tutor's existing individual work with students, and developing and extending his or her skill repertoire, students may be encouraged to see the tutor as an available source of help who can be freely approached; and

b) that each student warrants the right of individual access to a concerned and interested adult who is prepared and able to help that student to meet, cope and manage the issues related to being on the course, and associated with the stages of selection, induction, experience (including assessment), and transition.

The skills of tutoring ... are all very apposite here, and will not be elaborated further. Instead, attention will be focused on the physical setting, and the phases of a tutoring interview.

116.   i) Physical setting
As with group-work, the right to privacy is a very important consideration in individual work.   Students are unlikely to feel at ease discussing issues related to themselves if the discussion takes place in a snatched meeting in a corridor between classes. This does not mean there is no place for such 'brief encounters'; they can be useful to make an appointment to meet, or to check on progress since last meeting.

117.   Privacy implies a private location. Although few tutors have the luxury of an office, it is desirable if at all possible to find a space where distractions and interruptions can be minimised, if not completely obliterated.

118.   It is also important for both student and tutor to know what the time constraints are for the session. In group tutorials, negotiation over time is usually not necessary, because the institution 'thinks' in terms of particular units (e.g. single hours), and the staff and students have been 'conditioned' by them. In an individual setting, such external conditioning usually does not apply, and it is very easy for the student to assume that the tutor has 'all the time in the world'; indeed, some tutors may even say that, when it is blatantly not true. Therefore, the boundary of time around the interview needs to be fixed at the outset, and adhered to – there can always be another meeting. The structure that this gives can offer support both to tutor and student; both are likely to be more relaxed, and more is likely to be achieved.

119.   It is preferable for both participants to be physically comfortable both in terms of the quality of seating (although it is often a case of 'making do') and also in terms of the direction they are facing. There is nothing worse than realising that a cricked neck is developing! Such small matters can be surprisingly significant in practice.

120.   ii) Phases of a tutoring interview
It is possible to identify a series of phases through which a task-oriented tutoring interview is likely to pass. It is important to recognise that in practice these phases are not as clear as they may appear on paper, and that some interviews miss out on some of the phases altogether. They are identified here not as a check-list to be followed slavishly but as an aide-memoir to assist understanding of the process involved.

121.   (a) *Establishing a sound working relationship*
In this phase, the tutor strives for rapport, puts the student at ease, sets clear boundaries of time and space, and generally attempts to foster clear communication, thus helping to build the contract for the meeting.

122.   (b) *Defining and exploring the nature of the task*
Here the tutor and student consider the variety of issues that they may need to deal with – in other words, to establish 'Why are we here?' Since much tutorial work initially takes place at the request of the tutor, this issue of being clear of what the task is has vital significance: if it is not resolved, such tutorial work can easily fall into the trap of being seen as manipulative ('We are here for the tutor's purposes') rather than enhancing ('We are here to assist the student').

123.   Example 14A illustrates this point.

Example 14A

The tutor has determined that a particular student's performance has fallen in a number of subjects, apart from catering, and decides to take time to explore this with the student. The primary task being performed here is one of 'monitoring'. The tutor sees the student after a class, briefly explains the purpose of the meeting she wants to have, and arranges a time and place.

At the interview, the situation is briefly described from the tutor's perspective: that the student's work is in decline in several subjects, except catering; that the tutor is concerned that this is happening and would like to help work it out if necessary; and that she would like to invite the student to say what has caused it and whether it is causing concern to him.

The student has had little real choice about being present at the interview, and may counter with 'It's no business of yours'. Hopefully, however, the tutor's careful approach will encourage the student to be as open as possible about the situation, reflecting the openness of the tutor. There are, after all, a variety of possible reasons for the drop in performance, and if the student's initial resistance has been overcome, the tutor will be able to attend to the reasons as stated by the student (see Example 14B).

Example 14B

Possible reasons for the student's decline in performance include:

i) '. . . I just can't seem to keep up with the rest in other subjects . . . I don't like the other teachers very much . . .'

ii) '. . . Well, I've got this offer of a full-time job starting next month at the cafe where I work part-time . . .'

Continued...

> *iii) '. . . I dunno, nothing seems to make any sense any more . . . what's the point, anyway . . .?'*

In the case of (i) and (iii), the exploration might involve the student and tutor in gaining greater insight and understanding of the situation; in this case, the skills of responding to content and feeling, and of identifying themes, may be particularly useful. In the case of (ii), a move to the next phase might be immediately called for.

124.   (c) *Exploring the consequences of the various options available*
For each option available in a given situation, there are likely to be both beneficial and costly consequences. In the case of response (ii) in Example 14B, the consequences of relying on the promise of a job next month may be that, if the job falls through, the student might be too far behind to make up the work on his present course, and therefore might have wasted an opportunity. There are other options available to the student: e.g. continuing with the course, on the basis that other components of it could be useful; or checking with the cafe and getting 'something in writing'. Each of these options similarly may have consequences for the student, that will need to be taken into account.

125.   The focus of this phase is, then, on identifying the range of options available, both for the student and for the tutor, and on discussing the consequences of each, including the effect that each option might have on the student's relationship with parents, friends, etc. The 'options for the tutor' include *referring* the student to a more expert helper: for example, response (iii) in Example 14B may indicate a depressed student who might usefully be referred to the college counsellor. They also include *liaising* with other members of staff – for instance, where the problem the student experiences is one of low levels of literacy, and a joint recognition by teaching staff of the student's difficulty could be helpful. Both these options describe tasks performed 'on behalf of' the student rather than tasks performed 'alongside' the student...

126.   (d) *Helping the student make a decision*
This is the crux of the matter: since the aim is to promote self-reliance, it is important for the student to have the strongest possible say in any decision, not only in terms of what the student him/herself needs to do, but also in terms of agreeing on any actions to be performed by the tutor. If the option of referral is suggested, for example, the student should agree to the validity of such an option, after considering it alongside other options, before any action is taken. Many students need help in this process of deciding, and here again there is a possible link back to group tutorials where individual goal-getting, action-planning, and choosing skills can be explored and practised.

127.   (e) *Assisting the student to take the agreed action*
This includes offering support and follow up where appropriate. The purpose is to encourage the student to take action without feeling isolated in so doing. The tutor

can help by encouraging the student to map out the steps to be taken and to attach clear time checks to each step. Follow-up can be through brief informal encounters, but also through specific follow-up meetings to see how things are going.

128. *Discussion*

There is a danger of presenting these phases in over-neat terms, but the identification of phases is useful in suggesting the desirability of any individual tutorial having a clear *beginning* in which its purpose is clarified; a *middle* where some hard work, using many of the skills identified, is done; and an *end* where a sense of purpose, however limited, is achieved. It is also worth noting that as part of the closing phase of an interview, a simple checking question, such as 'Have we dealt with everything you wanted to say to me?', is useful. Many students leave from a tutorial having worked through some issues but leaving their main concerns undeclared, and the end of a session is often a time when such concerns will be expressed, if invited. These may then need to be taken up on a subsequent occasion.

3)   Organisational settings

129.   The task of referral warrants a special mention because, as identified above, it illustrates a task in which the tutor works 'on behalf of', rather than 'alongside', the student. In the same way, the tasks of liaising, representing, and refereeing involve acting for the student, and some of the issues involved in referral are common to all these tutoring tasks.

130.   If the tutor values openness, there is unlikely to be a major difficulty here, because the tutor and student will explore together the need for referral, liaison, representation, etc. The confidentiality of the information exchanged between tutor and student is then clearly negotiable, and is not absolute as is the case between lawyer and client, or priest and parishioner.

131.   The need for the exercise of these tasks is usually indicated by a recognition that the issues posed by the student are too complex or are beyond the ability of the tutor to handle in isolation from the organisation in which both tutor and student work. An example is discussion regarding possible changes of course where the involvement of other people inside the college is required to implement such a change. The three issues that need to be borne in mind when working for a student in this way are described in the following paragraphs.

132.   (i) *Knowing when to switch task*

This refers to the point at which the tutor realises that, to help the student, it may be appropriate to move into an 'acting for' stance through referral, liaison, etc. This realisation may stem from one or more of a variety of factors: a recognition of being out of depth; an acceptance that to continue to work alone with the student is an inefficient use of time; and an understanding that some students need long-term help to resolve their situation. There is, however, a danger in referring a student *too soon*, perhaps due to the tutor's own anxieties, as in Example 15.

> **Example 15**
>
> Student: *'I don't talk it over with my parents . . . I never speak to my parents.'*
>
> Tutor: *'I don't think we should talk about that here: perhaps you should see the counsellor.'*

There is also danger in holding on to the student for too long despite being aware that there has been no move toward resolution of the difficulty, as in Example 16.

133.   (ii) *Knowing who to involve*
This issue can be picked out of Example 16.

> **Example 16**
>
> Student: *'I always feel better for just talking it over with you. I know nothing can be done about my getting more money . . . and it is a worry . . . But you are very helpful.'*
>
> Tutor: *'I am glad I can be of help . . .   Same time next week?'*

The student with a money difficulty is unlikely to be helped by the tutor. To be able to work one's way around the national and local benefits scene is a skill in its own right, and it is important that the tutor has clear and easy access to a person possessing this skill, either within the college or outside the college.

134.   It can be useful to establish a directory of such resource people... Such a directory is particularly useful if the list of agencies is supplemented by the names of individual contact people within these agencies. To refer the student to someone is, in effect, recommending the student to trust that person. If the tutor has met the people and talked with them, it will be easier to make such recommendations with confidence; also, students are often more likely to follow up named people than impersonal agencies.

135.   Knowing the contact person or the agency implies a knowledge of factors such as the value system on which their work is based, and the availability of the service. These issues are particularly important where outside-college referrals are to be made on matters of a personally sensitive nature, such as sexuality, pregnancy, etc.

136.   (iii) *Knowing how to involve the other person or agency*
This involves a recognition that it may sometimes be more appropriate for the tutor to seek help than for the student to be simply 'moved on'. The advantage is that the other person or agency becomes a resource to the tutor, enabling the tutor to develop his or her skills and experience, rather than using the agency simply as a one-off resource to one particular student. It is an approach that may be particularly relevant within college, and it can be useful in terms of achieving supervision and support for tutors.

137.   It is also important to understand that the tutor's own values may colour the range of referral agencies and contact people the tutor is prepared to recommend to the student.   For example, a tutor may think a particular college counsellor is a 'trendy lefty' and may refuse to refer students to him or her. The result may be that the students do not get the help they need.

138.   All these issues are related particularly to the tasks of referral and liaison, but they are also relevant, as was stated earlier, to all those tasks where the tutor acts on behalf of the student – in boards of studies, disciplinary hearings, courts, etc.

Reference

Further Education Unit (1978) *Experience, reflection, learning* London: FEU

Part Three – Managing Difference

Several of the contributions to this Part are taken from texts written for professional counsellors, and as you read them you will need to understand 'tutor' and 'student' in places where the authors have written 'counsellor' and 'client'. We have already made the case in Part One that there are a number of counselling and related skills which it is appropriate for tutors to acquire, and these are enumerated more fully here in Part Three. We should also acknowledge the enormous range of different people involved in learning and teaching, as in counselling, and recognise that we all need to be able to understand and work within the frame of these differences, whether of race, sex, class or – in its very widest sense – culture.

The theme of communication is introduced by Colin Lago and Joyce Thompson in their exploration of 'transcultural counselling' and the way in which all aspects of communication are culturally determined. They present the work of two significant researchers in this area: Edward Hall, who identified five categories of cultural difference in communication (space, time, verbal behaviour, non-verbal behaviour and context); and Geert Hofstede, who found four sets of criteria or 'dimensions' which helped to mark the differences between national cultures (power distance, uncertainty avoidance, individualism/collectivism, and masculinity/femininity). Paul Pederson, in the next extract, takes Hofstede's four dimensions as applied to an educational context and related to teacher-student and student-student interaction.

The ways in which we link gender differences with specific expectations of the way men and women speak and behave, and how in turn these influence communication patterns, are explored by Deborah Tannen. She presents many examples of children at play, students in class and committee members in meetings to support her argument that women are disadvantaged in the majority of contexts where men and women meet and communicate. The research which she quotes shows how important it is for the group leader or teacher-tutor to be prepared to intervene and structure the communication activities within mixed groups. Like Hofstede, Tannen demonstrates that conversational 'styles' have a cultural as well as a gender dimension.

In the final contribution to Part Two, Patricia d'Ardenne and Aruna Mahtani present research into the varieties of language and non-verbal communication used in transcultural counselling. Once again, the cultural rules and conventions which they apply to counselling and therapy are of immediate relevance to situations in which tutors and students interact. Of particular interest is their own experience of working in the East End of London, where there is the extra dimension of social class, and non-standard forms of English are often spoken by those for whom English is their first and only language. Throughout the chapter many examples are given of the points made.

The principal theme running through all of the contributions to Part Three is that it is crucial that counsellors and, by implication, tutors are aware of the issues of perception and expectation raised by the published research and of the conclusions, which demonstrate that differences of race, sex, social class and culture can significantly affect the nature of the communication between counsellors and clients, and between tutors and students.

5.   Cultural Barriers to Communication

Colin Lago & Joyce Thompson

People carry culture with them. When they leave one group setting for another they do not shed its cultural premises.

(Becker & Gear, 1960)

We are all culturally conditioned. We see the world in the way we have learned to see it. Only to a limited extent can we, in our thinking, step out of the boundaries imposed by our cultural conditioning.

(Hofstede, 1980)

Introduction

... The intention here is to offer ideas on the huge range of cultural differences that can be present when two people meet in the counselling setting.

The process of counselling is quintessentially based upon sensitive, understanding and accurate communication between counsellor and client... Counselling research has led the way in highlighting specific skills and styles of being that can lead to optimal outcomes for clients.

While communication constitutes part of the visible and audible aspects of people's behaviour, the inner origins of such messages come from the complex inner workings of our minds, our emotions, our memories, our relationships and so on. This book encourages counsellors to understand more fully their inner complexities and, specifically, their own cultural barriers to communication.

This chapter moves from an account of a training exercise – that provides a range of ideas generated by many participants on courses – to offering [two] different perspectives of differences between cultures: the work of ET Hall, [and] the work of G Hofstede... Inevitably, not all theoretical perspectives or indeed cultural differences are listed here. However, the views that are offered provide a resounding range of ideas and phenomena, sufficient to make us dwell deeply on the following question: with so many potential and actual differences between us, will we ever be able to communicate satisfactorily – has transcultural counselling any chance whatsoever?

A training exercise

The authors have often used the following training exercise as a way of helping groups think more about what cultural barriers to communication might be. Two stick figures having been drawn on the board, the group is invited to brainstorm as many cultural barriers to communication that they can think of existing between any two people who come from differing cultures. In quite a short time, an amazing array of ideas can be presented. Initially, the exercise is introduced in terms of the general barriers to communication any two people would experience.

A further development is to consider that the two figures, described as being culturally and racially different from each other, are a counsellor/client dyad. This secondary brainstorm can then produce further specialised ideas relating to cultural barriers affecting the counselling process.

Figure 1 (opposite) very quickly provides us with a huge range of issues that are potentially present in any meeting between two people who are culturally and racially different. The complexity of this situation is further realised when one takes into account that person A, already having all these aspects, attitudes and attributes is trying to communicate with person B, also possessing these aspects, though differently constituted. Each is different from the other. Each also then proceeds to see, perceive, attribute and project on to the other from their own understanding of the world. Let us illuminate this with an example.

Person A is tall. She comes from a society of tall people and is thus used to conversations with others of a similar height. However, when confronted with person B, a shorter person, she has to significantly change her posture to communicate. The change in posture thus affects her attitude towards the other person as it reminds her of sayings she heard in her childhood about never trusting shorter people.

Thus person A, within her own culture, is fine. On meeting person B, she develops a set of reactions based upon her own culturally determined system of interpretation. Likewise person B, from their perspective, perceives the tallness of person A as potentially threatening and becomes fearful of her potential power. This leads B into being somewhat timid and withdrawn in A's company.

> A perceives B
> A judges B on A's system of categorising people
> A's behaviour and communication is thus likely to be affected.

> B perceives A
> B judges A on B's system of categorising people
> B's behaviour and communication is thus likely to be affected.

This apparently very simple example of just one difference, of relative tallness, offers an insight into the potential complexity of the impact of difference upon communication. If the two persons were to be meeting for counselling, the scenario presented above indicates that whoever was counsellor, their capacity to be accepting of and non-judgmental towards the other, as client, is already limited. This demonstrates that the counsellor may have considerable difficulty in fully offering one of the core therapeutic conditions as defined by Rogers (1987) for successful therapy to occur, that of acceptance or non-judgementalism.

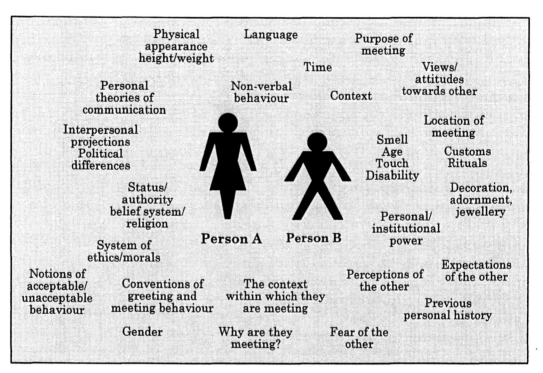

Physical appearance height/weight

Language

Purpose of meeting

Time

Views/ attitudes towards other

Personal theories of communication

Non-verbal behaviour

Context

Interpersonal projections
Political differences

Location of meeting

Smell
Age
Touch
Disability

Customs
Rituals

Status/ authority belief system/ religion

Person A

Person B

Decoration, adornment, jewellery

Personal/ institutional power

System of ethics/morals

Notions of acceptable/ unacceptable behaviour

Conventions of greeting and meeting behaviour

The context within which they are meeting

Perceptions of the other

Expectations of the other

Previous personal history

Gender

Why are they meeting?

Fear of the other

Figure 1: Cultural barriers to communication

The work of Edward T Hall

Edward Hall has written a series of books which are concerned to stimulate the view that in addition to learning other's languages we must also grasp the need for what he calls 'cultural literacy'. Broadly speaking, this is the ability to be sensitive to, and understanding of, the ways of being that are determined by different cultures.

For example, Triandis (1975) relates how an American visitor asked his Greek acquaintance what time they should come to his house for dinner. The Greek villager replied 'anytime'. Now in American usage, apparently, the expression 'anytime' is a non-invitation that people give to appear polite but which they hope will not lead to anything. The Greek, however, actually meant that the American would be welcome any time, because in Greek culture, putting limits on when a guest can come is deemed insulting (Furnham & Bochner, 1986: 206). The consequences of such misunderstandings can lead to the attribution of negative values upon the other person and inevitably contribute towards a deterioration of the relationship. Edward Hall's books are full of anecdotal accounts from all over the world of such breakdowns in communication. Based on this wide experience and knowledge of differences between cultures, he has attempted to construct a set of hypotheses on how cultures differ (Hall, 1959; 1966; 1976 and 1983).

He proposes five major categories of difference between cultures. These propositions are supported by considerable research literature. The categories are space, time, verbal behaviour, non-verbal behaviour and context. These are detailed below.

Space (proxemics)

> *People's feelings about being properly oriented in space runs deep . . . such knowledge is ultimately linked to survival and sanity. To be disoriented in space is to be psychotic.*
>
> (Hall, 1966)

Edward Hall subdivides this category on space into five subsections:

Interpersonal space

Cultures have different conventions about the space between individuals in social situations. For example, people from certain cultures stand and converse at much closer distances than British people. Feelings of discomfort can soon be generated in such circumstances by the person who feels their space is being 'intruded'. However, they are often not fully aware of why they are experiencing such discomfort!

Olfactory space

Cultures have different ways of using the sense of smell. In Middle Eastern countries it can be a way of sensing the other person, whereas in Britain, perfumes and talcum powders are used to screen out natural smells.

Thermal space

The experience of space can be sensed through thermal sensations, e.g. 'feeling hot under the collar' or blushing.

Visual space

We use space visually to gather and convey information.

Sociofugal and sociopetal space

These terms relate to the different ways in which cultures use furniture arrangements and room designs, for example, that either enhance or inhibit interactions between people.

Time

Hall divides time into two broad categories, monochronic and polychronic.

Monochronic time

This refers, in general terms, to the increasingly dominant world view of the 24-hour day in which only that time system for measurement exists, e.g. 'The train leaves at 9.35 a.m.' or 'Come to dinner at 8.00 p.m.'

Polychronic time

This is a much less well-known view of time but is practised by certain cultures. Hall cites the example of the Hopi Indians in the United States who have a belief in each thing, each person as having their own time. This concept is therefore very rooted in an individual's own experiencing.

Beyond those broad divisions, we are also informed of subdivisions of monochronic time that could have enormous implications for the relationships between counsellors and culturally different clients.

Appointment times. If the counsellor sets the appointment for 7.00 p.m., does the client turn up ten minutes before, or 'on the dot', or an hour later? Different cultures have different expectations and practices. 7.00 p.m. does not necessarily mean 7.00 p.m. exactly as determined by monochronic time. Cultural time modifies the precise time indicated, adding or subtracting so much time as is culturally understood and agreed.

Acquaintance time. This is the time considered polite in which to establish acquaintanceship before moving on to the matter that is the purpose of the meeting. This convention might have considerable implications for the counsellor in terms of their behaviour in the early part of an interview.

Discussion time. In business meetings, who is involved, who takes the decisions, how can decisions be taken and when? If we transpose Hall's conception of business meetings into counselling sessions, there are implications as to who makes decisions, the counsellor or the client, and who else is or should be involved in the process (e.g. family and friends, etc.).

Visiting time. How long meetings or social gatherings last is also determined culturally. The counsellor, within their interview rooms, might offer 50-minute sessions. If they were to visit a client in their own accommodation it might be considered more appropriate for the client to determine (culturally) how long they should meet. This aspect has a potential clash of interests now embedded in it.

Time schedules. The creation of time schedules, also, is an area full of difficulty if the persons involved have different cultural origins and, therefore, have different notions of how long things should take.

The term 'chronemics' has been applied to the timing of verbal exchange during conversations. British people normally expect people with whom they are having conversations to respond fairly quickly to their statements. In some other cultures, people time their exchanges to leave silences between each statement. For British people this can be unnerving and leads them to judge the other as shy or inattentive or bored. As a way of coping with this discomfort British people can end up repeating themselves, paraphrasing, talking louder and using other strategies to cope with the apparent silences of the other (silences incidentally that are absolutely appropriate and conventional from their own cultural domain).

Verbal behaviour

This is a much more obvious division between cultures, especially where languages differ. However, even in the case of both participants using the same language, the use of similar words may have different meanings or there will be different conventions for expressing opinion, etc. The capacity to which empathy may be extended to culturally different others may be quite limited.

Also not only what is said but how things are said (paralinguistics) have significantly different meanings for different cultures. Ums, ahs, sighs, grunts, accent, intonation, stress, pitch, are all culturally determined. Similarly, how the information is structured, who manages the conversation and who says what and when, falls within culturally determined conventions.

Non-verbal behaviour

Cultural differences in non-verbal behaviour can be categorised as follows:

Kinesics

These are movements of various parts of the body. Gestures in one country may well be quite inappropriate in another country.

Oculesics

This refers to the use or avoidance of eye-to-eye contact. The British use eye contact as a sign of listening behaviour. Research in the United States has demonstrated that many American black people listened with their ears and looked elsewhere, which proved disconcerting for white speakers who considered they had not been heard! The white Americans were not aware that they listened with their eyes as much as their ears. In many countries there are elaborate patterns of eye avoidance which are often linked to considerations of deferential respect for elders, those in authority and so on.

Haptics (touch)

Where, how and how often people touch each other while conversing are culturally determined patterns of behaviour.

The differences of role, class, and status are also arenas for considerable confusion between cultures because the various signals and cues to infer these positions are often quite invisible to outsiders.

Context

Hall draws broad definitions between what he terms high context and low context cultures. Examples of high context cultures are the Chinese, the Japanese and some Middle Eastern countries. Low context cultures tend to be in the west.

In low context cultures words are presumed to carry all meaning. In some cultures, words and meaning do not have such a direct connection. Notions of truth, consequently, are relative and culturally based. In low context cultures, there is also a tendency towards fragmentation of experience evidenced by the development of all sorts of experts and a proliferation of legalistic documents and contract.

By contrast, high context cultures tend towards conservative, rigid class structures where individual needs are sacrificed to group goals. However, these are cultures in which 'a person's word is their bond'. The context of a meeting carries the meaning, not simply the words used.

The work of Geert Hofstede

The following data represent the outcome of research carried out by Hofstede among employees of subsidiaries of one large US-based multinational corporation in 40 countries around the globe. 116,000 questionnaires were sent to a range of employees, from unskilled workers to top managers. Twenty languages were used in different versions of the questionnaire. This research (1967-73) was cross-referenced with other cross-cultural research studies and statistically significant similarities were achieved.

... Hofstede (1980) defines culture as the collective mental programming of a people in an environment. Culture is thus not a characteristic of individuals; it encompasses a number of people who were conditioned by the same education and life experience.

Hofstede (1980) argues strongly that because culture is characterised through collective mental programming, cultural change may only ever occur with difficulty and will take time. This is explained by the fact that it has become crystallised by the people within the wide variety of institutions and practices they have constructed together. These include educational, legal, governmental, religious, work, social and other organisational settings as well as their scientific theories.

For a set of 40 independent nations Hofstede tried to determine empirically the main criteria by which to judge how their national cultures differed. He found four such criteria, which he labelled dimensions; these were power distance, uncertainty avoidance, individualism/collectivism, and masculinity/femininity. They are described more fully below.

Power distance

The first dimension of cultural difference Hofstede called power distance. It indicates the extent to which a society accepts the fact that power in institutions and organisations is distributed unequally. It is reflected in the values of the less powerful members of society as well as in those of the more powerful ones. A partial picture of these different value assumptions is shown in Figure 2. (There are many more examples in Hofstede, 1980).

Small power distance	Large power distance
Inequality in society should be minimised.	There should be an order of inequality in this world in which everybody has a rightful place; high and low are protected by this order.
Hierarchy means an inequality of roles, established for convenience.	Hierarchy means existential inequality.
The use of power should be legitimate and is subject to the judgement as to whether it is good or evil.	Power is a basic fact of society that antedates good or evil. Its legitimacy is irrelevant.
All should have equal rights.	Power holders are entitled to privileges.

Continued...

The way to change a social system is to redistribute power.	The way to change a social system is to dethrone those in power.
People at various power levels feel less threatened and more prepared to trust people.	Other people are a potential threat to one's power and can rarely be trusted.

Figure 2: The power distance dimension

Uncertainty avoidance

The second dimension, uncertainty avoidance, indicates the extent to which a society feels threatened by uncertain and ambiguous situations and tries to avoid these situations by providing greater career stability, establishing more formal rules, not tolerating deviant ideas and behaviours, and believing in absolute truths and the attainment of expertise.   Nevertheless, societies in which uncertainty avoidance is strong are also characterised by a higher level of anxiety and aggressiveness that creates, among other things, a stronger inner urge in people to work hard (see Figure 3).

Weak uncertainty avoidance	*Strong uncertainty avoidance*
The uncertainty inherent in life is more easily accepted and each day is taken as it comes.	The uncertainty inherent in life is felt as a continuous threat that must be fought.
Ease and lower stress are experienced.	Higher anxiety and stress are experienced.
Aggressive behaviour is frowned upon.	Aggressive behaviour of self and others is accepted.
Less showing of emotions is preferred.	More showing of emotions is preferred.
There is more willingness to take risks in life.	There is great concern with security in life.
The accent is on relativism, empiricism.	The search is for ultimate, absolute truths and values.
If rules cannot be kept, we should change them.	If rules cannot be kept, we are sinners and should repent.

Figure 3: The uncertainty avoidance dimension

Individualism/collectivism

The third dimension encompasses individualism and its opposite, collectivism. Individualism implies a loosely knit social framework in which people are supposed to take care of themselves and their immediate families only, while collectivism is characterised by a tight social framework in which people distinguish between in-groups and out-groups; they expect their in-group (relatives, clan, organisations) to look after them, and in exchange for that they feel they owe absolute loyalty to it. A fuller picture of this dimension is presented in Figure 4.

Collectivist	Individualist
In society, people are born into extended families or clans who protect them in exchange for loyalty.	In society, everybody is supposed to take care of him/herself and his/her immediate family.
'We' consciousness holds sway.	'I' consciousness holds sway.
Identity is based in the social system.	Identity is based in the individual.
There is emotional dependence of individuals on organisations and institutions.	There is emotional independence of the individual from organisations.
Belief is placed in group decisions.	Belief is placed in individual decisions.
Value standards differ for in-groups and out-groups (particularism).	Value standards should apply to all (universalism).

Figure 4: The individualism/collectivism dimension

Masculinity/femininity

Measurements in terms of this dimension express the extent to which the dominant values in society are 'masculine', that is, whether they show assertiveness and approve of the acquisition of money and things, in contrast to 'feminine' values of caring for others and showing concern for the quality of life or people. The former values were labelled 'masculine' because, within nearly all societies, men scored higher in terms of the values' positive sense (for example, they were more assertive than women), even though the society as a whole might veer towards the 'feminine' pole. Interestingly, the more an entire society scored to the masculine side, the wider the gap between its men's and women's values (see Figure 5).

Feminine	Masculine
Men need not be assertive, but can also assume nurturing roles.	Men should be assertive. Women should be nurturing.
Sex roles in society are more fluid.	Sex roles in society are clearly differentiated.
Quality of life is important.	Performance is what counts.
You work in order to live.	You live in order to work.
People and environment are important.	Money and things are important.
Interdependence is the ideal.	Independence is the ideal.

Figure 5: The masculinity/femininity dimension

... Hofstede's work has been immensely influential in the field of international management but, as yet, it seems not to have filtered into this particular discipline. Counsellors who are actively engaged in transcultural work might be assisted immensely in their attempts at understanding specific clients through consulting Hofstede's original work. The graphic representation of culturally determined values that depict the relative positions between one culture and another, provide a unique and readily accessible mechanism for hypothesising the potential value differences that lie between the counsellor and their client.

Nevertheless, this material, however useful, must also be used cautiously: ... these ideas are generalised findings gleaned from wide research. They, therefore, cannot be attributed, unthinkingly, to every particular client, or indeed counsellor.

The above work, then, may be used most appropriately as a further background information source to assist the counsellor in their task. However these models must not be used as diagnostic or predictive tools. They can support an overall attempt at understanding but they cannot replace the moment to moment, attentive counselling relationship that is focused upon each client's specific and unique difficulties...

Summing up

On the one hand we believe strongly that all forms of counselling are cross cultural, that cultural issues need to be seen as central to cross-cultural counselling (not ancillary) and that by focusing just on ethnic minority issues, we may be 'ghettoising' the problem. Yet, we believe that multicultural counselling is a speciality area as well. Although all of us are racial, ethnic and cultural beings, belonging to a particular group does not endow a person with the competencies and skills necessary to be a culturally skilled counsellor.

(Sue *et al.* 1992: 478)

This chapter has offered a very wide range of ideas concerning cultural differences in behaviour. This considerable range of information has deliberately been included to demonstrate the enormous extent of the potential behavioural differences that could occur between counsellors and their culturally different clients.

In Britain, for example counsellors working with recently arrived nationals from other countries (refugees, international students, victims of torture, asylum seekers, international business persons etc.) may find this information extremely useful and applicable.

Where counsellors are meeting clients who have lived in the dominant culture a significant proportion of their lives (or indeed all of them) yet have culturally different origins, then the subtleties of cultural identity and behaviour might become more obscure. Indeed, such clients may be biculturally competent and feel very comfortable operating out of both sets of cultural assumptions (those of the dominant culture and those of their own root culture). On the other hand, phenomena may occur in the interview that are confusing and misleading to both parties, and the counsellor might profitably gain from trying to understand these as cultural phenomena in action.

Counsellors must also be aware that cultural differences, however useful as a way of contributing understanding to interpersonal dialogue, can be used to conceal from the counsellor their own prejudiced and racist tendencies.

References

Becker HS & Gear B (1960) 'Latent culture: a note on the theory of latent social roles' *Administrative Science Quarterly* 5: 304–13

Furnham A & Bochner S (1986) *Culture shock: psychological reactions to unfamiliar environments* London: Methuen

Hall ET (1959) *The silent language* New York: Anchor Press/Doubleday

Hall ET (1966) *The hidden dimension* New York: Anchor Press/Doubleday

Hall ET (1976) *Beyond culture* New York: Anchor Press/Doubleday

Hall ET (1983) *The dance of life* New York: Anchor Press/Doubleday

Hofstede G (1980) *Cultures, consequences: international differences in work-related values* Beverly Hills CA: Sage

Rogers CR (1987) *Client-centred therapy* London: Constable

Sue DW, Arrendondo P & McDavis RJ (1992) 'Multicultural counselling competencies and standards: a call to the profession' *Journal of Counselling and Development* March/April 70, 477–86

Triandis (1975) 'Culture training, cognitive complexity and interpersonal attitudes' in RW Brislin, S. Bocher & WJ Lonner (eds) *Cross cultural perspectives on learning* New York: Wiley

6. Cultural Systems: Teacher-Student and Student-Student Interaction

Paul Pederson

The four cultural dimensions in Hofstede's model describe patterns of preference... The practical implications of each cultural tendency are indicated by Hofstede (1986: 312–314 Figures 5.2–5.4) as they might apply to the educational setting.

Although no individual or group can fairly be labeled by one or another extreme on the four dimensions, individuals will construct their own identity about self and cultural relationships, incorporating and combining responses similar to these lists of preferences.

Differences in Teacher-Student and Student-Student Interaction Related to the Power Distance Dimension

Small Power Distance Societies	*Large Power Distance Societies*
• Stress on impersonal 'truth' that can in principle be obtained from any competent person	• Stress on personal 'wisdom' that is transferred in the relationship with a particular teacher (guru)
• A teacher should respect the independence of his or her students	• A teacher merits the respect of his or her students
• Student-centered education (premium on initiative)	• Teacher-centered education (premium on order)
• Teacher expects students to initiate communication	• Students expect teacher to initiative communication
• Teacher expects students to find their own paths	• Students expect teacher to outline paths to follow
• Students may speak up spontaneously in class	• Students speak up in class only when invited by the teacher
• Students allowed to contradict or criticize teacher	• Teacher is never contradicted or publicly criticized
• Effectiveness of learning related to amount of two-way communication in class	• Effectiveness of learning is related to excellence of the teacher
• Outside class, teachers are treated as equals	• Respect for teachers is also shown outside class
• In teacher-student conflicts, parents are expected to side with the student	• In teacher-student conflicts, parents are expected to side with the teacher
• Younger teachers are more liked than older teachers	• Older teachers are more respected than younger teachers

Note: In contrasting small power distance societies with large power distance societies, it is useful to consider the importance of power relationships in counseling across cultures. The importance of power relationships across cultures has already been identified. It is important to recognize that an equal distribution of power is preferred in some but not all cultures and that other cultures are quite comfortable with an unequal distribution of power.

Differences in teacher-student and student-student interaction
related to the power distance dimension.

Differences in Teacher-Student and Student-Student Interaction Related to the Uncertainty Avoidance Dimension

Weak Uncertainty Avoidance Societies	*Strong Uncertainty Avoidance Societies*
• Students feel comfortable in unstructured learning situations; vague objectives, broad assignments, no timetables	• Students feel comfortable in structured learning situations; precise objectives, detailed assignments, strict timetables
• Teachers are allowed to say 'I don't know'	• Teachers are expected to have all the answers
• A good teacher uses plain language	• A good teacher uses academic language
• Students are rewarded for innovative approaches to problem solving	• Students are rewarded for accuracy in problem solving
• Teachers are expected to suppress emotions (and so are students)	• Teachers are allowed to behave emotionally (and so are students)
• Teachers interpret intellectual disagreement as a stimulating exercise	• Teachers interpret intellectual disagreement as personal disloyalty
• Teachers seek parents' ideas	• Teachers consider themselves experts who cannot learn anything from lay parents and parents agree

Note. In contrasting weak uncertainty avoidance societies with alternatives, it is important to recognise that some cultures appreciate and function well in a highly structured setting whereas others require more spontaneity. The counselor will need to function differently in these two contrasting cultural settings, applying more or less structure appropriately.

Differences in teacher-student and student-student interaction related to the uncertainty avoidance dimension.

Differences in Teacher-Student and Student-Student Interaction Related to the Individualism Versus Collectivism Dimension

Collectivist Societies	*Individualist Societies*
• Positive association in society with whatever is rooted in tradition	• Positive association in society with whatever is 'new'
• The young should learn; adults cannot accept student role	• One is never too old to learn; 'permanent education'
• Students expect to learn how to do	• Students expect to learn how to learn
• Individual students will only speak up in class when called on personally by the teacher	• Individual students will speak up in class in response to a general invitation by the teacher
• Individuals will only speak up in small groups	• Individuals will speak up in large groups
• Large classes split socially into smaller, cohesive subgroups based on particularist criteria (e.g. ethnic affiliation)	• Subgroups in class vary from one situation to the next based on universalist criteria (e.g. the task 'at hand')
• Formal harmony in learning situations should be maintained at all times (T-groups are taboo)	• Confrontation in learning situations can be salutary; conflicts can be brought into the open
• Neither the teacher nor any student should ever be made to lose face	• Face-consciousness is weak

Continued...

Collectivist Societies	*Individualist Societies*
• Education is a way of gaining prestige in one's social environment and of joining a higher status group ('a ticket to a ride')	• Education is a way of improving one's economic worth and self-respect based on ability and competence
• Diploma certificates are important and displayed on walls	• Diploma certificates have little symbolic value
• Acquiring certificates, even through illegal means (cheating, corruption), is more important than acquiring competence	• Acquiring competence is more important than acquiring certificates
• Teachers are expected to give preferential treatment to students (e.g. based on ethnic affiliation or recommendation by an influential person)	• Teachers are expected to be strictly impartial

Note. In contrasting the collectivist societies with the individualist societies, we are examining the differences between the United States and Third World countries. Individualism has an important function in the theory and practice of counseling. It is useful to identify the specific ways in which a collectivistic and contrasting perspective may construct quite a different reality in which to live.

Differences in teacher-student and student-student interaction related to the individualism versus collectivism dimension.

Differences in Teacher-Student and Student-Student Interaction Related to the Masculinity Versus Femininity Dimension

Feminine Societies	*Masculine Societies*
• Teachers avoid openly praising students	• Teachers openly praise good students
• Teachers use average student as the norm	• Teachers use best students as the norm
• System rewards students' social adaptation	• System rewards students' academic performance
• A student's failure in school is a relatively minor accident	• A student's failure in school is a severe blow to his or her self-image and may in extreme cases lead to suicide
• Students admire friendliness in teachers	• Students admire brilliance in teachers
• Students practice mutual solidarity	• Students compete with each other in class
• Students try to behave modestly	• Students try to make themselves visible
• Corporal punishment severely rejected	• Corporal punishment occasionally considered salutary
• Students choose academic subjects in view of intrinsic interest	• Students choose academic subjects in view of career opportunities
• Male students may choose traditionally feminine academic subjects	• Male students avoid traditionally feminine academic subjects

Note. In contrasting the societies displaying characteristics more traditionally associated with a feminine role from those societies traditionally associated with a masculine role, it is important to suspend value judgments. This dimension is perhaps the most controversial of the four dimensions and to the extent that one seems more natural the opposite extreme may seem less appropriate.

Differences in teacher-student and student-student interaction related to the masculinity versus femininity dimension.

A personal-cultural orientation

Rather than labeling persons according to their culture, it might be more functionally useful to understand the ways that different cultural influences lead individuals to behave in a particular way through constructing a personal-cultural orientation toward the situation or event. Accuracy in assessment and interpretation requires that we understand each person's behavior in the sociocultural context in which that behavior occurred. Behaviors are frequently interpreted and changed without regard to their sociocultural context, resulting in misattribution and inaccurate data. Perhaps the most important reason for understanding a person's cultural context is to facilitate accuracy in the assessment and interpretation of a person's behavior...

It seems clear that culture is not an external force but an internalized perspective of reality as we know it.

Reference

Hofstede G (1986) 'Cultural differences in teaching and learning' *International Journal of Intercultural Relations* 10, pp301–320

7.   Men and Women Talking

Deborah Tannen

When is sexism realism?

Many work settings, just like families, come with ready-made roles prescribed by gender, and the ones women are expected to fill are typically support roles. It was not long ago when medical offices and hospitals were peopled by men who were doctors and orderlies and women who were nurses and clerical workers, just as most offices were composed of men who ran the business and women who served them as receptionists, clerks, and secretaries. All members of Congress were men, and women found in the Capitol Building were aides and staff members. When a woman or man enters a setting in an atypical role, that expectation is always a backdrop to the scene.

All the freshmen [sic] women in Congress have had to contend with being mistaken for staff, even though they wear pins on their lapels identifying them as members. For her book *A Woman's Place*, Congresswoman Marjorie Margolies-Mezvinsky interviewed her female colleagues about their experiences. One congresswoman approached a security checkpoint with two congressmen when a guard stopped only her and told her to go through the metal detector. When Congresswoman Maria Cantwell needed to get into her office after hours, the guard wanted to know which member she worked for. But her press secretary, Larry West, has gone through the gate unthinkingly without being stopped. When Congresswoman Lynn Schenk attended a reception with a male aide, the host graciously held out his hand to the aide and said, 'Oh, Congressman Schenk.'

You don't have to be in Congress to have experiences like that. A woman who owned her own business found that if she took any man along on business trips, regardless of whether he was her vice president or her assistant, people she met tended to address themselves to him, certain that he must be the one with power and she his helper. A double-bass player had a similar experience when she arrived for an audition with a male accompanist. The people who greeted them assumed she was the accompanist. A woman who heads a research firm and holds a doctorate finds she is frequently addressed as 'Mrs', while her assistant, who holds only a master's degree, is addressed as 'Dr'.

One evening after hours, I was working in my office at Georgetown University. Faculty offices in my building are lined up on both sides of a corridor, with cubicles in the corridor for secretaries and graduate-student assistants. Outside each office is a nameplate with the professor's title and last name. The quiet of the after-hours corridor was interrupted when a woman came to my door and asked if she could use my phone. I was surprised but glad to oblige, and explained that she had to dial '9'. She made the call, thanked me, and left. A few minutes later, she reappeared and asked if I had any correction fluid. Again surprised, but still happy to be of help, I looked in my desk drawer but had to disappoint her. Since my typewriter was self-correcting, I had none. My patience began to waver, but my puzzlement was banished when the woman bounded into my office for the third and final time to ask if I was Dr. Murphy's secretary, in which case she would like to leave with me the paper she was turning in to him.

I doubt this woman would have imposed on my time and space to use my telephone and borrow correction fluid if she had known I was a professor, even though I would not have minded had she done so. At least she would probably have been more deferential in intruding. And the experience certainly gave me a taste of how hard it must be for receptionists to get any work done, as everyone regards them as perpetually interruptible. But what amused and amazed me was that my being female had overridden so many clues to my position: my office was along the wall, it was fully enclosed like all faculty offices, my name and title were on the door, and I was working after five, the hour when offices close and secretaries go home. But all these clues were nothing next to the master clue of gender. In the university environment, she expected that professors were men and women were secretaries. Statistics were on her side: of the eighteen members of my department at the time, sixteen were men; of the five members of Dr. Murphy's department, four were men. So she was simply trusting the world to be as she knew it was.

It is not particularly ironic or surprising that the student who mistook me for a secretary was female. Women are no less prone to assume that people will adhere to the norm than are men. And this includes women who themselves are exceptions. A woman physician who works in a specialty in which few of her colleagues are female told me of her annoyance when she telephones a colleague, identifies herself as 'Dr Jones calling for Dr. Smith,' and is told by Dr Smith's receptionist, 'I'll go get Dr Smith while you put Dr Jones on the line.' But this same woman catches herself referring to her patients' general practitioners as 'he', even though she ought to know better than anyone that a physician could be a woman.

Children seem to pick up norms as surely as adults do. A woman who was not only a doctor but a professor at a medical. school was surprised when her five-year-old said to her, 'You're not a doctor, Mommy. You're a nurse.' Intent on impressing her daughter, she said, 'Yes, I am a doctor. In fact, I teach other doctors how to be doctors.' The little girl thought about this as she incorporated the knowledge into her worldview. 'Oh,' she said. 'But you only teach women doctors.' (Conversely, male nurses must deal with being mistaken for doctors, and men who work as assistants must deal with being mistaken for their boss.)

Another of my favorite stories in this mode is about my colleague who made a plane reservation for herself and replied to the question 'Is that Mrs or Miss?' by giving her title: 'It's Dr.' So the agent asked, 'Will the doctor be needing a rental car when he arrives?' Her attempt to reframe her answer to avoid revealing her marital status resulted in the agent reframing her as a secretary.

So long as women are a minority of professional ranks, we cannot be surprised if people assume the world is as it is. I mention these stories to give a sense of what the world is like for people who are exceptions to expectations – every moment they live in the unexpected role, they must struggle against others' assumptions that do not apply to them, much like gay men and lesbians with regard to their sexual orientation, and, as Ellis Cose documents in his book *The Rage of a Privileged Class,* much like middle-class black professionals in most American settings.

One particular burden of this pattern for a woman in a position of authority is that she must deal with incursions on her time, as others make automatic assumptions that her time is more expendable, although she also may benefit from hearing more information because people find her 'approachable'. There is a sense in which every woman is seen as a receptionist – available to give information and help, perennially interruptible. A woman surgeon complained that although she has very good relations with the nurses in her hospital, they simply do not wait on her the way they wait on her male colleagues. (The very fact that I must say 'woman surgeon' and 'male nurse' reflects this dilemma. All surgeons are presumed male, all nurses presumed female, unless proven otherwise. In other words, the unmarked surgeon is male, the unmarked nurse female.)

Expect the expected

We approach new perceptions by measuring them against our past experience. This is a necessary process that makes it possible for us to get through life without regarding each incoming perception as brand-new. It works very well when the world we encounter is behaving as the world has done in the past but leads us astray when the world is new. And right now, we are all learning to deal with a world that is changing much faster than our expectations can keep up with.

What I am getting at is that there is no point in blaming those who expect the world to continue as it has been in the past, but we should not let anyone off the hook either – including ourselves. We must continually remind ourselves that the world is changing, and women and men no longer can be depended upon to stay in the narrowly prescribed roles we were consigned to in the past. But we must also be on guard for signs that such expectations are getting in our way. One of the major ways that expectations impede us is in the strong associations we have of how women and men should speak and behave. With women entering situations that were previously all male, where established norms for behavior are based on the ways men behaved in those roles, expectations must give way – either expectations for how someone in that role should behave, or expectations of the women who move into those roles. Which will it be? Will women change their ways of talking to fit existing norms, or will they change the norms – establish new expectations for the roles they come to fill?

'Your style or mine?'

There is a mountain of research attesting that when females and males get together in groups, the females are more likely to change their styles to adapt to the presence of males – whether they are adults or children. Psychologist Eleanor Maccoby cites studies by Linda Carli and by Judith Hall and Karen Braunwald showing that when women are with men, they become more like men: they raise their voices, interrupt, and otherwise become more assertive. But, Maccoby continues,

> there is also evidence that they carry over some of their well-practiced female-style behaviors, sometimes in exaggerated form. Women may wait for a turn to speak that does not come, and thus they may end up talking less than they would in a women's group. They smile more than the men do, agree more often with what others have said, and give nonverbal signals of attentiveness to what others – perhaps especially the men – are saying (Duncan & Fiske, 1977). In some writings this female behavior has been referred to as 'silent applause'.

Psychologist Campbell Leaper observed girls' tendency to adapt to boys' styles in his study of 138 children playing in pairs at the ages of five and seven. Although 'collaborative' speech accounted for the majority of all the children's speech, whether or not they were talking to other children of the same sex, there were nonetheless differences in degree. He found collaborative and cooperative exchanges to be more frequent when girls played with girls, and controlling and domineering exchanges more frequent when boys played with boys, especially when the children were older. Boys were less likely than girls to adopt strategies typical of the other sex when they played co-ed. When girls played with boys, they used more controlling speech than when they played with girls. Leaper suspects this occurred because the boys tended to ignore the girls' polite speech. Again, we get a glimpse of the ritual nature of conversation. The girls' strategies worked best when used with other girls who shared the same strategies. When they used these strategies with boys, they didn't work as well, so the girls had to adapt to the boys' style to get results.

The tendency of women to adapt their styles to men's has been found even on the most small-scale and personal level. Donna Johnson and Duane Roen examined peer-review letters written by graduate students to fellow students whose term papers they had evaluated. The results showed that women students used slightly more positive evaluation terms, such as 'interesting' and 'helpful', than the men, but the most striking finding was that the women offered positive evaluation terms far more frequently *to other women* than they did to men, whereas the men offered only slightly more such terms to women than to other men. In other words, the women adjusted more in response to whether they were addressing another woman or a man. (An indirect result of this pattern was that men received the least praise, whether they were talking to other men or to women)…

The unfairness of unstructured groups

Elizabeth Sommers and Sandra Lawrence were interested in investigating the benefits of the wonderful-sounding 'cooperative learning', by which students in composition classes meet in small groups to respond to each other's writing. Sommers & Lawrence studied the talk that went on among the students in the composition classes they taught, but since the two of them had different teaching styles, the results of the group process were different for their students. One teacher gave her students explicit instructions about how to structure their discussion, whereas the other teacher allowed the students to determine their own structure. I think many Americans would feel that allowing group members to determine the structure of their own groups is preferable; it seems more democratic, less authoritarian. Ironically, though, women fared better in the 'teacher-directed' groups, in which females and males participated almost equally. In the student-directed groups, females made 17% fewer comments and took 25% fewer turns.

Sommers & Lawrence show how this happened. When the structure was prescribed, each student spoke in turn, while the others remained silent. Free discussion followed only if time remained after each student had taken a turn. In other words, the opportunity to speak was handed to each student. In this structure, the young women took their turns just as the young men did, showing that they had things to say and were willing to say them. In contrast, in the free-wheeling discussions of the other groups, speakers had to get the floor for themselves in order to speak. In this situation, the young women 'tended to acquiesce more, to be interrupted more, and to initiate less.' Whereas the young men in these groups interrupted each other as well, they were more likely to persist in the face of those interruptions until they made their points, whereas the young women usually just backed off and gave up when their attempts to speak were met with interruptions...

Simply counting up how much individuals speak does not tell much about group dynamics at a meeting. What each person says is just as important, if not more. Sommers & Lawrence examined the contributions of a woman, Meredith, who was the only female in a group of four students in a composition class. Not only did she make few comments, but when she did speak, she spent most of her time affirming the three men in the group. She agreed with their observations, reassured the writer, and remarked on the process of group interaction or the process of writing. Half her turns were agreements. For example, when Bob said, 'You just got to . . . elaborate more on it,' Meredith said, 'Yeah, I mean, you need to elaborate.' There were also times that Bob echoed Meredith's words, to reassure the writer:

> Meredith: It wasn't *bad*.
> Bob: It wasn't . . . no . . .
> Meredith: It wasn't bad.
> Bob: I really liked the conclusion.

Meredith's own comments were often interrupted or drowned out. Six times she tried to make a contribution but backed off when interrupted:

> I think . . .
> . . . The change . . . should . . .
> Cause . . . cause . . .
> . . . Cause right on that account . . .
> . . . Or else you will be . . .
> Yeah, I . . .

Again, it would be easy to blame the young men in Meredith's group for interrupting or even 'silencing' her. Clearly, they did that. But the process by which interruption occurs is very complex. Like everything else that happens in interaction, it is the doing of two people, not one. For an interruption to occur, one person has to start speaking and another has to stop. Sommers & Lawrence observe that the young men in their study also interrupt each other. When interrupted, they continued to try to speak until they got their ideas out. But Meredith gave up five out of the six times she was interrupted.

I do not know if her fellow students interrupted Meredith in the same way that they interrupted each other. (Studies have shown more *attempts* to interrupt women than men.) And Sommers & Lawrence point out that even when Meredith persisted, her voice was drowned out by the others', as it was the highest in pitch and the lowest in volume. Whether or not Meredith's own way of speaking played a part in her not speaking equally, it is clear that she did not have an equal opportunity to speak.

Another, quite similar, example comes from a colleague who wrote to ask my advice about how to avoid just such a pattern in his own classes, also apparently resulting from his nonauthoritarian teaching style. He wrote to me after the class was over, but he wanted to avoid anything like this happening in the future. He explained that the students in his graduate class divided into two groups, to analyze a linguistic phenomenon in two languages.

> About half the class chose analyzing French and half worked on Spanish. Richard, the only man in the class, got in the French group. He almost immediately took over and would ask me to announce that the group was meeting after class, or even for time during class when he could take the French group aside. One time they went out in the hall, and when they came back, some of the women in the group were making wry jokes about 'executive decisions'.

> At the end of the term, they were doing course evaluations, so I left for ten minutes. On the way back, I was stopped in the hall for questions from two students who were working on Spanish. While I was talking to one of them, one of the women in the French group burst out of the room and walked past us looking straight ahead with a grim look on her face. The student I was talking to said, 'She seems disgusted.' When I went into the room, there was Richard, up at the board expounding while the women in the group sat in a little circle around him.

My colleague commented, 'I think my natural inclination just to let people alone might not have been the right thing this time.'

A similar irony emerged in the companies where I observed. For example, one manager, a woman, typically ran meetings by throwing major decisions back on the group. In a highly democratic way, she asked her team, 'Where should we go from here?' But in a somewhat undemocratic way, this opportunity tended to be seized by two of the eight team members, both men who habitually spoke up and hence disproportionately determined the direction the group would take.

'How did I get here?'

An important point to keep in mind is that the men who end up taking over do not necessarily want or exult in that role (although they may). I had the privilege to glimpse the feelings of a young man who apparently did not enjoy the role he took. I had asked the students to keep notebooks in which they commented on their own experiences and observations communicating with others, as well as their analyses of them, and to hand them in at the end of the term. This articulate young man wrote about his reaction to finding himself caught in the pattern I have just described. He was a student in a very large undergraduate class I taught on cross-cultural communication. Since there were nearly eighty students in the class, I frequently divided them into smaller groups of four or five and asked them to discuss topics in their groups and then designate one member to synthesize the group discussion for the entire class. There were far more women in the class than men, so most small groups had only one man in them, if any. Yet just about without fail, when it came time to present small-group findings to the class, each group that included a man had chosen the man to stand up and be the spokesperson. This is what the young man wrote in his notebook:

> We worked in small groups today, and for the second time out ... I ended up being the spokesperson for the group. And I find this bizarre. I don't 'like' being the spokesperson – or so I say. So if I'm exuding 'not wanna do the synthesis,' how come I seem so perfect to be elected for the task. Maybe it's by default; no one else wants to. I don't think I buy this. Oh, well, that's all fairly immaterial anyway.

It is anything but immaterial, to those of us who want to understand what goes on when women and men get together in groups. Why was this young man repeatedly chosen against his conscious will? What I find most interesting is that he himself didn't know how it happened – and wasn't especially pleased that it did. This is how he described the experience:

> I also wonder why I feel relatively calm in a small group. I feel like I'm myself, like I'm a personality. But when I tell the class about the small-group discussion, I feel like an abstraction.

I love this description of the alienation of speaking to a large, faceless crowd, not knowing how they are responding – and how different it is from speaking in the small group in which this young man said he felt quite comfortable. And it is interesting to me that even though he ended up being the one to address the group, he did not feel comfortable doing it.

This young man's experience is useful to bear in mind, to remember that if you are not happy with the role taken by someone else in an interaction, it is not necessarily the case that the other person is happy with that role or necessarily set out to take it.

The joy of free-for-all styles

Another researcher, Carole Edelsky, poses the question: *'Under what conditions* do men and women interact ... more or less as equals and under what conditions do they not?' Sommers & Lawrence's research provides a partial answer. When the floor is handed to participants in turn, women and men are more likely to interact as equals. Another partial answer is provided by Edelsky in her own study of talk at meetings.

Edelsky taped and analyzed five complete meetings of a standing university department faculty committee composed of seven women (of which she was one) and four men. When she set out to measure how much women and men spoke at the meetings, she realized that the meetings broke into two different types of interactions. At times, interaction followed what one thinks of as meeting structure. One person spoke while others listened or responded. But there were times when the nature of interaction was quite different: they seemed like 'free-for-alls' in which several people talked at once or seemed to be 'on the same wavelength'. In order to answer the question of who talked more, she first had to ask which type of interaction was going on. She found that men took more and longer turns and did more joking, arguing, directing, and soliciting of responses during the more structured segments of meetings. During the 'free-for-all' parts of the meetings, women and men talked equally, and women joked, argued, directed, and solicited responses more than men. In these parts of the meeting, no one person held the floor while others sat silently listening. Instead, several voices were going at once as people either talked over each other or talked to their neighbors at the same time that other parallel conversations were going on.

This is a very different lack of structure than that of the self-structuring student writing groups, where one person at a time held the floor, but the group determined for itself who would get it. Although the question of why women talked more in the free-for-all parts of meetings is outside of Edelsky's focus in her study, I think it may be that those parts of the meetings are more like the interactional style to which many women have become accustomed in same-sex conversations.

At many different companies where I observed or taped, there happened to be meetings made up of women only. At all these meetings, there were more 'multiple floors', more laughing, teasing, and overlapped speech than I observed in meetings where most or all of the participants were men. A university professor wrote to me about her experience at meetings in her university. She said that she found university-wide meetings difficult, but department meetings pleasurable. In fact, she wrote: 'the most enjoyable conversations seem to be those characterized by a lot of interruption and overlapping; lack of interruption seemed to be characteristic of conversations I would characterize as stilted and uncomfortable.' Two major distinctions seem to be how large the meeting is, and whether or not the people taking part in the meeting 'are all fairly comfortable socially with one another' – which is the case for her with her immediate colleagues.

Shifting alignments

Individuals' participation in groups can change according to context and over time. One woman reported a transformation of her status over a year in an organization. At the beginning, she would make contributions at meetings and see them passed over. Occasionally, they were picked up and attributed to others. But by the end of the year, the tables had turned. She was taking part in a meeting at which a man made a comment that she thought very important, but it was ignored. So she repeated it, giving full credit to him. The group then listened to it and took it up, referring to it thereafter as her idea.

This suggests that it is not only the fact that an idea is picked up by a man that makes it listened to, but simply the fact that it is picked up. If a number of individuals agree to pick up and repeat each other's ideas at meetings, they may be able to increase the impact of all their contributions.

Those who speak up in one setting are not necessarily talkative in others. Although gender is only one of a range of influences on conversational style, the differing socialization patterns of boys and girls makes meetings a very different environment for most men and women. As previously mentioned, there has been a great deal of research by psychologists, anthropologists, and sociologists on how children speak and interact in their peer groups. I have summarized these differing styles as 'report talk' versus 'rapport talk'. Meetings are often a paradigm case of 'report talk', and therefore situations in which many men feel more comfortable speaking up than many women. In other words, the ways many men have learned to speak in a group – trying to take and keep center stage – better prepare them for talking at meetings.

It is crucial to bear in mind that not all boys excel at these skills. Since boys' groups are made up of high- and low-status boys, those who are able to hold center stage and those who can't, not all boys do well as children and not all men are comfortable or successful at getting heard at meetings. In her study of students working on a science problem in small groups, Jacqueline Madhok found that in the all-male groups there was a wide range of participation. Some boys talked a lot, while others talked very little. Recall too that Maccoby observed more passive behavior when boys played together in pairs than when girls did. But their socialization patterns as children gave men a better crack at learning the skills that are rewarded in this setting, and some men learned them well.

The skills girls are more likely to have learned, such as linking one's comments to those of others, waiting to be recognized rather than speaking out, making suggestions rather than demands, supporting others' remarks rather than making all one's comments sound original, are very constructive when everyone at the meeting is observing those rituals. But they may not help a speaker stand out – or even get the floor – at a meeting. And there are good reasons why speaking up and being the center of attention in a group, especially a group that includes men, is a more difficult and complicated matter for women, since so much of their socialization has taught them *not* to attract attention. All these patterns make meetings more congenial for more men than women.

A pilot study

I have observed many of these dynamics at work in my own classes. One year, my graduate class in analyzing conversation had twenty students, eleven women and nine men. Of the nine men, four were foreign students: two Japanese, one Chinese, and one Syrian. With the exception of the four Asian men, all the men spoke in class at least occasionally. The biggest talker was a woman, but there were also five women who never spoke in class at all, only one of whom was Japanese. I decided to do something to examine and restructure patterns of participation.

I divided the class into small groups to discuss the issues raised in the readings and to analyze transcripts of conversation they had recorded. I had often used the small-group format in my teaching, but in the past I had simply told class members to count off, or to form groups with those around them. This time I devised in advance three ways of dividing the students into groups: one by the degree program they were in, one by gender, and one by conversational style. In attempting to group the students by conversational style, I put Asian students together, big talkers together, and quiet students together. The class split into groups six times during the semester, so they met in each grouping twice. I told students to regard the groups as examples of discourse, and to note the different ways they interacted in the different groups. Toward the end of the term, I gave them a questionnaire asking about their participation in the groups and in class.

I could plainly see from my own observation that women who never opened their mouths in class were talking away in the small groups. In fact, the Japanese woman commented on her questionnaire that she found it hard to contribute to the all-woman group because 'I was overwhelmed by how talkative the female students were in the female-only group. So I couldn't say much.' These were the same female students who never spoke in class. To add to the irony, one of the Asian men commented that the Japanese woman had been too talkative in the all-Asian group. This example is particularly important because it shows that the same person who can be 'oppressed' into silence in one context can become the verbose 'oppressor' in another. No one's conversational style is absolute; everyone's style changes in response to the context and the styles of the others in the group.

In answer to my questions, some of the students said they preferred the same-gender groups; others preferred the same-style groups. (No one preferred the grouping according to degree program.) And it was not only the quiet speakers who could feel 'silenced'. One woman said that when she was in a group with quiet students, she felt she had to hold herself back so as not to dominate.

Another striking outcome of this study was that, on the whole, the women in the class were more dissatisfied with their participation. In answer to the question 'Would you have liked to speak in class more than you did?' six of the seven who said yes were women; the one man was Japanese. Most startlingly, this response did not come only from quiet women; it came from women at every level of class participation and included women who had indicated they had spoken in class never, rarely, sometimes, and often. Even the woman who had talked the most of anyone in the class said that she would have liked to talk more. Of the eleven students who said the amount they had spoken was fine, seven were men. Of the four women who checked 'fine', two added qualifications indicating it wasn't completely fine. One wrote 'maybe more', and one wrote, 'I have an urge to participate but often feel I should have something more interesting/relevant/wonderful/intelligent to say!!' In other words, of the eleven women in the class, nine indicated that they would have liked to talk more than they did.

The experience of separating into groups, and of talking about patterns of participation, raised everyone's awareness about classroom participation. After we had talked about it, some of the quietest women in the class made a few voluntary contributions, though sometimes I had to ensure their participation by interrupting the students who were exuberantly speaking out to recognize someone sitting silently with her hand raised. I believe both of these procedures could be useful in a work setting. Discussing how people feel about their participation in meetings can raise everyone's awareness and make it easier for some individuals to speak up, for others to speak less, and for the person running the meeting to elicit participation from some who otherwise might not say what is on their minds. These different ethics of participation are opaque to others, so those who speak freely assume that those who remain silent have nothing to say, and those who are reining themselves in assume that the big talkers are selfish and hoggish. It may come as a surprise to some that quiet group members have something to say, and it may come as a surprise to others that the big talkers want to hear what they have to say.

Getting heard

What can be done to ensure that people with varying conversational styles, including both women and men, are heard at meetings, and that companies take advantage of and recognize the contributions of all their employees? One strategy would be for quiet people to change their styles, becoming more aggressive about talking up their own ideas. This will work for some. But it may be unpleasant to others and may go against their notions of being a good team member – or a good person. And the results will not always be positive. The most important point is for managers to become skilled at observing group process and noticing the role that each group member takes. It is their job to notice, as in fact the leader of the focus-group I discussed did, that the ideas that found their way into the report originated with one employee and were picked up by another.

Another possibility for those who lead meetings is to devote a portion of the meeting to going around the table and inviting all those present to express their thoughts in turn. There are drawbacks to this procedure, though. For one thing, those who speak first are likely to influence the ones who follow. Anyone planning to make comments that seem to go against what every preceding speaker has said may well decide upon a different course before speaking. And, again, once someone of high status has expressed an opinion, it may be less likely that others will express dissenting views. A way to correct for that would be to invite individuals to submit their opinions in writing either before or at the meeting, so they will not be unduly influenced by what others say before their turn comes.

References

Cose E (1994) *The rage of a privileged class* NY: Harper Collins

Duncan SS & Fisk DW (1977) *Face to face interaction: research, methods and theory* Hillsdale NJ: Erlbaum

Edelsky C (1981) 'Who's got the floor?' *Language in Society* 10, pp383–421, reprinted in D Tannen (ed) (1993) *Gender and conversational interaction* Oxford & NY: Oxford University Press, pp189–227

Johnson D & Roen D (1992) 'Complimenting and involvement in peer reviews: gender variation' *Language in Society* 21 (1), pp27–57

Leaper C (1991) 'Influence and involvement: age, gender, and partner effects' *Child Development* 62, pp797–811

Maccoby E (1990) 'Gender and relationships: a developmental account' *American Psychologist* 45 (4), pp513–20

Margolies-Mezvinsky M with B Feinman (1994) *A woman's place: the freshmen women who changed the face of Congress* NY: Crown

Sommers E & Lawrence S (1992) 'Women's ways of talking in teacher-directed and student-directed peer response groups' *Linguistics and Education* 4, pp1–36

8.   A Common Language

Patricia d'Ardenne & Aruna Mahtani

... Effective communication is common to all counselling but clearly raises very particular issues for the culturally skilled counsellor. In the first instance a common language must be found. As counsellors, we all select and adjust our mode of speech to what we perceive as the client's intellectual, social and emotional level. We are hardly likely to talk to a professor of law in the same way as a teenage rock star. An effective counsellor assumes responsibility for finding a shared language with the client.

Similarly, in a cross-cultural setting, we need to select and adjust our mode of speech sensitively to our clients' needs. Some counsellors have interpreted this to mean shouting at their clients – a practice we do not endorse! Transcultural counsellors use clear, precise language, and request feedback from the client as to whether communication is effective. Communication occurs at many levels: linguistic, grammatical, gestural, postural, attitudinal and conceptual...

Non-verbal communication accompanying speech

There is evidence (Argyle, 1981) to show that therapists can greatly improve their effectiveness with clients if they pay attention to clients' non-verbal cues. These include eye contact, gestures, proximity to the client, bodily orientation, facial expression, head movements and bodily contact. Furnham & Bochner (1986) have shown that in a transcultural setting, people from different cultures have different ways of:

- sending and receiving information;
- expressing their wishes and commands;
- demonstrating feeling.

When two people of differing cultures meet, they will need to negotiate their varied modes of communication. Furnham & Bochner further point out that this task becomes more difficult when the two parties share the *same* language. They argue that this is because the language similarities may mask differences that exist in their cultures. For example, the American who travels to London may succumb to a false sense of being at home when she hears a language familiar to her. She speaks effusively with the proprietor of a wine bar, who interprets this behaviour as flirtatious by his cultural standards. Unless one or both of them negotiate their messages accurately, there is likely to be misunderstanding. The main ways in which non-verbal signals assist communication are by:

- elaborating on what is said;
- providing feedback from listener to sender;
- giving messages about when it is time to speak or listen.

Furnham & Bochner use the example of how Arabs and Latin Americans have high levels of mutual gaze when compared to Europeans. In practical terms, this would mean that counsellors seeing a client from these cultures would need to adjust their own gaze accordingly to establish non-verbal congruence.

In addition Henley (1979) points out the critical role of feedback. She makes the important observation that non-verbal behaviours may provide you with information about how much language has been understood (or not) in the interview. She cites the following examples: a glazed expression, a change of behaviour, for example, shifting in chair, a fixed smile, a look of embarrassment, or a repeated 'yes'.

In general it seems that facial expressions and gaze are more important in the communication of feeling than spatial behaviour. Transcultural counsellors learn the particular rules and conventions of the culture of their client and ensure that these are reciprocated in the counselling process.

Furnham & Bochner (1986) also refer to evidence about members of a dominant section in a particular society. For example, white people in South Africa experience fewer problems in meeting socially, as measured in a social situations questionnaire, than their black counterparts. This is because white people have more opportunities to learn mainstream socially skilled acts.

In our experience in East London, transcultural clients from a less powerful section of society are doubly disadvantaged in communication. Their right to be understood is affected in two ways:

- Their first language is other than English. They are therefore unable to communicate outside their own community and influence their wider world.
- Racism affords them fewer opportunities to learn the unspoken rules and conventions that accompany the English language.

You will be more effective counsellors if you understand and are sympathetic to these disadvantages. Furthermore, you can help your clients by valuing them and their culture enough to learn their major rules and conventions accompanying speech. Good examples of these are:

- learning non-verbal rules governing 'please' and 'thank you';
- the appropriate volume with which you speak;
- etiquette, for example, rules concerning social invitations;
- values about time-keeping.

Standard and other forms of English

There are many forms of English in the world. We assume that our readers have no difficulty in following us in what we judge to be standard written English. The spoken word, however, is more subject to variation. English-speaking counsellors expect their clients to share their manner of speech. When they do not, counsellors may devalue their clients, either by believing that they are intellectually slow or that they are uneducated.

Black clients who speak another form of English, for example, are even less likely to be understood by their counsellors than those who speak another language and require interpreters. Sue (1981) quotes a lively example of a black adolescent in New York who is totally misunderstood by his counsellor, who is unable to understand his street talk and takes every word uttered quite literally.

Also in the United States, Thomas & Sillen (1972) noted that language differences among black clients were judged as deficits by social scientists and educators. Black youngsters were also seen as having restricted opportunities for cognitive development because they had 'restricted' language forms. Thomas & Sillen quote early work that challenges the stereotype of verbally destitute lower-class black children. On the contrary, they found the language and abstract thinking of these children were fully developed in their own form of English. What the children had to contend with was English speakers who did not understand their form of English, and judged it as inferior to their own.

Wong (1986: 121) makes the important point that Patois and Creole are languages that developed because they were necessary for intra-community communication that excluded others. The language became at once a source of pride as well as a barrier behind which the community survived. In practice, transcultural counsellors who speak to their black clients in standard English will appreciate why that barrier exists and respect the reasoning behind it.

Milner (1983) states that young West Indian children living in the UK are frequently corrected for speaking 'bad' English, even though their English is grammatically consistent and culturally correct. No assistance is given to them to learn a form of English which is new to them. Instead they are castigated as 'poor' speakers and are seen as cognitively impaired. This experience is carried into their adult lives and may be reawakened when they meet the standard English-speaking counsellor. In practice, then, we are faced with a situation where any client who speaks an alternative form of English will often be disadvantaged by prejudice.

[We can give an example.] *Clifford* does not speak standard English. He speaks with an accent, vocabulary and sentence structure that reflects his own Nigerian culture. English is his first language, but when he first comes to see his counsellor he faces someone who speaks standard English and who may judge him, as others have done, to be uneducated or unintelligent.

Counsellors with cultural sensitivity will appreciate that standard English is not spoken by all, and that it may indeed impose an additional barrier to client-counsellor communication. Further, they will be looking at their own prejudices about language, and allowing for them when listening to alternative forms of English.

Of course language disadvantage is not only experienced by people from another culture. Class and education are just as likely to produce alternative forms of English which promote prejudice among listeners. [We can give as another example *Fred*, a white, working-class client, and his] initial discomfort in speaking with a Cockney accent to a black, educated counsellor. He is particularly sensitive to people whom he sees as 'better' educated than himself, especially when he believes that they are in some way judging his behaviour. Our contention is that Fred may have suffered in this respect, but not as much as if he had been black. People from other cultures suffer additional barriers to communication because of prejudice both about their colour, their culture *and* their language.

Working across languages

... Clients whose first language is not English have to learn the majority language as a matter of necessity. When they approach an authority such as the social services, health services or the police, they *have* to communicate on the terms of that authority. What is more, that communication often concerns vital and distressing material. Even people working in their first language might find this information difficult to communicate clearly.

In counselling across cultures, these same factors still apply. The client approaches the counsellor – an authority figure – for help with concerns that are distressing, vital and very personal. The counsellor rarely assumes responsibility for learning the client's language, for finding a common language, or even for learning about the problems that clients face in communicating in another language.

Henley (1979) makes the point that even when clients speak excellent English, everyday stress reduces their fluency. Similarly, clients who have little English may lose it altogether when exposed to similar stress. This is not a phenomenon peculiar to the English tongue. We all lose our skill in a second language when fatigued, stressed or angry.

When clients have no choice about language, they are distanced from expressing themselves fully. If clients are counselled in their first language they gain easier access to important cultural and familial experiences. Transcultural counsellors, working across languages, understand the limitations imposed on their clients by this lack of choice. In practice, this may mean that counsellors need to take longer to explore significant feelings and experiences. A way of doing this is to approach a particular topic in a number of different ways in order to help the client elaborate more clearly.

Furnham & Bochner (1986) consider that the acquisition of the majority language is the single most important aspect of integration in a majority culture. Inability to do this, they suggest, usually leads to decreased social mobility, increased ghetto living and increased disruption between parents and children.

In our view the picture is more complex than this; language is a necessary but not sufficient condition for increased social change. The xenophobic attitudes of the majority culture ensure that members from other cultures are 'kept in their place'. Counsellors from the dominant culture must recognise that their attitudes are part of their cultural inheritance. Effective counsellors are those who are aware of the many subtle forms in which this inheritance is revealed.

Bilingualism

Counsellors and clients who are bilingual have an additional resource which enriches transcultural counselling. They have a greater choice in terms of language, as well as insight into the difficulties of moving from one given language to another.

Although local community groups in the UK use bilingualism as a resource, there have been no nationwide attempts to harness counsellors' language resources. There does, however, exist a training programme in the US (Pedersen, 1985; 1988) whose objective is to prepare culturally effective counsellors to work with bilingual, multicultural populations. It has produced bilingual counsellors in English and Spanish, Portuguese, Chinese, Italian and Creole...

Linguistic equivalence

Our clients cannot enjoy the right to be understood unless the English language has some degree of equivalence with their own. By this we mean that there has to be a degree of correspondence of meaning when translating from one language to another. Rack (1982) observes that English is a very rich language for the expression of mood and feeling. However the language is limited in other ways.

For example, English is more limited in defining family relationships when compared with languages from family-centred cultures. Just as the Laplander has over twenty different words for something as important as snow (Rack, 1982), so Hindi speakers have separate words for family relations. In English there are only the words 'aunt' and 'uncle'. In Hindi, there are different words for your mother's sister and brother-in-law, and your mother's brother and sister-in-law. The same is true for your father's relatives. There are thus four different words for 'aunt' and four different words for 'uncle'. In counselling a client from this family-centred culture, the counsellor working only in English is limited in her understanding of the subtlety of family relationships. By asking questions and using many words, the counsellor may be able to identify which of her client's aunts is being referred to. But she will not be able to appreciate that 'chaachi' denotes more than your father's brother's wife. 'Chaachi' carries a particular status for every member of the family. For example, the eldest 'chaachi' is the wife of the oldest son in the household, and is afforded the privilege of being the senior woman of that generation. There is quite simply no equivalent term in English for this. English culture does not distinguish relationships in this way as family structures are organised differently. The meaning of 'chaachi' is therefore lost.

Counsellors may not be able to speak Hindi, but at least they should be aware of some of the more significant values that the language connotes. The client loses all this meaning when working in English.

In another Indian language, Bengali, there is no gender usage either for common nouns or pronouns. Therefore when Bengali-speaking people use English, they are unaccustomed to words such as 'she' or 'he', and may use them interchangeably. This is not to be confused with a lack of fluency in English, or as a sign of intellectual impairment!

How, then, can you as counsellors acquaint yourselves with so many nuances in other languages? Cultural knowledge comes in many forms. Counsellors need to use their personal and institutional resources to the full in order to learn about their clients' language and culture. Specifically, we have found that reading the translated literature of a culture, from religious classics to popular novels, seeing films that depict that culture, talking to people sensitively about their culture and travelling to different countries will all help you to understand and communicate more effectively...

Non-racist language

Counsellors' speech also reflects the attitudes and beliefs they hold about other cultures that set a particular tone to the counselling process. The counsellor's choice of language sends messages continuously to the client about the counsellor's values. Language is more than 'getting your credentials right'; it pervades the entire counselling process and will betray you if you do not genuinely respect your client's culture.

Even more than this, your thinking affects your language outside the counselling relationship. When you speak to your colleagues about your clients, you will need to reflect on which words you employ when describing people from a culture different from your own, and what you reflect about yourself when you do so.

Words change their meaning and connotation over time. Effective counsellors are aware of changes in terminology and why they have come about. For example, it is not so very long ago that people with learning disabilities were called 'idiots' and 'cretins'. When these words became used as terms of abuse, other terms such as 'mental retardates' or the 'mentally handicapped' were employed. Each new definition tries to achieve a more accurate definition of the person it describes without prejudice. Similarly, in cultural terms, words change in their connotation. For example, the words 'negro' and 'coloured' featured in general and academic use until the late 1960s. In the wake of the civil rights movement, and the work of Martin Luther King, these terms became increasingly unacceptable to black people, and fell out of use.

Counsellors need to acquaint themselves with how their transcultural clients refer to themselves and their own communities. For example, terms like 'Asian' are not only imprecise, but can give offence. Other terms such as 'immigrant', 'indigenous', 'alien', 'native', 'foreigner', 'ethnic minority', may all seem to the white counsellor as innocuous, but may have strong emotional connotations for black people. In historical terms, these words have been used in a derogatory and discriminatory way. Take the trouble to find out...

In conclusion, we have seen that the client's right to be understood makes many demands of the transcultural counsellor. It is only when a common language has been established that the full work of counselling can take place.

References

Argyle M (ed) (1981) *Social skills and health* London: Methuen

Burke A (1986) 'Racism, prejudice and mental illness' in J Cox (ed) *Transcultural psychiatry* London: Croom Helm

Furnham A & Bochner S (1986) *Culture shock: psychological reactions to unfamiliar environments* London: Methuen

Henley A (1979) *Asian patients in hospitals and at home* London: King Edward's Hospital Fund

Milner D (1983) *Children and race: ten years on* London: Ward Lock International

Pedersen P (1985) 'Intercultural criteria for mental health training' in P Pedersen (ed) *Handbook of cross-cultural counseling and therapy* Westport: Greenwood Press

Pedersen P (1988) *A handbook for developing multi-cultural awareness* Alexandria: American Association for Counseling and Development

Rack P (1982) *Race, culture and mental disorder* London and New York: Tavistock Publications

Sue DW (1981) *Counseling the culturally different: theory and practice* New York: John Wiley and Sons

Thomas T & Sillen S (1972) *Racism and psychiatry* Secaucus: The Citadel Press

Wong A (1986) 'Creole as a language of power and solidarity' in D Sutcliffe & A Wong (eds) *The language of black experience* Oxford: Basil Blackwell

Part Four – Interpersonal Skills

In Part Four we turn to a consideration of the more specific skills that tutors need to acquire and practise in dealing with people both as individuals and in groups. The contributions here extend our sphere of interest to include working with colleagues as well as with students; as John Miller indicated in the first extract in this Reader, the tasks of the tutor include negotiating, liaising, referring, representing and feeding back, all of which involve dealing with others.

Meg Bond's account of the notion of being assertive in the making and refusing of requests sets the scene. Though the context of her succinct summary is that of the health professional, the article will equally well apply to the work of the college tutor. The table of the characteristics of aggressiveness, submissiveness and manipulation in comparison with assertiveness is particularly helpful.

John Miller's third extract describes the skills that tutors will use in working successfully in encounters with others, especially in developing their guidance work with students. He makes the point that most of us already have most of the skills of helping others that he identifies:

- *multiple skills*: attending, observing, listening, responding;
- *specific skills*: questioning, managing silence, appropriate timing and pacing, awareness of emotional attachment, identifying themes, personalising, target-setting, immediacy, confrontation;
- *ancillary skills*: record-keeping, self-evaluation.

It is interesting that Miller uses the word 'confrontation' in a way that is very different from what he calls the 'day-by-day use of the term'. The context of the next reading from Mick McManus is that of the classroom rather than the tutorial, and McManus outlines the skills involved in dealing positively with confrontations that arise from conflict and the choices and strategies that are available to teachers in responding to them.

In the next section Colin Turner provides a very accessible introduction to the principles and practice of transactional analysis (TA), a psychological approach to the ways in which we interact with other people particularly in relation to the meanings that participants attribute to one another's verbal and non-verbal behaviour. It is an approach which underpins a number of the ideas explored in this Reader. Among the basic concepts which Turner analyses are:

- being OK or not-OK;
- the three ego states of Parent, Adult and Child;
- 'games people play';
- 'stroking'.

Throughout the chapter he illustrates these with examples from the world of further education. An understanding of the nature of different transactions will illuminate many encounters between tutor and student as well as between tutor and colleague.

In the final, brief, contribution to this Part Derek Marsh uses the principles of TA to offer four practical steps for resolving interpersonal conflict:

- who owns the problem?
- making a choice;
- confronting the issue and the problem;
- handling the response.

The themes of conflict and disruption and their prevention or resolution are continued into Parts Five and Six.

9.   Assertiveness: Methods of Making and Refusing Requests

Meg Bond

Stress can be caused by not getting what you want or need, and from the consequences of an unassertive approach. Assertiveness should not be confused with aggressiveness. It is an *alternative* to aggressiveness and manipulation (both involve not respecting others' rights) and submissiveness (not respecting one's own rights). These four approaches involve not only respect, or lack of it, but verbal and non-verbal features (Table I).

	Aggressive	Submissive	Manipulative	Assertive
Content of speech	Demanding, blaming, making threats, firmly stating own point of view as the right one. Attacking, giving orders when it is not appropriate. Deciding for others and they know it. Being pushy, trying to force others to do things.	Repeating, 'I'm sorry' and 'I'm afraid'. Waffling and avoiding the point. Backing down frequently. Putting oneself down. Complaining behind the scenes. Not saying what you want. Going along with others to keep the peace or to be liked. Agreeing to do things you don't want to do without negotiating, (and doing them resentfully, badly, late or not at all.)	Insincere ego-boosting. Veiled threats. Beating about the bush before getting to the point. Conning others to do what you want. Being two-faced. Appearing to put others up but in fact putting them down. Deciding for others though they may not realise.	Honest, open and to the point, saying no when you want to, giving praise and criticism, sharing and taking responsibility for own feelings. Giving and accepting valid praise and constructive criticism, rejecting inappropriate feedback. Stating what you want clearly, gently and firmly; acknowledging your own right (and that of others) to state what you want, standing up for yourself and those dependent on you.

Continued...

	Aggressive	Submissive	Manipulative	Assertive
Eye contact	Glaring, staring, hard gaze. Looking down from a height.	Avoiding eye contact. Looking up from a lower position.	Looking out of the side or top of eyes or avoiding eye contact. Direct eye contact may also be used.	Gentle, direct, relaxed gaze. Being at same eye level whenever possible.
Posture	Solid stance, perhaps hands on hips, feet firmly apart. Moving uncomfortably close to emphasise points. Trying to get physically higher, standing when other is sitting.	Round-shouldered, head down, chest cramped, slumped. Staying at a lower level, for example, sitting when other person is standing.	Not facing directly but sideways. Coming too close in an over-chummy way. Looking coy, flirtatious movements.	Relaxed, upright, well-balanced, facing the other person directly at a distance acceptable to the other's cultural background.
Gestures	Pointing, waving, poking with finger. Clenched fist. Sharp flicks of the wrist. Hand-crunching handshakes. Over-hard jocular slaps on the back.	Nervous fiddling. Generally hands and arms turned in on self.	Flirtatious hand movements. Exaggerated elegant movements. Patronising touching or patting.	Balanced, open, relaxed gestures to emphasise points.
Facial expression	Tense, clenched teeth, frown, superior, indignant or angry expression.	Nervous smile. Apologetic, hang-dog or blank look.	Over-nice, over-innocent looking. Coy, full of smiles. Appearance of intense listening.	Relaxed, open, firm and pleasant.
Timing	Interrupting, leaving no time for others to have their say. Incessant chatter while bulldozing.	Hesitating, leaving lots of gaps where others can butt in, waffling for a long time or keeping quiet.	Appearing to listen, but interrupting and not leaving enough time for others to have a say. Incessant chatter while shepherding.	Concisely putting own point of view and allowing others to have their say.
Voice tone, volume, etc.	Loud, sharp, firm and threatening.	Quiet, strained and childlike.	Exaggerated, sing-song tone, smarmy and over-sweet.	Low pitched, relaxed, firm, medium volume and gentle.

Table I: Characteristics of aggressiveness, submissiveness, manipulation and assertiveness

Being assertive is not easy, because our culture conditions us to be otherwise. Women, in particular, are encouraged to be non-assertive in the process of learning to be a woman. Christine Webb (1982) and Bush & Kjervik (1979) have suggested that nurses are conditioned to be subservient to doctors; while Donna Moniz (1978) has claimed that nurses are caught in the compassion trap (believing that a tender, submissive, permissive, compassionate approach must be used with everyone all the time).

A developed skill

Male nurses and doctors have also expressed difficulty in being assertive. However, the fact that it is a challenge does not mean that it cannot be learned and developed as a skill by nurses of both sexes...

Everyone has the right to make requests and refuse them. If you clear your mind of anxieties about being turned down (you are not being rejected as a person, but merely having a request turned down), you will feel more confident about asking. After all, if you are not getting what you want or need, you have nothing to lose by asking. You may be surprised how often your requests can be granted.

You are more likely to get what you want or need if you ask for it specifically, directly and gently but firmly. Dropping hints or hoping that someone will know you well enough to guess what you want is seldom effective. If you do not ask for what you want or need, you are denying your own importance.

When making requests, avoid saying 'I'm sorry', 'I'm afraid', 'Would you mind . . .' and other redundant phrases because these can place you in a submissive position. Decide *exactly* what you want, rather than what you do not want, and be specific. For example, if nurse A would like her colleague nurse B to pull her weight when they are on duty together, she specifically wants nurse B to return on time from lunch so she can take her full break.

Timing is also important. Instead of giving a long list of wants, spread them out and ask at appropriate times. Use *short* sentences which state what you want, starting with 'I'd like . . .' or 'I want . . .'; for example, 'I'd like you to come back from lunch at 1.15 so I can get my full break before the ward round.' Use the verbal approach and body language outlined in the 'Assertive' column of Table I.

You could receive one of several responses:

- immediate agreement, in which case you are home and dry;
- a direct refusal, which you accept or negotiate;
- a blustering explanation of excuses;
- an attempt to sidetrack you;
- ignoring your request;
- aggressiveness.

One method of coping with the last four responses is to use the 'broken record', whereby you repeat the request calmly until you've been heard and understood properly. You could preface it with a phrase such as 'Let me say it again . . .', 'I don't think you heard me . . .', 'Perhaps I'm not being clear . . .', 'But the point is . . .' or 'That's really not relevant to the main point, which is that . . .' For example, nurse A could say, 'Let me say it again, I'd like you to come back at 1.15.'

Let the other person have their say and listen carefully. Show that you have listened by prefacing your broken record phrase with words that indicate you have understood exactly what the other has said. This phrase could start with, 'I understand . . .', 'I realise . . .', 'I can see . . .' or 'I can appreciate . . .' For example, in response to nurse B, nurse A could say: 'I understand that the queues in the canteen are long at this time of day. Nevertheless, I'd like you to come back at 1.15'; or 'I can see that you're resentful about my making this request, but nevertheless I'd like you to come back at 1.15.'

Difficult to refuse

Refusing requests can be more difficult, while the compassion trap can lead to guilt. Tenderness and compassion, at appropriate times, are important elements of the nurse's caring approach to people, but if they are taken to extremes the nurse can degrade herself as well as the other person.

Saying 'yes' when you mean 'no' can make you feel used, resentful, powerless and angry for being so weak. According to Bush & Kjervik, if this is done often enough, the nurse will have a poor self-image and be less effective as a professional. These authors have also suggested that it is insulting and patronising to assume that other people are too weak to cope with your assertiveness, such as your gentle but firm refusal.

One method of learning to refuse requests is to practise being aware of your immediate gut reaction to requests. This can be a good guide to what you *want* to do rather than what you think you *ought* to do. If you are not sure, give yourself time to clarify what you want by stalling; ask for more information or for time to consider. Again, avoid 'I'm sorry' and 'I'm afraid' as well as long explanations, white lies and citing others' displeasure as an excuse (for example, 'The nursing officer wouldn't like it'), but take responsibility for your own decision.

Listen carefully to the other person's requests and reasons. Show that you have listened by starting with the 'I understand/realise/appreciate/can see . . .' approach; for example, 'I understand you've left your purse at home again, but no I won't lend you £5.'

End by saying 'no' clearly. If the silence is embarrassing, count to 20 before you back down. If you feel you have to explain the reason (you have the right not to), try to end with '. . . so the answer's no'. Beware of the expert manipulator who can pick holes in your excuses, sidetrack you and try to make you feel guilty. Don't crumple at the occasional aggressive response designed to frighten you into submission. Cut across the sidetracking or aggression with a broken record lead-in such as 'I don't think you heard me, the answer's no.'

Again, you must stay calm and use the appropriate body language and gentle voice tone.

This approach to refusing requests can be useful in many situations, particularly if your usual method has failed. Practise these methods of making and refusing requests whenever appropriate.

If you are seldom assertive and people close to you are used to your ways, take it gently at first. Start practising with comparatively unimportant situations and people, gradually building up to those closer to home. This will give you the confidence, skill and sensitivity to change your approach slowly without turning your established relationships upside down. With new relationships, be as gently assertive as possible.

Practising assertiveness will help you to make your life less stressful, to know what you want or need, to communicate this gently and directly to others, to negotiate at an adult level and to cope with aggressive, manipulative or submissive behaviour. It does not guarantee that you will always get what you want, but that you will succeed more often. In any event, you will feel better about trying and you will be in a better position to help your patients assert themselves, and if necessary act as their advocate.

References

Bush MA & Kjervik DK (1979) 'The nurse's self-image' *Nursing Times* 697, April 26

Moniz D (1978) 'Putting assertive techniques into practice' *American Journal of Nursing* 1713, October

Webb C (1982) 'The men wear the trousers' *Nursing Mirror* 29, January 13

10.   Skills for Effective Tutoring

John Miller

[Editor's note. The numbering of paragraphs and illustrative examples in this extract is from Section 5 of the 1982 FEU publication: *Tutoring*.]

60.   A key section in any manual on tutoring must be a description of the skills that may be appropriately used by the tutor in helping the student. It is important to recognise that the same skills may be used in a variety of different ways. For example, in controlling a class, the teacher might use the non-verbal technique of eye-contact, looking fixedly at the cause of disturbance until it ceases; so too, in an interview with a student to explore a difficulty, the tutor may use eye-contact to indicate that the student is for the time being the centre of attention for the tutor. The point is that because the purpose of the two situations is different, the way in which the skill is performed and experienced will be different, too. In the classroom setting, the teacher may be concerned to exert his/her will over the class to bring order out of potential chaos. In the guidance role, on the other hand, the tutor is concerned with developing students' self-reliance, self-control and self-management, and, therefore, the values [of the tutor and the quality of the relationship with the student] will be the foundations that will define the manner in which the skill is exercised. It is vital to recognise this difference, as in tutoring it is all too easy to use skills borrowed from teaching and other roles in inappropriate ways.

61.   This said, however, the intention of this section is to encourage tutors to realise that many, if not most, of the skills identified are recognisably those already used in the tutors' roles at work, in their family lives, or in their leisure time. The hope is that tutors will use the skills identified here not as a daunting check-list through which to chastise themselves for failing to meet its demands, but rather as a way of identifying how the skills of helping others are *transferable* from one situation and setting to another. Thus the aim is to describe rather than to prescribe.

62.   A mere list of skills is not sufficient to convey the complexity of the interaction between a tutor and a student. As has already been indicated, the purpose of the intervention, the qualities the tutor offers, and the values the tutor espouses, all blend together to influence this interaction. The list of tutoring skills has been borrowed and adapted from the literature on helping skills, in particular the work of Pietrofesa *et al.* (1979) and Egan (1976). The skills relevant to tutoring have been grouped here under three headings:

1) **Multiple skills**, where a series of specific skills can be identifiably related to one overall objective.

2) **Specific skills**, where individual skills can be identified and used within a variety of tasks.

3) **Ancillary skills**, where the skill may not be related directly to the face-to-face work with students, and yet is a necessary adjunct to that work.

4) Multiple skills

63.   *(i) Attending*

This group of skills relates to the manner in which the tutor gives evidence of paying attention to the student. It is perhaps the most fundamental set of skills in guidance and in tutoring. Like many of these multiple skills, it appears almost too obvious to merit description. In day-to-day life, however, it is not difficult to cite instances of other people's inattention to us: for example, the doctor in a great hurry to finish a surgery, colleagues who have something on their minds, our spouse reading the paper while we try to tell them something important, etc.

64.   Attending goes a long way towards meeting the need of the student to feel accepted and respected by the tutor. Attending skills can be divided into the following components:

a) Eye-contact. The tutor looks at the student: not the fixed stare that tends to indicate battle is about to commence, but in a supportive way which indicates that nothing else is on the tutor's mind. The student may not keep in eye contact as the search for the right words or expression of feeling proceeds, but when he/she checks back to the tutor, there is nothing more disconcerting than to find the tutor apparently concerned with something else. It is important, though, to recognise cultural differences in eye contact, as in some cultures it is a sign of respect to avert one's gaze; the consequences of this may need to be explored with the student, and certainly will need to be considered by the tutor.

b) Posture. A tutor indicates, by facing the student and by sitting or standing in a relaxed way, that the student is the centre of attention.

(c) Head movements and facial expression. Facial expression needs to be appropriately related to the emotional content of the interaction, and nodding at relevant times indicates that the tutor recognises the importance of the occasion and is attending to what is being said.

(d) Suspending value judgements. It is all too easy to be put off a person at first sight, by making a judgement based simply on appearance perhaps; the student then has to prove him/herself unworthy of that judgement ('You're guilty until you prove yourself innocent'.) Expressions of shock and dismay ('You didn't say that to Mr. Brown, did you?') can block communication between the tutor and the student, often leading to the subsequent criticism, on both sides, that 'They did not understand'.

(e) Avoiding or minimising distractions. Often tutors are unaware of the ways in which their mannerisms – pen clicking, hair twirling, nose rubbing etc. – tend to distract the student.

(f) Distance and position. How people position themselves can have a strong influence on how they interact, though again there will be cultural differences here. In general, too much space can indicate more than just a physical distance. Inappropriate positioning can foster inattention. For example, the tutor who meets a group of students in a lecture room where the students cannot face each other is paving the way for failure if the intention is to encourage interaction and involvement amongst the students themselves.

65.   *(ii) Observing*

If attending is evidenced in, primarily, the tutor's non-verbal behaviour, then the corollary to this is the way in which the tutor can observe and helpfully make use of the student's non-verbal behaviour. Observation of the student can provide a wealth of information to which a tutor may respond and which he/she can use in a way that can encourage and facilitate a student's self-awareness.

66.   There are, however, pitfalls here to which attention needs to be drawn. People tend to see what they want to see, and often disregard evidence to the contrary. Thus, a student can be seen in very negative terms – rudeness to staff, lateness to classes, unruly behaviour, untidy appearance – and it can be quite a shock for a tutor to discover, perhaps on a residential weekend, the extent to which the student is concerned for others and the hard work he or she willingly exerts, for example, in helping put up tents, cooking, etc.

67.   In addition, it is important to note that our culture emphasises communication through words, both spoken and written, and the skills of reading non-verbal behaviour are under-developed in many people, perhaps particularly in those who have had an academic training. This can seriously handicap our ability to make acute observations, and indicates a need for most of us to practise our observation skills.

68.   Such skills have two main components: the recognition of a *behavioural* cue – a sudden smile, shining eyes, a shift of position – together with the drawing of an *inference* based on that and (perhaps) other cues. The latter can be approached in an open-ended way, as in Example 3.

Example 3

Tutor: *'I have noticed that each time you describe the work you are doing in mathematics, you clench your fists and your eyes water . . .'*

The point being made in this example is that the two behaviours described – clenching fists and eyes watering – seem to indicate a conflict of feelings. They may indicate, for example, anger at the mathematics teacher, frustration with self, despair at ever being able to cope, or even all three. The use of observation can hopefully allow those feelings to be explored.

69.   *(iii) Listening*

Perhaps the most precious set of skills that a tutor can offer a student, and yet perhaps the skills in shortest supply, are those of listening. Most people can only identify one or two people who are prepared simply to listen to them, rather than give advice or to say how 'when that happened to me, I . . .', which is usually more comforting to the listener than the person being listened to.

70.   Listening is not easy. Firstly, it requires an ability to focus on a student without bringing into the interaction anxieties and thoughts that are related to the tutor's own life, either from work or from other areas.

Example 4

The tutor has a difficult class to take in an hour's time, and is unable to put aside thinking and worrying about that class.

Thus, in Example 4, if the anxiety is too great – in other words, if the tutor's need to focus on himself is stronger than the ability to focus on the student – it might be better, if possible, either to postpone the meeting, or at least to explore with the student the tutor's difficulty in focusing exclusively on the student's needs.

71.   Secondly, listening requires an ability to listen to the whole of the message communicated by the student, rather than to select only bits and pieces. This point is illustrated in Example 5.

Example 5

A student is telling the tutor about his work-experience placement and what it involves. The tutor knows the purpose and work of the firm, and therefore, switches off for a few moments. The student goes on: '. . . And she slammed the door in my face'. The tutor is left vaguely recognising the student's feeling of rejection but is not sure how it has emerged from the discussion on the placement and whether it is a significant cue to pick up.

Such sustained focusing on and listening to another person is very demanding and tiring, despite the not-uncommon myth that people who get paid for spending time listening to others have landed themselves a soft option...

72.   Thirdly, listening requires the ability to be alert not just to the words being expressed, but also to the feelings infusing the words, since it is the combination of words and feelings that will help the tutor to understand the importance that is attached by the student to the issue concerned. Thus, at face value, Example 6 implies that the student, having had other aspirations, is now ready to take anything that turns up.

Example 6

A student is talking to the group about her hopes for the future, after the course at college has ended. 'You know, I don't really care about what I do next . . . I'd always wanted to work outdoors with animals . . . but it really doesn't matter to me now . . . at the moment, anything is better than nothing . . .'

It may not, however, be as simple as the words suggest; the student may be expressing disillusionment and sadness or perhaps resignation. The tutor might infer that the student means that the situation is simply one to be coped with, that the aim is to survive, that life obviously does not offer people a chance to be what they want to be, and that this is accepted. Alternatively, the tutor might infer that the student is depressed and needs help.

73.   The ability to draw such inferences accurately has been called 'listening with the third ear'. This implies that such nuances of meaning are just not 'heard' but are picked up by a mixture of the senses, including, very importantly, 'gut reaction'.

74.   *(iv) Responding*
What the tutor says to the student in response to anything the student has said, or indicated non-verbally, is critical. Any inferences the tutor may make need to be recognised for what they are — inferences, not facts — and thus need to be checked out before being explored or discarded. The main skills of responding can be divided into two groups: those of responding to content and to feelings.

75.   *(a) Responding to content.* This is a response where the tutor picks up and reflects to the student in some way the essence of the content of the student's story. The illustration in Example 7 seems banal in written form, but its intention is to communicate to the student crisply and clearly that the tutor has heard and understands the information that the student has offered.

Example 7

Student: *'The difficulty is getting from my special mathematics group which doesn't finish until 11 o'clock and is on the top floor of A block to joining the rest of the group for the bus that is supposed to leave for the sports centre at 10.50.'*

Tutor: *'So there is a real timetabling problem for you here.'*

Student: *'Yes, because I get blamed for being late and holding everyone up, yet I can't leave the maths group early because the teacher reckons I should stay 'til the end . . .'*

The point of checking it out is that it gives the student a chance to clarify it where necessary, and to add to it where appropriate. The essential skills are those of recognising the central core of the information disclosed, and of summarising this information concisely and accurately. A possible pitfall is that, because it tends to elicit more information from the student, it can mean that the student and tutor get caught in the trap of exchanging information in a fairly superficial way, and are unable to get through to possible underlying issues.

76.   *(b) Responding to feelings.* This is a response where the tutor picks up and reflects back to the student the feelings that the student appears to be experiencing. The usefulness of this skill is that the tutor can check out tentatively any inference made from the student's statement.

> **Example 8** *(continuing Example 6)*
>
> Student: *'You know, I don't really care about what I do next . . . I'd always wanted to work outdoors with animals . . . but it doesn't really matter to me now . . . at the moment, anything is better than nothing . . .'*
>
> Tutor: *'You say you don't care about what happens to you next, yet I sense that you're pretty unhappy about it.'*
>
> Student: *'Well . . . at school they used to say "Work hard and you'd get a good job" but that isn't true . . . I know lots of my friends who . . .'*

It may well be that the tutor is incorrect or only partially correct, because the level of recognition and articulation of feelings in our culture in general, and our educational institutions in particular, tends not to be very high. The benefit of using such a skill is that the student feels understood, and recognises that in the interactions between tutor and student a concern with feelings is an accepted part of the currency of exchange.

77. The skills of responding to content and feeling are the prime ways of indicating that the tutor is attempting to appreciate and understand the complex world of the student, thus giving tangible evidence to the quality of empathy. These skills also help the tutor to avoid the trap of prematurely defining the issue presented – e.g. the student's poor classroom work – as the root issue rather than as the indicator of a more important issue yet to be explored. In other words, the 'presenting' issue may not be the 'real' issue.

2) Specific skills

78. *(i) Questioning*

This is one of the most ensnaring of all guidance skills, especially for a teacher. In classroom instruction the question-and-answer session is a mainstream activity, in which the teacher usually knows the answers and, therefore, the questions are chosen skilfully to lead the student to the 'correct' answer. In tutoring, on the other hand, the tutor is unlikely to know what the answer is. Hence, questions which help exploration are more helpful than questions which provide only for one or a restricted set of answers. It is important, however, to recognise that students often expect the tutor to ask questions which lead to known answers, and that they may well be initially confused by the tutor's use of questions that can elicit a variety of responses, all perfectly valid or 'correct'.

79. Tutors need to avoid the over-use of questions, and to recognise that their main use in the guidance component of tutoring is to provide opportunities for students to respond openly. Questions such as 'Do you like college?' have limited use; to elicit the information that will help the student rather than the tutor, 'What do you like/dislike about college?' would be of much greater value.

80.   An alternative way of viewing the issue of questioning is to consider who is the primary agent in tutoring. If restrictive or closed questions are asked – e.g. 'You haven't been working hard, have you?', to which the correct answer may be 'No' – the focus remains firmly on the tutor to work out what to say next. If, however, a more exploratory question is asked – e.g. 'What part of the work do you find most difficult?', to which there are a variety of answers – the focus is on the student, and the tutor is released from the pressure of thinking of the next question to ask. Many tutors, especially those new to the role, find that the pressure to know exactly where they are going is quite unbearable. Thus, tutorial sessions which really need time for exploration often end after a few minutes, with neither tutor nor student feeling very good about the outcome.

81.   Another pitfall in the use of questioning is the tendency to ask more than one question at a time. Many people engaged in this type of work, partly due to the pressure identified in the previous paragraph, find themselves asking a question which fails to elicit an immediate response, and, therefore, asking a supplementary, or two. The skill of a good question is that it encourages a student to think before answering. The need for this thinking time addresses attention to another skill in the tutor's repertoire, managing silence.

82.   *(ii) Managing silence*
Perhaps the most productive silence in tutoring is that when the student is taking time to consider what has been explored. But this requires the tutor to be comfortable with the silence, and possibly to extend his or her usual 'silence threshold' – that is, his or her ability to sustain silence. The tutor needs to try to be aware of the nature of the silence and its cause, and then, if it seems to be one in which the student is 'working', to allow it to run its course without anxiously breaking in to 'put the student at ease'. This sensitivity to the atmosphere of the tutorial session requires the tutor again to use all available 'antennae', especially those of eyes, ears and 'gut reaction'.

83.   *(iii) Appropriate timing and pacing*
Knowing when to avoid breaking into a student's exploration is one indicator of the skill of appropriate timing. Not everyone works at the same pace; for example, the tutor may talk and think quickly while the student talks and thinks more slowly. At a time when the student is being encouraged to explore issues, it is appropriate to work with a slower, more reflective, pace than when the student is perhaps simply giving information on courses studied, home address and so on. It is, therefore, important for the tutor to be flexible in relation to pacing.

84.   *(iv) Awareness of emotional attachment*
Most teachers will recognise the young person who develops a particularly close attachment to them; they are always there at the end of the class, always seem to need to talk and be with the teacher. This closeness of relationship can also find expression between tutor and student, in both directions. It can be evidenced, for example, by a tutor's reluctance to refer the student elsewhere because 'Nobody else can do as much as I can – all that can help the student is my continued support'. It is important for a tutor to recognise the ease with which all people can fall into a trap of

'being needed', and to realise that this might prevent the resolution of issues that the student needs to work through.

85.   (v) Identifying themes

In working with students in a tutorial role, it is often the case that themes tend to emerge and re-emerge, though perhaps in different guises.

Example 9

A group of students meet to talk about their progress through the course. Their initial reaction is to go along passively with the discussion, but avoid talking about anything important – 'Oh, it's OK'. When pressed to talk about particular elements of the course, they say 'Everyone asks us about the course . . . Discussions in this group are always like this'

Thus, the negative and even hostile flavour of the passivity in Example 9 can give the tutor some evidence to work on in terms of identifying an underlying theme. For example, if the group gets on well while they are on their own, without a teacher present, the theme may be that of 'Can you trust authority figures?'

86.   (vi) Personalising

This refers to the skill of helping students to talk about themselves without hiding behind, for example, a generalised 'they'. For instance, 'Everyone knows that parents never understand you' may not be correct as a general statement, but indicates a belief that the student's own parents do not understand. To help the student focus on the personal meaning behind the statement is important, and can be done by asking the student to rephrase the statement, referring to 'I' or 'my' instead of 'everyone'. Helping students to speak for themselves is an important tutorial skill, as it helps them understand, for example, what their own beliefs and values are.

87.   (vii) Target setting

Tutoring, as described here, is task-oriented, and, therefore, one of the skills of the tutor is to be able to help a student to make plans, to set targets and goals, and generally to translate talk into action. The target for each student will obviously depend on the task. For example, in a tutoring session focusing on monitoring, it may be discovered that the student has real difficulties in basic reading skills. If it is agreed that the target is to improve such skills, the tutor and student may work out together the most appropriate steps required to meet this target.

88.   (viii) Immediacy

This is a skill that uses the tutor's sensitivity to the immediate dynamics of the interaction. For example, a student might be describing, tentatively and hesitantly, the difficulty of getting on with someone – for instance, with a supervisor on a work-experience placement. The very way the student describes the difficulty may exasperate the tutor – 'Why can't he tell me exactly what the problem is?' This experience of exasperation that evolves from the interaction between student and tutor may be exactly the same experience that others working with the student face – for example, the supervisor. To be able to express this experience to the student in a constructive way may be a very productive use of the tutorial session. Thus, the tutor might say 'I find myself getting frustrated – I am not sure exactly why – perhaps it is because you seem to be skirting around what you really want to say'.

89.   This form of response illustrates what is often referred to in the jargon as using the 'here and now', and is particularly important as, in the example given, it provides a rare opportunity for the student to get feedback in a safe setting, enabling – if wished – something to be done about it. The skill also indicates the importance of the tutor being prepared to disclose some of his or her own thoughts and feelings to the student. Such self-disclosure is an important indicator of the tutor's authenticity and genuineness.

90.   *(ix) Confrontation*
This is a skill that can be used by a tutor to identify and explore with the student any apparent inconsistencies or conflicts in his or her expressions or behaviour. It differs from the day-by-day use of the term 'confrontation', which often evokes the imagery of anger and aggression. Confrontation in tutoring needs to be not aggressive but assertive, and in some ways is a combination of the 'observing' and 'immediacy' skills identified earlier as in Example 10.

Example 10

'I remember that you said how much you like reading, but you have just said that you never read anything at all'.

The purpose of confrontation, as with all the skills identified here, is to aid students to be more aware of themselves and thus increasingly to take charge of their own development.

3)   Ancillary skills

91.   There are several other skills that tutors may use surrounding and supporting their work with students. The two discussed here are those of record-keeping and self-evaluation.

92.   *(i) Record-keeping*
Students will inevitably have some records kept on them, and the issue for tutors is to what *extent* their work with students should be recorded. The answer to this is not simple; tutors have a variety of roles to perform ... which will involve access to records and even responsibility for recording achievement and progress. Two crude rules-of-thumb in record writing may well be 'Can I stand by what I say?' and 'Am I prepared to discuss what I've said with the student?' Certainly verifiable information (e.g. 'She is often late') has a stronger claim to a place in a record than does opinion (e.g. 'He is unmotivated'), particularly if such a record is to be accessible to others. Issues that need to be considered here include: 'Why are records kept?'; 'What is contained

within such records?'; 'What system is it most appropriate to adopt?'; and 'Who should have access to such records?' Such questions need to be carefully considered and discussed within any college or scheme.

93.   *(ii) Self-evaluation*
Tutors need to be prepared to evaluate their own performance and skill, putting themselves in the position their students are in – as learners. There are many ways in which such self-reflection can be achieved... But the essence of evaluative processes seems to be:

• increased awareness of what the role of the tutor entails and the ways the role can be performed,

• support to share information about tutoring and its skills between tutors, and

• training to develop existing skills and to learn new skills.

94.   Issues such as those of record-keeping and self-evaluation also identify the need for discussion within a college of a wide range of issues relating to tutorial work with students. These may include the need for a common form of student profile and an agreed procedure for how it is to be used (see, for instance, Pearce *et al.* 1981). Such discussions will also need to include the tutors' links with the work of counsellors within the college and with careers officers, probation officers, etc. outside the college.

References

Egan G (1976) *The skilled helper: a model for systematic helping and interpersonal relating* Monterey, California: Brooke/Cole
Pearce B, Varney E, Flegg G & Waldman P (1981) *Trainee centred reviewing* London: MSC
Pietrofesa J, Hoffman A, Splete H & Pinto D (1979) *Counselling: theory, research and practice* Chicago: Rand McNally

11.   Confrontations

Mick McManus

For whosoever exalteth himself shall be abased; and he that humbleth himself shall be exalted.

(Luke, 14:11)

Coping in situations of confrontation and severe conflict is an extension of the earlier discussions on understanding pupil motives and controlling teacher reactions. This section concerns confrontations that the teacher has not provoked and does not wish for. It is assumed that everyone understands that unwanted confrontations can result from pupils being subjected to humiliation or sarcasm, and therefore such a style is best avoided. From time to time it may be judged desirable to confront a pupil and risk, or even hope for, a crisis. Where a teacher has shown patience and tolerance over a considerable period, presenting a pupil with some harsh truths can provoke the sort of crisis that becomes a turning point in the pupil's efforts to reform. Laslett & Smith (1984: 87) suggest that occasional confrontations of this sort can benefit the pupil, the class and the teacher's management. This kind of confrontation is controlled and most effectively managed by a teacher who knows the pupil well and for whom the pupil has respect. The points that follow apply to situations where conflict is unlooked for and in danger of being uncontrolled.

Avoid being manipulated

The first sign of approaching trouble is the cue to be on guard against slipping into an habitual or automatic response. It is necessary for the teacher to accept responsibility for his or her actions and to accept that they are in control and able to avoid knee-jerk reactions: the serene, dispassionate professional, not a puppet of the pupil's capricious emotions. The warning signs include a feeling of personal hurt resulting from both one's positional authority as a teacher being attacked and one's attempt at reasonableness – there has invariably been one (Pik, in Cohen & Cohen, 1987). In the first stages of a conflict, both the office and person are rejected: two blows which are often sufficient to preclude the possibility of the teacher retaining equanimity or recovering control.

Confrontations always take place with at least one of three possible audiences in attendance, whose effect on the actors is to heighten tension and drive judgement off the stage. There is invariably an audience of pupils present. The teacher therefore feels constrained not to lose face and often feels that, for the sake of the others, there is no alternative but to stand firm, irrespective of consequences. From the pupil's point of view, the presence of others hinders any inclination or opportunity to back down from a public act of defiance. If the audience can be removed, or the teacher is able to remove the pupil or allow a retreat, serious conflict is less likely. The two other possible audiences are often absent but are none the less influential. The teacher may feel constrained to stand his or her ground on principle, perhaps having in the past declared such principles to colleagues and friends. These people constitute a shadow audience, constraining the teacher's actions. Wagner, in a chapter of Calderhead (1987), terms the conflicts resulting from 'self-imperated cognitions' as 'knots'. The suggested remedy for the problems that arise from refusing to see things as they are but only as they should be is: stop being ruled by 'musts' and determine to accept responsibility for choosing anew in each situation. There is an apparent contradiction in advising that one must not be ruled by musts, but a rule about rules has a different logical status to a rule about things. The pupil may have a parallel audience, who similarly give him or her 'no other choice'. The third possible audience consists of those persons who will inevitably appear on the scene if the conflict does not evaporate. For the teacher, this audience consists of colleagues and superiors; for the pupil, parents, and friends from other groups.

All three audiences contribute to the fear, embarrassment and tension and put accurate perception and balanced judgement at risk. Pik (in Cohen & Cohen, 1987) includes the sadness teachers often feel in such unlooked-for conflicts as another factor confusing wise judgement. To be aware of the effect of these audiences is the first step in understanding and controlling one's reactions. If the audience of pupils is to be encouraged to accept the reintegration of the pupil into the community, care must be taken to define the crisis in a way that makes this possible. For example, saying 'Helen is not herself today' is preferable to 'Helen will not be able to stay in this school if she does not improve'. The words and actions of a teacher who is highly regarded by pupils will influence the troubled pupil's view of self and the class's view of him or her, too. Future harmony depends on words being carefully chosen.

Identify the pupil's point of view

Unlikely as it may seem, a time of acute stress is a time to try to step into the pupil's shoes and understand and possibly accept the reasonableness of their behaviour from their point of view. Another way of looking at the situation is to see the confrontation as the pupil's particular distress, not the teacher's. As Hanko (1985: 80) puts it, what others think about us is their problem; our reaction to this is ours. Wills (1967) tells a story about a Quaker who was the victim of a murderous hold-up on a lonely road. With a gun at his head there was good reason to be alarmed but his distress was directed elsewhere, for he said to the robber: 'Dear fellow, what has brought you to this?' It may be that the teacher has carelessly or unintentionally provoked an outburst, and most teachers are able to accept this and restore calm with a placatory or apologetic statement. The attempt to grasp what is driving the pupil's action helps to distance the teacher from the feelings of personal hurt and professional incompetence. The pupil's feelings may be a mirror image of the teacher's and the latter may often be used to discover the former. The teacher may also reflect on the influence the pupil's audiences are having upon his or her behaviour and the possible reasons for the pupil investing so much in what may have begun as a trivial exchange or minor offence. Often, the open discussion of these audience effects can stop a confrontation situation developing. For some teachers, who habitually show patience and have good relations with a pupil, a sudden aggressive confrontation can be exceptionally distressing and undermine the teacher's confidence in his or her understanding. A distressed pupil may finally lose control when faced with a teacher who is, from the pupil's point of view, unusually kind. This contradiction, perhaps added to several lessons of failure and frustration, can be the trigger that causes the pupil to relinquish self-control. To be selected in this way may be seen as a confirmation of one's importance in the pupil's eyes. To worry about it is inappropriate, just as it would be for a specialist surgeon to worry because all the most hopeless cases were pushing at the door.

Avoid ratchet statements

Ratchets turn only one way and any threat or remark that cannot be abandoned or withdrawn inevitably carries the dispute forward and raises its temperature. Threats of force or removal are particularly effective in bringing a crisis to a violent climax. There should always be some physical or interactional escape route for both pupil and teacher. Assaults upon teachers sometimes result from physical attempts to block doorways to escaping pupils. The feeling, and subsequent claim, that 'there was no alternative' is an example of the tyranny of 'musts' discussed by Wagner (1987). There is always an alternative to every imperative except this present one. Confrontations are times when hurtful things are said. Laslett & Smith (1984: 104) describe a case in which the teacher shouts insults and threats. These are difficult to withdraw and there is greater than normal danger that a pupil may store and live up to any deviant labels that have been applied. Some pupils even have difficulty separating corrections of their work from personal criticisms of themselves. Caspari (1976) gives examples of this. It is much more difficult to separate comments on one's behaviour from attacks upon oneself. The primary offence must be prevented from becoming the focus of later, secondary action as the pupil seeks to live up to the deviant designation (see Lemert, quoted in Hargreaves *et al.* 1975: 5).

Accept or divert an attack

It sometimes costs nothing in terms of esteem or control simply to accept an insult or act of defiance. This is to apply one of the principles of judo to verbal contests: go with the opponent's force rather than resisting it, and use it to unbalance him or her if possible. One teacher in a school for maladjusted pupils recalled how a pupil noticed the wedding ring on her finger and said: 'I don't know how you ever got a fella, with a face like yours.' She admitted that such remarks can be hurtful but she was not wounded by it, for as she said: 'I had long ago come to much the same conclusion myself, and I told the pupil so.' Kohl (1986) suggests diverting attention from the threat by giving misused objects a name. For example, as a chair is lifted ready to be thrown, 'Don't do that to Boris, he cannot stand heights.' Another example given in Robertson (1981) concerned a teacher who entered a classroom to find a pupil about to hit another with an iron bar taken from the gym: 'Right, pokers away, books out.' These examples are not merely evidence for the common belief that a sense of humour helps in a crisis: humorous judo is more than a facility for easy jokes. Turning the other cheek is a strategy with a long pedigree.

Try procrastination

A straightforward technique is simply to refuse to become embroiled at the particular moment chosen by the pupil. The dispute is postponed without surrendering any other issue. Kohl (1986) advises putting the burden of choice on the pupil:

withdrawing from the struggle and leaving the pupil to decide when he or she is ready to resume co-operation. In this case, the teacher specifies what the pupil must do to mend the breach and then withdraws. There is no need to specify a time limit and the importance of the conflict may rapidly diminish; with luck, postponement becomes cancellation. Inflammatory or ratchet statements can sometimes be withdrawn in a graceful and humorous way by being put off till later. For example, teachers sometimes say: 'I shall ask you once more and then . . .' A threat follows. To be sure, the teacher will have to ask once more and no doubt the prospect of having to carry out an impossible threat, or abandon it, increases the tension by another notch. One way out is to add, having paused, an absurd date and time in the future when the pupil will be 'asked once more'.

Repair the relationship

Where a confrontation has occurred and does not end in a satisfactory way, the pupil should be seen alone before the next timetabled meeting takes place with its attentive audience waiting breathlessly to be entertained. A private, face-to-face talk can be disarming – particularly if it begins with conciliatory remarks from the teacher. A closeness and openness is possible face to face that is often unachievable in classrooms: 'in the face-to-face situation, the other's subjectivity is available to me through the maximum of symptoms . . . no other form of social relating can reproduce the plenitude of symptoms of subjectivity present in the face-to-face situation' (Berger & Luckmann, 1971: 43). More succinctly:

> If thy brother shall trespass against thee, go tell him his fault between thee and him alone.
>
> (Matthew, 18:15)

People who are unsure of themselves find apologies embarrassing and shaming; those who have authority can sometimes use apologies to confirm and enhance it. It is therefore important for teachers to feel confident in their expertise and to understand that 'it is not demeaning to make an apology' (Laslett & Smith, 1984: 102). Some schools, determined to succeed with disturbing pupils, ensure that such meetings follow conflict and may emphasise their importance by setting aside the headteacher's room for them. In rare cases the pupil will decline to co-operate, but it is still possible for the teacher to indicate that the matter is closed by a light comment. One teacher suggested that it was always possible to offer a brief apology for an offensive remark if she had made one, or a self-deprecatory gesture and a wink and a smile in passing.

Confirming continued co-operation

Despite protestations to the contrary, and in the face of all the evidence, most confrontational pupils do not want to be rejected. Some may even be using confrontations to test, in a socially inept way, the reliability and sincerity of their teachers. They must therefore be assured that, despite what may have been said during the conflict, and irrespective of future behaviour, they are expected to continue following the same timetable at the same school with the same teachers. For many pupils this will be unexpected, for they may frequently have been threatened with banishment from both home and school. It also reassures them that perhaps they have found someone they can trust to forgive them and with whom they are sure of a welcome even if they fail: till death us do part, if necessary.

References

Berger P & Luckmann T (1971) *The social construction of reality* Harmondsworth: Penguin

Calderhead J (ed) (1987) *Exploring teachers' thinking* London: Cassell

Caspari I (1976) *Troublesome children in class* London: Routledge & Kegan Paul

Cohen L & Cohen A (eds) (1987) *Disruptive behaviour* London: Harper & Row

Hanko G (1985) *Special needs in ordinary classrooms* Oxford: Basil Blackwell

Hargreaves DH, Hestor KH & Mellor JM (1975) *Deviance in classrooms* London: Routledge & Kegan Paul

Kohl H (1986) *On becoming a teacher* London: Methuen

Laslett R & Smith C (1984 & 1992) *Effective classroom management* London: Croom Helm

Robertson J (1981) *Effective classroom control* Oxford: Blackwell

Wagner AC (1987) 'Knots in teachers' thinking' in Calderhead *op. cit.*

Wills D (1967) *The Hawkspur experiment* Harmondsworth: Penguin

12. Transactional Analysis: the Basic Concepts

Colin Turner

Introduction

How can we as individuals try to make sense of the various relations or transactions we have with other people?

Most of us feel that we want to improve our skill in relating to other people and have many moments of feeling inadequate in a particular transaction. We might, for example, as Heads of Department be approached by a member of staff who wants to talk over some kind of problem, or we might get involved in a major row with the Principal. Outside our work life, we are likely to experience many more moments of clumsiness or inadequacy in transactions – with our adolescent sons and daughters, our spouses, our in-laws, our neighbours, our friends.

One of the difficulties of analysing and so improving our everyday behaviour with other people, is that the theories and writings of psychologists and social behaviourists have been very difficult for the layman to follow, both because of the language used and the complexity of the conceptual ideas. Read for example some Freudian or Gestalt theory.

The beauty of Transaction Analysis (or TA as we will now call it) is that its language is very simple, even colloquial – and, ironically, that in itself makes people very suspicious of it. We have been conditioned to expect to use long words to describe the way we relate to ourselves and other people. Not only is TA language simple, but its concepts are based on common sense, everyday observation of what we see and what we feel. There is very little underlying theory such as there is in Freudian psychology. The basic concepts of TA can be taught to anybody of average understanding in a few hours. It is true that, like all simple effective tools, TA concepts can be used to search deeper and deeper into human behaviour, but a useful level of understanding which can be put to practical use is available straight away.

There is nothing that can be said about the human condition that has not been said many times before over the last three millennia, and it would be wrong to make that claim for TA. Each age however has its own voice, and it was the particular gift of Eric Berne (1964; 1975) in his formulation of transactional analysis that he seemed to express the particular state of the late 20th century. It has proved a potent aid in individual and group therapy, in various forms of management training, and in all those professions which involve particularly close interpersonal relations – nursing, social work and teaching, for example.

TA is at one and the same time a method of analysing communications between people and a theory of psychological development. This dual function gives TA great flexibility and may account for the rapid spread of its use in recent years.

The underlying assumption

TA assumes that all the events and feelings that we have ever experienced are stored within us, as though on video-tape, and can be replayed. We can re-experience the events and, more importantly, we can re-experience the feelings of all our past years. Of particular significance, because they were so crowded with new feelings and experience, are the tapes from our childhood. We can relive the feelings we had of a child's joy or frustration, or our childhood perceptions of parental behaviour and commands. These feelings from our own childhood state and from our parents as experienced by us as children we carry around within us, and they are frequently reactivated. It is absolutely basic to TA, however, that all individuals have the capacity for change. Ultimately, the way we are is because that is the way we have chosen to be, and whatever the difficulties in so doing, we are free to make new choices. We are responsible for ourselves and cannot blame other people and other things for the way we are. The belief in the capacity for change makes TA a psychology of optimism. Eric Berne expressed this metaphorically by saying that everyone was born a prince or princess. Most people are persuaded that they have become frogs and so start behaving in a frog-like way. But it is in their power to stop waiting for the magic kiss, and instead choose to reaffirm that they are really princes or princesses.

OK – not-OK

We will start with one of the simplest of concepts: that of being OK or not-OK. The assumption is that we are always in one state or the other, and most people seem to spend much more time feeling not-OK than OK.

Being not-OK is experiencing discomfort, embarrassment, worry, apprehension, fear, boredom, lack of confidence, shyness, impotency and other such feelings. We may feel these more when we are on our own or more when we are with other people, but the likelihood is that during the average day we will have these discomforts nagging away below the surface. For much of the time they will be in a relatively mild form that we can well cope with, and we may regard them as just part of the human condition, but on occasions they will acquire quite dramatic forms. To check the truth of this argument, work forward from the time you got up this morning trying to identify the states of feeling you had minute by minute.

Being OK needs little explanation. It is the feeling of comfort, of being at ease, of feeling confident with oneself, and of joy with the world. It is experienced at moments of intimacy, of wonder, of total relaxation, of oneness with nature. We all feel OK sometimes, but it is not a continuous state and it may be only rare moments in the day when we feel truly OK. One of the purposes of TA is to move us more often from the not-OK states to an OK state.

When we are considering relationships with any other person at work or elsewhere, it is clear that we must not only be aware that we are operating from a not-OK state, but that the other person is likely to be doing so as well.

It might seem odd that we spend so much of our time feeling not-OK, but such seems to be the case, and furthermore we often develop various strategies and mechanisms to stay with and reinforce such feelings. If we are feeling depressed, for example, we tend to look for things or set up situations to make us further depressed rather than do the apparently obvious thing of looking for ways of feeling better.

Rackets

We all at sometime experience all the following not-OK feelings.

Anger	Frustration	Stupidity	Fear
Guilt	Anxiety	Inadequacy	Clumsiness
Hurt	Loneliness	Rejection	Depression

One of these feelings however will be particularly familiar to each of us individually. It will have a special saliency. It is the one we know really well in all its shapes and contours and we have experienced the worst it can do. This is our racket, our favourite bad feeling. It is the feeling we will most commonly move into when we feel not-OK and its very familiarity gives us some comfort. So if we consider the varying reactions of a group of people to having a bump with another car, we would probably find one person straight away moving into anger, another feeling stupid, another feeling anxious about the other driver's reaction, another feeling guilt and so on. One stimulus will set off very different feelings in different people and it will happen in a patterned way. Likewise some feelings are very foreign to any individual. Just as he may be very familiar with guilt, he may hardly ever express anger and does not know very well what it feels like. Racket feelings are invariably inappropriate to the situation and must be clearly distinguished from genuine feelings clearly related to the external reality. It is, after all, very sensible to feel fear when an enraged bull is galloping towards you, but not when your boss is shouting at you. People will commonly set up situations to reinforce their rackets. Thus the Head of Department who has an anger racket will create situations several times a day when he can feel legitimately justified in being angry.

Rackets can be distinguished from genuine feelings by the fact that they are:

> Repetitive
> Inappropriate
> Manipulative

Rackets were learned in childhood. Whenever as a child we felt for various reasons not-OK, we had to find a behaviour which was accepted by the family and that was generally the racket modelled by parents. Thus, if during the bad times our parents tended to go off on their own and feel lonely and rejected, then that is probably what we learned to do. If they get angry, we will feel we have permission to be angry. And the more we get familiar with that feeling, the more we are likely to retreat to it.

Ego states

Fundamental to transactional analysis is the concept of ego states. If we look at the way people behave, we can observe them as appearing to exist in three separate discrete states, which we label the Parent, the Adult and the Child states. These states of behaviour seem associated with their own repertoire of vocal tones, gestures, expressions; attitudes and vocabulary which in turn seem to derive from different sources within ourselves.

To take an example: consider the staff member who comes bursting into a meeting with a broad grin on her face, and says, 'Hi, great to see you all again.' She sits down, looks towards the chairman [sic] and asks 'What is on the agenda today?' Then noticing the absence of one of the group, she says 'Don't say Bill is late again. It really is time he learnt to be on time.' Each of her three statements had its own set of expressions and gestures and seemed to come from different sources within her.

It was observation of these kinds of switches which led Berne into developing his theory of the three ego states. They are conventionally represented as shown in Diagram 1.

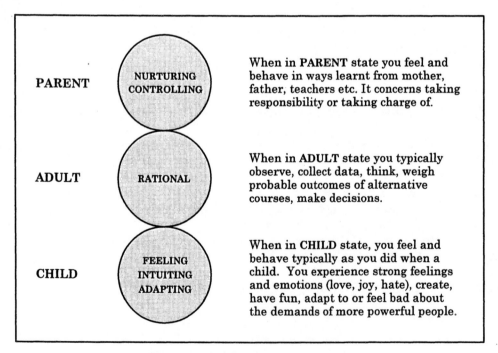

Diagram 1: The three ego states

It is very important to understand that these ego states are not abstract concepts (such as Freud's ego, super ego and id) but actual states which can be observed. They can never be hypothesised, but must always be demonstrably present. Of course, one's vision might be defective so the behaviour might be misinterpreted, but this does not alter the fact that the behaviour is there.

How can we describe the three ego states?

The Child. In the first few months of our lives we experienced the world almost totally by feeling – feelings of satisfaction and contentment when we were fed, frustration and anger when we were hungry. As we grew, so we explored the world with curiosity, joy, pain and love. Experiencing the world through feeling is the hallmark of the Natural Child and it remains with us for the rest of our lives. Our joy at meeting a loved one, or our anger at being thwarted in our desires, is the same whether we are six or sixty. As the baby grows he begins to experience the pressure of the world of grown-ups about him. He finds he must adapt his behaviour to please them rather than doing what he wants. Otherwise they cease to love him. He learns to be polite and submissive, and sometimes rebellious, and underneath he starts to learn about guilt and anxiety and other not-OK feelings. All the behaviour and feelings involved in adapting to other people we call the Adapted Child.

The toddler and youngster also learns to suss out what kinds of behaviour will get the responses he wants. He uses his intuition to guess that a smile to daddy will get him what he wants but it will not work with mummy. And as he gets older it is his Intuitive Child which enables him to 'feel' the right answer before he works it out logically. Artists and scientists rely heavily on their Intuitive Child for their most creative work. They work things out logically as well, but some of their most valuable work comes from the creative leap in the dark.

The Adult. When he is still very young the child begins to puzzle out things. He begins the process that he will continue all his life of taking in and processing information, and making informed judgements on that basis. This is his emerging Adult state. It has been referred to as the computer within us, and although this may give it a too limited role, it is an apt analogy. Whenever we are asking questions, giving answers, taking in or giving out information, assessing evidence rationally, judging between alternative actions based on likely outcomes, then we are in our Adult state. The Adult state goes through very rapid development between the ages of 6 and 12. It is a state which has little feeling in it. If we are experiencing strong feelings we cannot be in our Adult. This state has a capacity denied to the other two. It can view the activities of the Parent and Child, particularly if they are involved in some kind of tussle over what action you should take, and it can arbitrate between them. All of us who have experienced internal dialogues will be familiar with this process.

The Parent. As the young baby gets into childhood so she begins to incorporate from those older people around her feelings about what is right and wrong and how to help others. She begins to feel responsibility for other people, either by wanting to correct them or by helping them. Children at play can often be seen rehearsing these roles with their dolls or pets or younger siblings, by lecturing them on their misdeeds and by comforting them or bandaging them up. The Parent incorporates the moral and political codes, generally derived from mothers, fathers, school teachers and the like, and is concerned with what 'should be', what goals we ought to be aiming at. Its two aspects, therefore, are of the Critical Parent, which sets the rules and judges people against them, and of the Nurturing Parent, which cares for people. In a not-OK state the Parent is persecuting and prejudiced in its critical aspect. The not-OK side of nurturing is rescuing. In the TA world rescuing is not a good thing. It is defined as helping other people in order to help yourself feel better and to make the other person feel more helpless. It is really another form of persecution done under the guise of good deeds. Over-protection is a form of rescuing.

It takes relatively little practice to become proficient at diagnosing ego states because we are dealing with observable phenomena. We are looking for clues from the behaviour being engaged in, the vocabulary that is being used, the tone of voice, facial expression, gestures, postures and apparent attitude. Although we can most commonly listen to speech tone and content, it is easy enough to guess a person's ego state entirely from non-verbal clues. Imagine three people: one is standing very erect wagging his finger at a young child, his expression hard and stern. Another is standing in front of a machine pointing out to a workman he has with him the various operating devices. His expression is alert, his gestures active and decisive. A third is lying in the sun, absolutely relaxed, a smile of pleasure on his face. We do not need to know what is being said to be able to identify the three states of Parent, Adult and Child. The diagnostic chart (Diagram 2) does no more than suggest probabilities. It cannot be used conclusively to establish ego states, particularly when we are considering vocabulary. All the key words mentioned could be used in another ego state, though it would be less likely. All the clues when put together, however, should give a clear picture of the ego state being observed.

There are favourite arenas for ego states, though none is exclusive to one. We tend to be in our Child when we are in pubs, at sports matches, at the seaside, in bed. We tend to be in our Parent at church, at political meetings, when with our children (and perhaps too often in the classroom). We tend to be in our Adult in the lecture theatre, at our desk, or in the office.

What is useful for us in the concept of ego states?

It is a mark of a skilled and mature person that he or she can move easily between the states using whichever one is appropriate to the situation. It is important to understand that whatever the situation we face we have available to us responses from all the states. We can choose to respond from our Critical (Controlling) Parent, Nurturing Parent, Adult, Natural (Free) Child, or Adapted Child.

	Controlling Parent	Nurturing Parent	Adult	Free Child	Adapted Child
Behaviour	Criticises Commands Dictates	Protects Comforts Helps	Enquires Tests Reasons Gives and receives information	Cries Laughs Rages	Submits Accepts Rebels Reacts
					Continued...

	Controlling Parent	Nurturing Parent	Adult	Free Child	Adapted Child
Attitude	Judgemental Moralistic Authoritarian	Understand- ing Caring Giving Smothering	Interested Observant Rational Evaluate	Curious Fun loving Changeable	Compliant Ashamed Apologetic Demanding
Key Words	Must Ought Always Should Wrong	Love Good Splendid Well done Help	How What Why Consider Probable	Super Wow Want Fun Ouch	Can't Try Sorry Thank you
Voice Tone	Critical Condescend- ing Sarcastic Firm Dominating	Loving Comforting Helpful Sugary	Calm Clear Enquiring Precise Monotone	Free Loud Sexy Energetic Happy Angry	Whiney Defiant Placating Moaning Demanding
Gestures, Postures	Pointing finger Hands on hips Foot tapping Looking down on	Arm round shoulder Leaning forward	Erect Pointing (to demonstrate)	Active energy Cuddles	Slumped Pouting Cringing Foot stamping
Expres- sion	Frowning Set jaw	Smiling Sympathetic Accepting	Alert Interested Pre-occupied	Uninhibited Laughter Excited	Dejected Apprehen- sive Pleading

Diagram 2: Indication of ego states

Let us consider an example: you are a head of department and your senior lecturer has been for an interview for promotion. You meet her coming back from it looking very downcast. She says:

Well, that's another one I really messed up. What a shambles. I'm really mad at myself.

This clearly is a Child statement from a position of disappointment and frustration, very similar to the feelings we had as children in failing to come up to expectations or achieve well when we really wanted to.

You might make any of the following statements:

Never mind, come into my office and tell me all about it (sympathetically).

Well, you deserved it. I've always told you you ought to spend more time bothering about presentation.

Are you willing to spend some time analysing where the interview seemed to go wrong?

(nervously) *Oh – er – well, I – er – don't know what to say really.*

To hell with them all – let's go and get drunk.

Heh, I tell you what. Let's go and see Caroline.

It is the skill of the head of department to choose an approach that is appropriate for that person at that particular moment, and he needs to listen to his Intuitive Child for this. The likelihood, however, is that he, like the rest of us, is not able freely to move between the states and choose the most appropriate. That is because as we grow older we develop some ego states and diminish others. We have a favourite ego state and another which we seldom use. Maybe we find it easy to get into our Nurturing Parent on almost any excuse but do not use our Natural Child very often, or perhaps our Critical Parent and Adult are highly developed but our Nurturing Parent only makes the occasional appearance.

There is a useful device for examining this. It is called the egogram and was developed by one of Berne's colleagues, John Dusay (1980). It requires you to consider your activities either in total or in particular aspects, such as at work or at home, over a stated period of time. This can be over a single day or several years. Of the aspects of ego states on the diagram, consider which you have been in most often and draw a bar to indicate that. Then consider which you have been in least and draw a bar to show that. Then consider in turn, and show appropriately, the next most common and the next least common states, and the surviving one in the middle. You could end up with something like Diagram 3 (opposite).

A lot can be done in exploring egograms and Dusay explains this in his book. At the very least, however, we can look at our own egogram and ask ourselves whether this is how we want to be. There is no right and wrong. No one else has the right to say our pattern ought to be different. But if we feel we are too often in our Critical Parent and too seldom in our Natural Child, then we can set about changing that.

There is a strong likelihood that if we have a particular favourite ego state then that is the one we move into whenever we are under slight stress or face an unexpected situation. Thus the person whose egogram is shown in Diagram 3 would most likely use an Adult response to our senior lecturer who had failed to get her promotion.

One basic assumption behind TA, and indeed most other psychological and developmental theories, is that the amount of psychic energy we have is constant. We can redistribute it, use it in different ways, but we cannot increase or decrease it. What we are born with we have for life. So it is our choice how we distribute it round the ego states. If we increase one, we must decrease another.

For some people, their use of ego states gets totally out of balance. We probably all know:

- The Constant Parents, who do little else but criticise others, advise others or take care of others – they seem to have no Adult or Child.

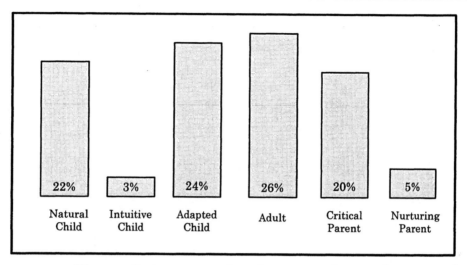

Diagram 3: An egogram based on one week at work

- The Constant Adult, who continually analyses, lives only with facts, distrusts feelings; avoids moral and political questions, cares for no one.

- The Constant Child who lives in his feelings all the time; consumed with anger, aggression or guilt, or always seeking fun or looking for kicks, or always feeling helpless, dependent or impotent.

The virtual absence of one or two ego states is referred to in TA terms as 'exclusion' and is a pathological state. For most of us it is a question of getting the balance right so that we can feel happy with our own lives and have the skill to relate sensitively to other people.

Ego states and the transaction

A transaction is a verbal exchange between two people (we will leave aside non-verbal transactions). One person speaks and the other responds. Transactions can be complementary and enable the conversation to continue, or they can be crossed and bring the conversation to an end or at least cause it to change its nature. To illustrate this let us consider the following simple transaction:

Head of Department (A): *Have you seen that MSC file?*

Secretary (B): *It is in the central registry.*

Here (A) spoke from his Adult to (B)'s Adult. This called for and received a reply from (B)'s Adult to (A)'s Adult. It was thus complementary and diagramatically would look like this (Diagram 4):

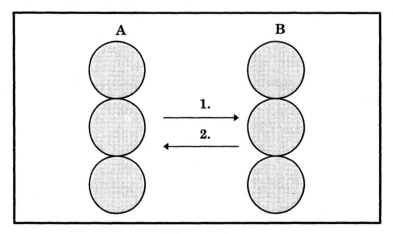

Diagram 4

Alternatively (A) might have said to (B):

> *Oh dear, I'm in awful trouble. You haven't seen the MSC report anywhere, have you?*

to which (B) might have replied

> *Don't worry, I'll hunt it out for you and make sure nothing goes wrong.*

Here (A) spoke from his Adapted Child hoping for a protective Parent to come to his aid. (B) obliged, and so we have another complementary transaction (Diagram 5).

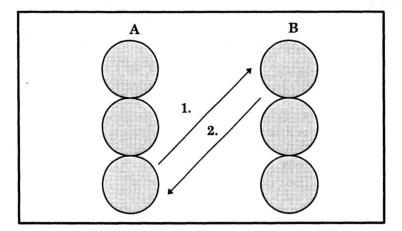

Diagram 5

A third alternative in the same situation is that (A) says to (B):

> *Where the hell is that damned file? I'm getting fed up to the teeth with this job.*

And (B) might reply:

> *Don't get at me. It's not my fault. I've got my own problems.*

Here the Child state of the one is complemented well by the Child response of the other (Diagram 6).

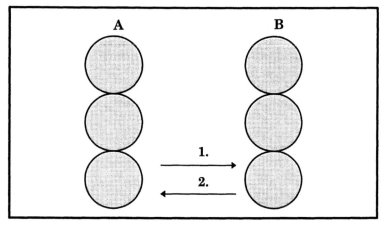

Diagram 6

All these are parallel transactions. The expected happens. There are no unusual responses and the conversations could carry on in that vein for quite a bit longer.

Suppose, however, that in, response to the first Adult comment of the head of department:

Have you seen the MSC file?

(B) had replied, flustered and tearful

Oh, don't say I've messed something else up.

Expecting an Adult response, the HoD is likely to be momentarily thrown by this emotional reaction from the secretary's Child (Diagram 7). At this point (A) has choices.

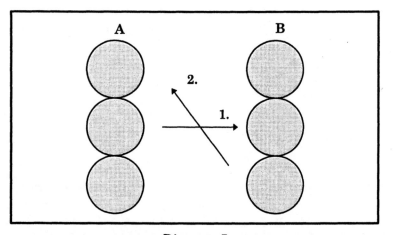

Diagram 7

(A) can carry on with Adult statements and try to pull (B) back to an Adult-Adult transaction. Or (A) can go into the Nurturing Parent role with a statement like:

There, there. Don't go getting upset. I'll go and find the file. You just forget all about it.

Alternatively (A) has the option of using the Critical Parent or Child roles. Whichever it is, the transaction has taken an unexpected line and is likely to land (A) in an undesirable position. If this happened once, it would not be of any concern but if it became a repetitive pattern and (A) was always being manipulated into the role of Nurturing Parent by (B), (A) ought to do something about it. After all, the pay-off for the secretary is that she does not have to be responsible and competent if she can always get someone to look after her.

So we need to be able to deal with crossed transactions when they happen to us. We also need to be able to make crosses when we want to switch the transactions we are in. For example, a particular type of Parent to Parent transaction is called the Blaming Parent, and it typically starts:

Isn't it awful what they are saying about the Principal?

and a typical response is:

Yes, I blame his secretary, you know.

If you do not want to join in this kind of transaction (which can go on for a very long time), then you can switch by an Adult response like:

What is the evidence?

It is unlikely the initiator will really want an Adult-Adult conversation, and will most likely simply close the transaction...

Ulterior transactions

There is a form of transaction where behind the spoken message is a clear and unambiguous second message. This is shown diagramatically by a dotted line. The classic ulterior message is:

(A)   *Come up and see my etchings.*
(B)   *That sounds a very interesting suggestion.*

On the face of it this is an Adult-Adult transaction but we all recognise it as a Child-Child. It is always the ulterior message that has the power.

Stroking

All people from the moment they are born need the stimulation of stroking. Without it babies can actually die, and adults will shrivel up as personalities and occupy our mental hospitals. A 'stroke' is a stimulation one person gives to another, and an exchange of strokes is one of the most important activities people engage in. Strokes are any act of recognition one person gives another. For babies and young children most strokes will be actual physical touching: with adults physical strokes are largely replaced by symbolic strokes such as praise or words of appreciation. Strokes can be either positive or negative – a kiss or a cuff. If the child cannot receive positive strokes from his friends or parents he will look for negative ones rather than get none at all. A blow is better than being totally ignored.

But it is the giving and receiving of positive strokes that develops emotionally healthy people with a feeling of confidence in themselves, trust of others and a general feeling of being OK.

The kind of positive strokes that give this OK feeling, of everything being well with the world, must spread across the three ego states.

> I require my Child to be stroked by being hugged.
> I require my Adult to be stroked by being congratulated on my work.
> I require my Parent to be stroked by being thanked for caring for someone.
> I need to stroke other people's Child.
> I need to stroke other people's Adult.
> I need to stroke other people's Parent.

And all these strokes should be positive. We can diagramatically represent this in the following way:

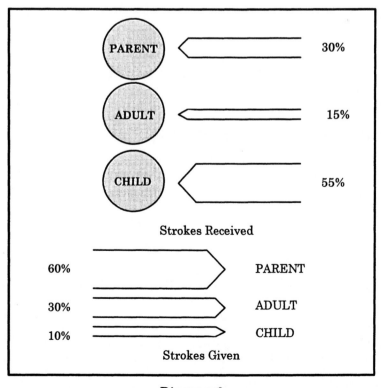

Diagram 8

If we look at our stroking pattern in the way it relates to a person or group of people, we can make decisions about whether that is the way we want it to be, and change it if it is not. For example, we might find we are giving a secretary plenty of strokes but they are invariably for her Child ('You look marvellous today'), when what she might most value is some strokes for her Adult ('That's an excellent idea') or for her Parent ('Thank you for looking after those visitors')...

Our stroke pattern of giving and receiving will be very much conditioned by what kind of strokes we received as a baby and child. If we became used to negative strokes, to being smacked, criticised, shouted at, and generally put down, we will probably go through life looking for and giving negative strokes from and to other people. If we received positive strokes of praise, love and rewards, but only conditional upon performing well or conforming to the rules, then we will tend to give and look for strokes based on performance or acceptable behaviour. If we did not get much physical stroking, we will probably find it difficult to give such strokes.

One of our major difficulties is our inability to accept positive strokes. We have all sorts of ways of turning away or discounting the good things said to us. We have been taught the virtues of modesty and it comes hard to us simply to accept and take in a compliment. In theory it is easy enough. All we need do is say, 'Thank you. I appreciate that.' In fact we have enormous temptations to 'discount' in some of the following ways:

1. Apply it to the giver:
   You handled those students very well, Eric.
   Oh, but not as well as you did.
2. Apply it elsewhere:
   Congratulations on getting your degree, Sonia.
   I owe it to my parents.
3. Globalise it:
   You have done a pretty good job on this project.
   Yes, the team did well. No one let the side down.
4. Don't see it (ignore it):
   That was a good speech – and your comment in question time was particularly valuable.
   Yes, it was a good speech.
5. Reject it:
   You did that very well.
   No, I didn't.
6. Discount the source:
   You look lovely today.
   You're bound to say that.
7. Unfavourable interpretation:
   That's a lovely dress you're wearing today.
   Didn't you like the one I wore yesterday?
8. Analyse it:
   Why do you think he said that to me?

Although there may be good reasons why you do not want to accept a stroke, and you certainly do not have to, it is worth remembering that a discounted stroke is a slap in the face for the giver. That may not be what the discounter intends, but that is how it comes out.

Strokes are very potent. One of the most powerful ways to use TA to change your own life is to look at your own stroke pattern and then change it by giving more positive unconditional strokes at work and outside work. The effect on colleagues, employees, partners, friends will always be beneficial to them and to you.

Life positions

The experiences of the baby and child during his first few years, particularly the strokes or lack of strokes, and the prescriptions and proscriptions he receives from parents, teachers and other adults, lead him to take basic positions about himself. These decisions become generalised into the basic OK and not-OK psychological positions. There are four of these positions:

I'M OK YOU'RE NOT-OK	I'M OK YOU'RE OK
I'M NOT-OK YOU'RE NOT-OK	I'M NOT-OK YOU'RE OK

The OK Corral

The child who comes to accept his own worth and that of other people, who can trust other people and feel confidence in himself, is in an I'm OK, you're OK position. Very few people seem to be able to operate in this position, but it is the most constructive, creative and healthy, and enables openness and intimacy to exist between people.

For most of us our early experience were of being put down, criticised, made to feel a fool, made to feel powerless or inadequate by parents, teachers, big brothers, etc. and we incorporate enough feelings about our own various inadequacies to carry though these feelings into our adult life and work from the position I'm not-OK, you're OK. If we think about our nervousness before making a speech or facing an argument with our boss, or our embarrassment when our colleague behaves strangely in public, or our apprehension when waiting for comments on our performance, we see the not-OK feelings of our Child within us. We can probably guess that about three-quarters of all people are generally in this position.

A few people have such a brutalised experience, physically or psychologically, in their childhood, that for their own survival they switch positions to I'm OK, you're not-OK, and as they take this into adulthood they are likely to display signs of megalomania, dictatorial or persecuting behaviour. At its strongest level it produced Hitler; at a more moderate level principals or parents who are forever getting angry with and putting down their subordinates or children. The I'm not-OK, you're not-OK position is one of black despair in which few people can be for very long without damaging their personality. It is the world of depressives and suicides.

Although we can move temporarily into another position, we are most of the time bound by the one which we were led to accept early in our life. Skilled therapy can certainly move people into more healthy positions, however, and TA therapists have had considerable successes in this.

Time

Everyone of us has the existential problem of what to do with the next few minutes or hours. For everyone of us time sometimes drags and sometimes races by, but one way or another we have to fill it. We have a limited range of choices. Berne suggested that we can pass time in one of the following ways:

1. **Withdrawal**. We can go into ourselves, detached from other people, and daydream, fantasise or meditate. If we are sitting on a train just watching the scenery go by, or in a lecture room thinking back to some enjoyable experiences the night before, we are structuring our time by withdrawal.

2. **Rituals**. We can pass the time by highly stylised exchanges with other people, where there is a minimum of content but interchanges of mutual recognition between people. It is typified by the greetings exchange:

   > *Hi!*
   > *Hello there!*
   > *How's things?*
   > *Fine, how about you?*
   > *Fine. Be seeing you then.*
   > *Sure. Cheers.*
   > *Cheerio.*

3. **Activities**. This is what we might normally call work. Giving a lecture, replacing a window, cleaning the car, operating the computer are all activities and may or may not involve us with other people.

4. **Pastimes** are ways of passing the time by pleasant cocktail party chat on safe subjects which require little thought and where responses are automatic. They have a somewhat repetitive quality and often start with a statement such as, 'What car are you driving now?', 'How's the baby getting along?', 'What recipe did you use for this cake?' They are, in Berne's words 'largely socially programmed by talking about acceptable subjects in acceptable ways.'

5. **Games** are sets of ulterior transactions with well-defined psychological gains and losses. These are discussed in the next section.

6. Finally, there is **Intimacy**, an open relationship of mutual free giving and receiving without exploitation. It is the most exciting, deep, rewarding, but for some people the most frightening, of the ways of passing time.

The six ways of time structuring are produced here in ascending order of risk. The total openness of intimacy involves risk, the total closedness of withdrawal gives almost total safety. We all pattern our time differently. There are people who spend much time in Withdrawal and Ritual, and when they do get more closely involved with people have to do it by Games playing. Other people spend most of their time in Activities and Pastimes. There are some mature, and fortunate people who can spend quite considerable time in Intimacy. An examination of your own time structuring over a week will enable you to decide whether you want to make changes or not.

Games

It was Eric Berne's analysis of psychological games in his best-seller *Games People Play* (1964) that first brought TA to the attention of the public. This was unfortunate in a way because a great deal of superficial interest in games developed without much serious thought as to what lay behind them, nor equivalent interest in the other areas of TA.

Games are transactions between people which are always destructive to at least one of the players and leave behind feelings of not being OK. They are compulsive and repetitive. People play the same games over and over again. Why do people engage in them?

Games provide for those taking part in them a number of 'rewards'.

- They satisfy our rackets – that is, they enable us to feel justified in feeling angry, stupid, incompetent or whatever our racket is.
- They reinforce our particular life position.
- They provide us with a lot of strokes of the kind we want – and for some games players these are negative strokes.
- They pass the time and thus avoid the need to spend it more constructively (e.g. in intimacy or withdrawal) but more threateningly.
- They have a pay-off in terms of some existential problem the player has.

Game playing is explained most easily by taking two or three examples.

Game 1
A lecturer comes into the Head of Department's office, looking worried.

Lecturer (A): *I wonder if you can help me? I've got a real problem.*
HoD (B): *Of course. Just sit yourself down and tell me all about it.*
(A): *I've been teaching for six months now and I am still making a mess of it. I'm just not making it as a teacher.*
(B): *Why don't you apply for one of the inservice courses for teachers?*
(A): *I'd love that, but my wife's pregnant and I don't want to be away from her more than I have to be the next four months.*
(B): *Well, how about the evening sessions the Professional Tutor is organising on teaching methods?*
(A): *Most evenings are really tricky for me just at the moment.*
(B): *You could read some of the books on teaching. They might help.*

(A):   *Yes, but I don't learn easily from reading things in books.*

(B):   *Why don't you go and talk to Jim? He's a very skilful teacher, and I'm sure he would be willing to help you.*

(A):   *I've thought of that, but what works for him, wouldn't work for me.*

(B):   *Well . . . why don't you take a tape recorder into the classroom. You could play it back and find out where you were going wrong.*

(A):   *I don't think I'd be at ease with a machine going.*

At this point the Head of Department runs out of ideas. She can do one of two things but neither of them will do any good because she is well and truly hooked.

1st variation

(B):   *I don't know. I can't really think of anything else. I'm sorry.*

(A):   *Well, I guessed you wouldn't be willing to help me.*

The HoD feels a sense of failure and criticism from the lecturer so she feels bad. The lecturer feels that if he doesn't get any help when he asks for it, it's not surprising he isn't teaching well, so he goes away confirmed in his racket of incompetence. He can carry on being bad and not have the responsibility of trying to get better.

2nd variation

(B):   (angrily) *Look, I keep on making suggestions and all you do is dismiss them. You've got to get a grip of yourself or you'll never make a teacher.*

(A):   *There you are, you see. I come to get help and all anyone can do is get angry with me. How can you expect me to get better.*

The lecturer goes away feeling justified in his incompetence. He has manoeuvred the HoD to appear to be unsympathetic to his problem, and the Head is left feeling bad.

This game is known as 'Why don't you – yes but', and is very common in organisations. The following are the points to notice about it:

1. The lecturer starts by hooking the Nurturing Parent of the Head of Department. If he cannot do that, the game won't work so he will only play this with someone with a strong Nurturing Parent. Games always require two players, and the initiator of the game looks round for the susceptible person. Once found, the game will be played over and over again in various forms.
2. There is a stage in every game when there is a cross over. Roles change and the knife goes in. In this case it occurs when the Head runs out of ideas and is likely to move either to Adapted Child or Critical Parent. This is what the lecturer is waiting for. He quickly moves into Critical Parent and leaves the scene.
3. The lecturer goes away not only feeling legitimated in his failure but also with an important pay-off – that he need take no responsibility for his performance. The most common kinds of pay-offs in games are: avoiding responsibility for your actions, avoiding intimacy, or avoiding the consequences of one's work (copping out).
4. The game was very stroke-rich. The lecturer got a lot of attention and concern which filled a need he had for strokes.

5. The way to avoid being dragged more than once into this game (almost everyone falls for it first time round) is to keep a firm check on your Nurturing Parent and respond to the initial hook by an Adult statement like:

> *Could you come back tomorrow at 10.00 with some ideas of what methods you might find useful, and we can discuss them.*

The Head will not be bothered with this games player again. The last thing the lecturer wants is a solution.

Game 2

A course team leader comes into the Vice Principal's office.

Vice Principal (A): *We have to have this course submission ready very quickly. Sorry about it but the committee have been on to me. What's the earliest you can get it done by?*

Team Leader (B): *If we cut all the corners and I work over the weekends I can let you have it in two weeks.*

(A): *Two weeks! Far too long. I cannot wait that long. I must have it in seven days. If not, believe me, some heads will roll.*

The team work very hard on the submission but still haven't finished after seven days. The Vice Principal then sends for them and demands angrily to know why they haven't finished and goes on to describe a whole series of faults, failings and unsatisfactory characteristics the incompetent and lazy team leader has, and discusses him with a whole series of undefined threats.

This is a simple version of the game known as NIGYSOB ('Now I've got you son of a bitch'). It consists of setting a person up to knock them down, in this case by giving an impossible task and then attacking someone for failing at it. It can equally well be set up by giving ambiguous instructions, conflicting instructions or changing the rules half way through. The pay-off for the Vice Principal is that he can legitimately satisfy his anger racket, and he can feel that failures are not his fault but those of his incompetent underlings. He can only play this with someone, however, who is prepared to take an Adapted Child role and who requires to be kicked in order to satisfy his racket. So he can go away feeling hurt, a failure, guilty or whatever his particular racket is. This is a complementary game in that a NIGYSOB player is looking for a Kick Me player, and when the two meet, they will cherish each other. The last person the NIGYSOB boss would ever want to sack is his Kick Me subordinate. The game is easily broken at the point where the Vice Principal's unreasonable time limit is given. A response could be:

> *I'm sorry. I cannot do it in seven days and you will have to accept that. I will finish it in 14 days but no sooner.*

Whatever the Vice Principal's response, he will realise he hasn't got a player for NIGYSOB.

Game 3

This is a game which normally takes place over a period of time, though it can refer to the activities of one day. A lecturer has made a very favourable impression since he was appointed a few months ago. He has worked very hard, often late into the evening and has several schemes in various stages of completion for improving the range and quality of the department's work. One of his colleagues goes sick for several weeks and he takes over her classes. He sits on several committees and has never yet turned down any request by the Principal that he involves himself in some new body. He is also in the middle of working for his MSc via a thesis on management. When one of the Vice Principals goes ill, he volunteers to take over some of her planning work. Everyone sees him as a dynamic, hard-working man for whom future promotion is inevitable, though a number wonder how ever he does it all.

Then just before his schemes come to completion, his thesis is written and his job application goes in for a Vice Principal's job, he collapses. Over-work, the doctor says, and orders him six months rest. He was a great chap, worked like fury, say his colleagues as they pick up the bits and pieces of his schemes and course submissions, committee memberships and the like. No one criticises him, everyone regards him highly. And yet what he has set up is a game, the purpose of which is to enable him legitimately to cop out, to fail to deliver or achieve what he is supposed to achieve. He is a person frightened of the responsibility of having to be accountable for his work, and so makes sure he never quite completes the projects. In the process he gets a very large number of strokes and can legitimately feel he is a highly competent person who would have achieved great things if only it had not been for his breakdown in health.

This is a common game among business executives, some of whom work quite hard to get their heart attack. It can be played in a small way over selected projects, such as the running of a conference or over the whole of one's work. It is a difficult one to deal with, but if it is recognised early enough colleagues can refuse to allow that level of over-work in so far as they have that power. This game is a version of 'Harried', and cop out or accountability-avoiding games are found in several manifestations...

There are many other variations of games and the reader is referred to the standard texts including Eric Berne's *Games People Play*.

Practical applications of TA in the college

We can apply TA to our working life in the college. Most obviously we can examine our own typical work transactions and see if they satisfy us as being flexible and appropriate to the situations we are in. Are we too often operating from our Parent or our Adult? We can examine our stroke pattern and see if we give as many strokes as we think we do, and whether our strokes are appropriate and freely given or conditional in some way. Are we set in certain stroke patterns where we always stroke the Child of our secretary and the Adult of our teaching staff? The rethinking of our stroke pattern is probably the most powerful single activity for change that we can undertake. Likewise we need to look at how we receive strokes: do we accept them or reject them? What difference will it make to our relationship with the givers if we start accepting strokes we have previously rejected?

With knowledge of our rackets, what kinds of games are we playing with those in charge of us and those we are responsible for? Are we initiating games or merely being hooked into them by those around us? How are we going to break out of our games?

With practice we can begin to apply TA to our interactions with other people, developing more flexibility and social control and reducing the amount of manipulation and the feeling of being not-OK.

If we look at our organisations as a whole, we can describe our college, department or section in TA terms:

It is very Parental – if so does this come out in nurturing, rule-setting, or controlling?

Does our organisation cope with the need to express the Free Child – is it sometimes a Fun organisation?

Is our organisation strokey or non-strokey? If it does seem to encourage a lot of strokes, are they positive or negative, conditional or unconditional?

Is our organisation in the position of I'm OK – You're OK? If not, what?

Whatever the situation, the important point is that we as individuals have the power to begin to change.

References and further reading

Berne E (1964) *Games people play* NY: Grove Press
   A best-seller in its day, but generally misunderstood and it needs to be read in the context of his other works.
Berne E (1975) *What do you say after you say hello?* Corgi
   At his most brilliant, and the culmination of his life's thinking. If you read only one of his books, this is it.
Birnbaum J (1997) *How to stop hating and start loving* Pan
   A popularisation of TA theory that is easy to read and with good examples. Its particular value is its concentration on hostility and anger.
Dusay J (1980) *Egograms* Bantam
   A very good exploration of the egogram as a technique for self-examination.
Steiner C (1974) *Scripts people live* NY: Grove Press
   This is an excellent book, which is centred on scripts.
Woollams S & Brown TA (1979) *The total handbook of transactional analysis* Englewood Cliffs NJ: Prentice-Hall
   A very good introduction, which assumes slightly more of the reader than some of the other books.

13.   An Interpersonal Skill: Handling Conflict

Derek Marsh

This paper summarises the principal skills and processes for effectively handling interpersonal conflict.

Effectively dealing with interpersonal conflict reduces stress, facilitates personal and work relationships, and reduces (or removes) dysfunctional behaviour, enabling the development of a more tolerable climate and achievement of tasks.

There are four principal rules to follow in managing conflict in such a way that you assert your rights without denying those of others.

1) Who owns the problem?

The person most concerned and discomforted owns the problem. Only the person who owns the problem can resolve it. In other words, if I am bothered by an issue I have the choice of either learning to live with it (if I do, then cannot complain), or resolving it. I empower myself if I handle it; I empower the other if I do not. If someone else owns the problem (e.g. they do not like my way of doing things, or their only response is aggression), then it is their task to handle the conflict. It is not up to me to change to meet their expectations. Conflict is generally internal in that there will be a mismatch between needs and wants, and the present situation.

2) Making a choice

If I decide to handle the conflict then I have to do two things:

a) Look at myself, that is, my beliefs, values, attitudes, prejudices, stereotypes, and standards and decide whether or not I can adjust these to remove the conflict. 'If all else fails lower your standards.' If I can alter my values sets without too much loss then it might be worth considering as a course of action.

b) If I cannot, then I have to decide on what precise issue will I make a stand to handle the conflict. It should be an issue from which I may reasonably expect, or be able to negotiate, a change in *behaviour* from the other person. (I cannot expect to change attitudes, beliefs, etc.)

3) Confronting the issue and the problem

Handling conflict involves taking action. Effective action comprises:

a) selecting a specific piece of behaviour about which you wish to confront the other; focus very clearly on one thing you wish to handle (there will probably be more than one you will wish to deal with, but take them one at a time always);

b) stating clearly that one piece of behaviour, using words which are non-judgemental, non-value laden;

c)   stating how you feel about that behaviour (feelings are facts);

d)   stating the effect that the behaviour has on you (and maybe others);

e)   stating what you would like to happen and invite co-operation;

f)   listening to the response;

g)   negotiating so that you both 'win'.

4) Handling the response

The response may be aggressive, critical, or refusing to listen.

Aggressive

In transactional analysis (TA) terms, aggression usually comes from the Parent (critical) or Child (adapted). At all times remain in Adult ego state and handle the transactions gradually to move the other from Parent or Child to Adult. Block games and do not allow the other to hook into your Parent or Child.

Reflect back, non-judgementally, the other's behaviour and accept it, but asking for a more reasonable, rational (i.e. Adult) response.

Critical

Criticism is either valid or invalid. When it is valid, accept it and agree not to behave in future in such a way. Thank for feedback.

When it is invalid, acknowledge the other's feelings and perceptions, and point out its invalidity.

Under a barrage response, respond by acknowledging the other's feelings and perceptions, and enquire whether or not there are further points the other would like to make since you would find their feelings and perceptions useful to you. Listen.

Agree, i.e. contract not to do certain things (focus always on behaviour by asking, e.g. what is it I do that makes you feel angry?) and then return to your confrontation to resolve your problem issue.

Refusing to listen

When someone refuses to listen, point out that refusal by reflecting their *behaviour* and repeating your confrontation (in Adult state). Having chosen to resolve your problem do not let go of the issue until it is resolved to your satisfaction.

Finally, do not sit on powerful feelings; acknowledge them and take action to handle them to remove the discomfort. Handling conflict is a learning, a growth, situation for everyone involved. Honest, authentic, and mature conflict management can only lead to more effective interpersonal relationships and institutions.

Part Five – Preventing Disruptive Behaviour

Part Five examines ways in which teachers and organisations can work together to minimise the occurrence of disruption in a teaching context. For obvious reasons, much of the literature is based on research in the compulsory phases of education, where issues of discipline and control are more urgent, but there is nothing in any of the extracts here which does not have relevance to the post-16 sector.

Mick McManus, while reassuring us that troublesome behaviour in the classroom is not a new phenomenon, critically considers some of the more recent definitions of disruption. He argues that that the classroom is a uniquely complex environment and that 'common-sense' approaches to discipline and punishment are of limited value. He maintains that pupil behaviour is a whole-school issue, and that the resolution of acts of aggression and disorder is to be found in the confident teacher's classroom management skills and understanding of the motivation and background of learners.

Judy Bradley considers the literature on disruption with particular reference to post-compulsory education and training. She advocates a 'multidimensional approach', which recognises the importance of considering individual students and their behaviour within the context of the classroom, the institution and of society itself. She affirms the importance of adopting both a curriculum and a style of teaching that are relevant to the needs and abilities of young people.

Colin Smith and Robert Laslett look more closely at what we mean when we talk about 'classroom management'. They question the 'charismatic' approach to successful teaching and present four very practical sets of skills that will help to achieve and maintain purposeful behaviour in the classroom. These are skills that all teachers can learn and they are brought together in the form of four 'rules'.

- Rule one: Get them in (greeting, seating and starting)
- Rule two: Get them out (concluding and dismissing)
- Rule three: Get on with it (content and manner)
- Rule four: Get on with them (who's who? what's going on?)

Smith & Laslett present this as a 'framework for analysing aspects of lesson-planning and management which contribute to a productive partnership between teachers and pupils'.

Several writers have drawn attention to the concept of 'mismatch' as a factor which contributes to troublesome classroom behaviour. In the last reading in Part Five Merillie Huxley examines mismatch between expectations and reality as a 'no blame' approach to the analysis of disruption. She defines the problem in terms of the needs and wants of different participants in the process and argues that disruption may result when needs of learners are not appropriately met. She, too, emphasises the responsibility of the institution for achieving a better match of expectations and thus an improvement in student behaviour.

14. Concerns, Causes and Remedies

Mick McManus

For playing truant he was caned. He tried to kick me, in fact he did kick me, and his mother then came to school and abused me in a most frightful manner.

(School Log of 1884, quoted in Porter, 1990)

Have times changed?

'The police believe themselves powerless before a rising tide of mischief and violence – particularly a recent serious increase in ruffianism among city youth.' This sort of statement is made every day and commands wide assent, but it is a quotation from a complaint voiced in 1898. In the 1890s a government enquiry was launched into the rising crime rate among young people; a century later, similar concerns resulted in the Elton Report (DES, 1989), which was the most comprehensive study of school discipline ever conducted in Britain. The report contains 138 recommendations addressed to every conceivable audience. Employers, parents, the Broadcasting Standards Council as well as teachers and even pupils are all the subject of advice as to how they can contribute to reducing bad behaviour in schools. Elton, unlike some of the experts we will consider ..., promised no miracles: 'Reducing bad behaviour is a realistic aim. Eliminating it completely is not' (paragraph 2/29: 65). The committee received extensive evidence, consulted research and commissioned some of its own, and came to the conclusion that 'any quest for simple or complete remedies would be futile'. Its own summary covers eight pages and the theme of the report is clear: discipline in schools is the responsibility of everyone and not only a matter for teachers. Nevertheless, it concludes that much indiscipline can be diminished by making teachers better at classroom management.

As the Elton committee discovered, the literature offers a bewildering collection of definitions, estimates of prevalence, claims about trends, historical evidence and speculations upon causes and cures. The popular view that disorder in schools, like disorder in society, is a recent phenomenon is easily contradicted by reference to historical sources. Curtis (1963) records some of the frequent disturbances at the ancient universities, whose students were in many respects the equivalent of present-day secondary pupils. For example, at Cambridge in 1261 there was a fight between scholars from the north and south; unlike twentieth-century two-nations disputes, this one led to plunder and burning. At Oxford, on St Scholastica's Day in 1354, a pub-fight ended with many dead and wounded; a similar riot broke out in Cambridge in 1381. School rules are a clue to what behaviour might be expected from thirteenth-century pupils: at Westminster, boys were forbidden to play tricks on townsmen and not allowed to carry bows, sticks or stones. The fifteenth-century Cambridge graduation ritual for a Master of Grammar, who sought a licence to teach, placed discipline on an equal footing with learning. After the candidate had 'argyude as shall please the Proctor' he was provided with a 'Rodde' and a 'shrewde', that is, mischievous, boy whom he then 'bete openlye in the Scolys'. In this way, says Curtis, 'the newly fledged master proved his ability to teach in a grammar-school' (1963: 65). Most sixteenth- and seventeenth-century pictures of school-masters, says Curtis, depict the master with a birch or rod. A number of serious disturbances followed the abolition of certain 'papist' holidays after 1565. In 1587, pupils used armed force to occupy Edinburgh High School, as had happened earlier in Aberdeen. In 1595, magistrates were called to regain control of the same school and a town councillor was shot dead in the process. Raikes was impelled to found his Sunday schools partly by the 'wild and mischievous behaviour' of children on their day of rest. Evidently some of it continued, for Raikes had discipline problems: in one incident, a badger was let loose in the schoolroom. The horrors of eighteenth- and nineteenth-century public schools have been described by Gathorne-Hardy (1977): for example, in an 1818 riot at Eton, pupils smashed the desk of their headmaster, Dr Keates.

It may be said in mitigation that these examples come from more brutal times, in which such incidents did not carry the horrifying implications that they would in the twentieth century. In the eighteenth century, Coram was moved to found his hospital to rid the streets of abandoned and dying babies, and even as late as the 1890s they were said to be a common sight (Schostak, 1986); there were twenty times as many child deaths then as there are today. However, there is evidence that past violence was not viewed lightly at the time. Concern about increasing disorder among the young led, in 1847, to the establishment of a House of Lords Select Committee to look into the operation of the criminal law with respect to children. Evidence included statistics showing a rising conviction rate among those under 21, and some witnesses blamed the ragged schools for it (Curtis, 1963: 302)...

What is troublesome behaviour?

Uncertainty about the amount of troublesome behaviour has always been a feature of the debate and is allied to the difficulty in arriving at a definition which all can agree is interpreted and applied consistently. Doyle says the key to understanding misbehaviour is to see it 'in the context of classroom structures'. He defines it, with a struggle, as 'any behaviour by one or more students that is perceived by the teacher to initiate a vector of action that competes with or threatens the primary vector of action at a particular moment in a classroom activity' (Wittrock, 1986: 419). In the effort to recognise the subjectivity and relativity of teacher perceptions, this definition makes anything potentially misbehaviour.

In a class which has been left to its own devices, so that the teacher can catch up with marking, a pupil who asks for some work to do would be misbehaving. Conversely, if the teacher does not notice the bored pupil cutting up his or her books, that is not misbehaviour. For, as Doyle's definition says, anything that interferes with the teacher's state of mind is misbehaviour. The definition of disruptive behaviour offered by Galloway et al. (1982) is similarly flawed: ... 'any behaviour which appears problematic, inappropriate and disturbing to teachers'.

Another attempt, which appears to remove the subjective element by defining disruption in terms of its effect upon (ordinary) teaching and the (normal) school, is that by Lawrence et al. (1977, 1984): 'behaviour which seriously interferes with the teaching process and/or seriously upsets the normal running of the school.' As many teachers say when asked for examples of such behaviour: it depends what you mean by 'seriously'. Distinctions between maladjustment and disruption are similarly problematic. There is a popular view that maladjustment is a pathological medical condition and disruption is rooted in moral deficiencies. Individual pathology plays a greater or lesser part in each pupil's behaviour, but there is no line between those who are typed as maladjusted and those typed as disruptive. Similar errors were made in identifying pupils with learning difficulties prior to the abolition of categories of handicap following the Education Act 1981. For example, many came to believe that pupils could be sorted into remedial, ESN(M) and ESN(S) types, but these categories evolved from historical and administrative arrangements. They encouraged the view that problems were solved because they had been identified, and where a pupil proved unamenable in a particular placement there was a tendency to seek a fresh place rather than a fresh policy.

More than twenty years ago, Hewett & Blake (1973) wrote that 'the most pressing need is for a reliable system of definition and classification of emotional and behavioural disorders'. We still do not have one, and they were wrong. To rely on definitions and categories to suggest remedies is to divert attention from observation of the individual and his or her circumstances. There are no easy solutions, so we have to think.

In a survey ... I asked fifty teachers to indicate on a list of thirty-eight items the pupil behaviours they thought were 'serious threats to good order'. There was total agreement on only one item: 'Hits teacher'. Five teachers ticked every item; five queried the meaning of 'serious' or declined to tick any. The difficulty of definition is captured in an autobiographical anecdote by Blishen (1980): 'There was a boy in class two who was, I had to conclude, an advanced delinquent – yet his offence was barely definable. The nearest I could come to it was to say that he turned sitting down into a comedy.' Becker (1963) was only slightly exaggerating when he wrote, more directly than Doyle, that: '... deviance is not a quality of the act a person commits, ... the deviant is one to whom that label has successfully been applied; deviant behaviour is behaviour that people so label.'

Labels and classifications spring from theories, often held implicitly, and it is true that they may tell us as much about the labeller as about the labelled. This does not mean that labels, categories and definitions are purely arbitrary: the distinctions, especially if they stick, must have something to do with that which is being observed. As Pring (1976) says, words like 'cats' and 'dogs' tell something about the classifier, but they also tell us something about the nature of cats and dogs. Defining and measuring the seriousness of misbehaviour is not a matter of applying such a simple distinction: it is more like trying to decide which dogs are light grey and which are not. No objective definition which would reduce the measurement of disruption to a simple counting process is possible. This definitional obscurity, unsatisfactory as it may be, is an important clue to one of the ways in which the problem of troublesome behaviour might be tackled. There are at least two parties to any disruptive incident. Both contribute to its being defined as serious or not, or indeed to whether it becomes defined as a disruptive incident at all...

Common-sense remedies

The dip into past indiscipline with which we began this chapter was intended to put present problems into a less stressful perspective. It also prompts us to consider the value of the simple solutions that are popularly offered for indiscipline in schools. Brutal punishments are as old as history: 'A boy's ear is in his backside' wrote one ancient Egyptian scribe (quoted in Tyldesley, 1994). In more recent times, it is questionable whether such punishments were effective. While some pupils were being flogged at school, some of their non-attending peers might be awaiting capital punishment or transportation for non-violent crimes. Spooner (1988) recorded a case of a boy who had been caned on eighty-nine occasions in a year in which he had attended school on only eighty-seven days. Even in countries where violent offenders are still violently dealt with, there remain those prepared to offend and earn the punishments. Naturally, in assessing the efficacy of a punishment, most of us consider whether we ourselves would be deterred. This is a mistake. We rightly feel that we would not risk punishment for a crime, neglecting the fact that we make this decision from our present, comfortable perspective; and since most of us eschew crime and violence anyway, we are not able to understand the motivation of those who ignore rules and who would not be deterred. There are, of course, considerations other than the efficacy issue: for many people, and most western governments, repaying violence with violence is not morally acceptable and no amount of evidence that such a policy works would change that view.

Even if rigid and complete discipline in a school were achievable by force, it would not necessarily transfer with the pupil to fresh situations. Goffman (1968) has documented the varied strategies available even to asylum inmates to enable them to protect themselves from unwanted influences: for example, withdrawal, rebellion, 'playing it cool'. We can be sure that pupils are at least as inventive. Wills (1967) hoped pupils would devise a moral system of their own which was 'not unacceptable to society' and which they would stick to and value: 'It is possible for a person under discipline never to display a single symptom and go out into the world untouched.' Davies & Maliphant (1974) conducted an extraordinary experiment to measure the effectiveness of 'distinctly unpleasant' electric shocks in teaching 'refractory' pupils and ordinary pupils a simple skill. The refractory individuals received significantly more shocks than their more amenable fellows but the effects were short lived. The authors suggest that this is typical of the ineffectiveness of punishment upon them in ordinary life.

Discussing troublesome pupils, Laslett (1977) points out that the cause and source of punishment are easily confused. Punishment does not discourage misbehaviour but rather reinforces the pupil's view of adults as treacherous. In a research review, Topping (1983) concluded that punishment was ineffective and could aggravate problems. For a few distressed individuals, seeking punishment may be a part of their problem not a solution to it; others are denied the opportunity to make amends. Laslett therefore suggests that management is a more useful concept than punishment. A pupil is put in the care and under the close supervision of one person, perhaps a personal tutor or senior member of staff, where difficulties can be sorted out without the interference of an attendant audience: close proximity encourages a helpful exchange of information. Wills (1945) also thought punishment took away the valuable opportunity for the offender to make restitution. He also suggested that punishment led to the exclusion of moral thinking in favour of book-keeping calculations related to the possibility of being caught, and the likely price to be paid. This encouraged the attitude that misbehaviour could be paid for, the slate being wiped clean for fresh villainy. A similar claim is sometimes made about the function of the sacrament of confession and it is equally unconvincing; in any case, the argument applies as well to restitution as it does to punishment. At the other extreme from punishment, permissiveness is equally unhelpful. In a pioneer study, Jackson (1968) noted that to survive in classrooms pupils needed to learn turn-taking and patience: teacher as gatekeeper created the experiences of denial, interruption and distraction for pupils. Delamont (1976) produces the often-quoted figure of one minute of teacher's time per pupil per forty-minute lesson and comments that research is needed into how pupils spend their minute. Many pupils need help in learning how to use the other thirty-nine. Something of this sort is implied in Laslett's (1977) suggestion that troublesome pupils should be exposed occasionally to adults less tolerant than their teachers.

Common-sense causes

The advice in this book is intended to be useful in the teaching of all pupils, from the naughty to the seriously disturbed. No one should assume that classroom management skills, or the social and institutional pressures of classrooms and schools, are irrelevant to the treatment of pupils believed to be severely disruptive or maladjusted. Many teachers take it for granted that the treatment of pupils who have behaved very badly over a long period is a medical matter. Certainly, any other form of approach may seem hopelessly time consuming and uncertain in its effects: to listen, think and help can be an open-ended, unrewarding and exhausting enterprise. It seems self-evident that some pupils have something bio-chemically wrong with them, and common sense to leave medical experts to find the most soothing cocktail of tranquillisers. Teachers have grown accustomed to deferring to experts of various kinds and take it as axiomatic that medical advice is safe, scientific and objective. Doctors have only recently lost the right to decide whether a child needed special schooling or not. Teachers are rarely cast in the confident role of experts and do not find it at all remarkable to be told to consult specialists.

Much of the drift of a book on disruptive behaviour, written by two doctors, is in this vein (Holman & Coghill, 1987). Members of powerful professional groups are accustomed to having weight attached to their views on matters outside their specialism: for example, a scientist's opinion of religion, a doctor's views on parenting, a university teacher's policy for primary school maths. We defer too easily. Part of my argument is that teachers need to increase their confidence in their own expertise and therefore to give only what limited credence is due to members of other professions when they pronounce upon school matters. Much of what they have to say is pure tautology. For example, we are told: 'The prime purpose of schools as places of learning can be furthered by reducing impediments to learning, especially in children unable to learn' (Holman & Coghill, 1987: 220). In another inconsequential passage we learn: 'A teacher of 35, 15 years in the profession, when told by the head to get her hair cut saw this as a threat to her identity'; and well she might. However, a more serious threat to teacher identity is posed by politely accepting any kind of flim-flam from outsiders. A healthy scepticism is needed: the observations of those who have distinguished themselves in other spheres can be every bit as insubstantial as comments from any other person stopped on the street. To say that teachers should have confidence in their own expertise and not accept other specialists' opinions uncritically is not to say that teachers should regard their own medical and psychological knowledge as complete and sufficient. Laslett (1977) warns against teachers as amateur psychologists but notes that teachers' contact with pupils is greater in duration and variety than that of any other professional. That being the case, teachers are best placed to understand pupils' problems and should take a central role in assessing the advice of others, whose contact with the problem can seldom be other than peripheral.

The notion that problem behaviour can be attributed solely to chemistry, whether internal in the genes or external in food additives or petrol-lead, has a powerful hold over the imagination, comfortably placing the responsibility elsewhere and offering an easy solution. It is important to be clear about the relationship between biology and behaviour, if only to rid ourselves of impossible dreams in respect of miracle cures. Biology cannot cause behaviour. We use the word 'cause' in many ways and easily deceive ourselves about the reasons why of things.

To make the argument clear, consider the relationship of biology to behaviour in a larger context. For example, a news report may say that famine, resulting from a crop failure, is causing starvation and food riots. In the wealthy countries we see such reports as fitting a well-known pattern: some countries have too many people, climates that grow too little food, and inefficient governments – it is a natural disaster. It is nothing to do with us, but having been moved by television coverage we will contribute what we can. But is the crop failure the cause? We know that the world is over-supplied with food and transport as well as the necessary botanical knowledge. A famine is not a result of natural events but of social ones: food could be redistributed and resources reallocated but we do not choose this uncongenial solution.

Behaviour problems are sometimes thought about in similar ways: a pupil has got into a wild state and gone berserk again; she has too much aggression, too little self-control and ineffective parenting – one of life's losers. It is nothing to do with us, but we will try to make sure she takes her tablets. It is tempting to let nature take the blame, but biological conditions cannot be any more than a background feature: their behavioural outcomes are the result of being channelled by experience. There is a view that we all have an aggressive drive that is essential to our independence (Storr, 1968): repression is therefore disapproved of and the solution is said to lie in encouraging positive aspects of aggression. But this view assumes what it seeks to explain. Aggressiveness does not have to be an innate drive necessary for survival: many people survive, and even command others, without being aggressive. To postulate an aggressive drive and then prove its existence by describing any sort of personal effectiveness as aggression is a circular argument. Aggression in schools is better understood as a strategy that a pupil has learned to use as an effective method of expression or a way of achieving his or her goals. The focus needs to be on individual perspectives, relationships and situational constraints, not the supposed defects in individual pathology. This is not to substitute what Dyke (1987) describes as psychoanalytical determinism for the biological kind. Bastide (1972) notes how a psychoanalytical focus on individuals leads to a sociological interest in relationships: early-life influences are social; for traumas of infancy to affect the present they must be reawakened and maintained in the present.

No one is born with a predisposition to hitting teachers: in a life of parental neglect and societal indifference, one pupil may find that violence is effective, another that teachers are a safe target for the hate they feel for their family and themselves. There is no genetic configuration that causes a particular misbehaviour: misbehaviour is social and exists not as a natural entity but only in a relationship, or potential relationship. Bastide (1972) argues this point even for insanity. In chronic and serious cases the use of drugs may be the only feasible strategy. Tablets are less labour-intensive than straitjackets, and the alternatives – full preventive, social and financial support for families at risk, and ready assistance for those who get into difficulty – are unthinkable. Often enough, it is more comforting for the parent, too: the belief that one's child has a medical problem is less threatening than accepting that our parenting is at fault. Of course, all treatments have a cost. Passed from one expert to the next, defined as a psychiatric or mental health problem, prescribed first this and then that, it is not surprising that some pupils grow dependent and anxious; and every recurrence of their problem behaviour confirms their growing and reasonable belief that they are not as others are and must face a life of troubles, isolation and possibly madness. Their problem is as much a result of our omissions as their flawed inheritance. It matters very much that we avoid the error of assuming that pupils receiving medical attention are beyond the reach of teachers' understanding and skills.

Our beliefs about the nature of a condition have real consequences. Bastide (1972) describes how a religious sect, the Hutterites, interpret bouts of depression as a visitation by the devil. They stay with the afflicted person and give social support until, as they see it, the demon gives up and leaves. Of course, unbelievers will point out that the companionship of others has lifted the spirits, not driven off a spectre. But that is not a point worth worrying about. Whatever their reasons, the Hutterites have settled on an altogether better treatment for depression than anything available on prescription. Most important of all, their strategy reintegrates the sufferer into the community; much medical or quasi-medical treatment abandons the victim to treatment in isolation. Schostak (1986) likens some drugs to riots: one acts inwardly to destroy the self, the other outwardly to destroy reality. In the matter of troublesome behaviour, medical interventions are like charity concerts and fun-runs for starving countries: a temporary relief and a welcome distraction from fundamental moral deficiencies in the way we exercise our social responsibilities... Some schools, like the Hutterites, view troublesome behaviour, and their responsibilities towards it, in ways that keep their pupils in their community.

Books and courses aimed at helping teachers manage disruption in the classroom generally fall into two groups: those that assume teacher skills are at fault and need remedying (for example, Chisholm *et al.* 1984); and those that assume that disruptive behaviour can be unlearned through a programme of behaviour modification (for example, Cheesman & Watts, 1985). Some blend both (for example, Galvin *et al.* 1990). Teachers can adopt the skills and strategies in these programmes without necessarily changing attitudes that may themselves be contributing to their problems and the stress they feel. Useful as these approaches may be, they are incomplete without consideration of the meaning of pupil behaviour and the hidden motives and anxieties that it may reflect. At a simple level, there is the testing of teachers' rules and resolution; the displaying and defending of personal identity; the establishment and maintaining of a place in a friendship or peer-group; and the straightforward relief of tedium and tension. Some teachers read these activities as personal attacks or as proof of a supposed rising tide of disorder. They may be disabused and reassured by the evidence in such texts as Beynon (1985), Denscombe (1985), Hammersley & Woods (1984), Schostak (1983) and Woods (1980).

At a deeper level, there are the influences of domestic and personal experiences which can dispose some pupils to unskilled and inappropriate strategies: struggles for attention, power or revenge; using the teacher as a safe target for feelings that belong to another person, place or time; seeking refuge from reminders of traumatic experiences in wild behaviour; camouflaged or inept attempts at friendship and destructive testing of any relationships that may be formed. Many teachers find themselves driven to pessimistic fatalism with severely disturbing pupils. Confrontations seem unavoidable and security may be sought in unbending and autocratic domination: pupils may be required to march in step or not to march at all. The result may be a synchronised but stressed and brittle atmosphere. Understanding may be gained through such texts as Balson (1982), Cronk (1987), Dreikurs (1957), Hanko (1985) and Stott (1982). Such knowledge permits a more dispassionate and analytical stance and can be used to produce an agenda for staff discussions focused on pupils or groups whose behaviour is causing problems. A possible list of tasks for such meetings might include: to retrieve and identify pupils' motives and strategies; to discover the sources of their need for attention or feelings of hostility; to uncover any teacher behaviour, classroom factors or school influences which may be unintentionally maintaining unwanted behaviour; to devise and agree a consistent, whole-school approach to particular problems.

This book is intended to provide a basis for teachers to begin their own casework discussions in their own schools. It is from a teacher and is addressed to teachers: the people who know and can help troublesome pupils. It is not intended to be a contribution from a 'tip and run' expert (Hanko, 1985). It is my hope that those who read it and begin to work in the ways described will integrate it into their practical experience: they should become unable to separate what they know from experience and what they read in the book. Sharing ideas, experiences and worries helps teachers become inured to and insulated from disruption; they may be less easily provoked and less likely to fall back on coercion and punishment. In a perfect example of the disarming approach, Kohl (1970) remarks: 'I like defiant, independent and humorous people and my preferences naturally come out in my teaching'. To be encouraged and enabled to use more detached and disarming strategies is to be able, should we so wish, to remain composed, dispassionate, impassive. And where such strategies predominate in a school the climate, ethos or atmosphere may be described as harmonious: many parts are played and varied tunes are possible. Pupils of every demeanour and disposition may feel valued in the care of serene and shatterproof professionals.

The deficiencies of explanations which rely on single causes are recognised in the more accessible guides that are now available – see Denscombe (1985), Docking (1980), Fontana (1985), Furlong (1985), Laslett & Smith (1984). Explanations for troublesome behaviour can be approached from two directions. On the one hand, we can begin with the pupil and his or her individual characteristics, personal perspectives and family circumstances; on the other, we can look at the social and cultural milieu in which schools and classrooms are maintained and teachers go about their work.

Whichever end we begin at, the quest for understanding leads us to glance towards, if not to travel to, the other. There is a similar range in the remedies offered for disruption in schools, but the fit is imperfect. Those focused on the pupil employ behavioural psychology, with its emphasis on straightforward rewards and punishments, or cognitive approaches which take account of the pupils' perspectives and motives. Those beginning at the societal end of the spectrum might emphasise the unequal distribution of chances in life, the social selection and allocation functions of schools, the shortages and competitiveness in the classrooms, and the resulting dilemmas and frustrations for teachers – many of whom see themselves as demoralised losers in a critical and unrewarding environment. Teachers stand on the boundary where pupils' problems and society's contradictions meet: to them falls the task of motivating those who have the skills that will be rewarded and mollifying those who do not. Some of the bad teachers blamed for indiscipline in schools are those who find this task beyond them. For some observers, confident that our social policies are fundamentally right, the weakness of such teachers renders them unfit for the profession.

In arguing for a broad and inclusive approach to problems in schools we are up against some terminology from which dangle simplistic theories and explanations. For example, the term 'disruptive' implies that the problem is caused by only one person. Sometimes the term is used in such a way as to suggest that it identifies a particular type of disorder – as distinct from maladjusted, delinquent or naughty. There is little to be gained in pondering these refinements. In general, I have used the phrase 'troublesome behaviour' and I do so, not to identify a specific syndrome, but in the hope that its neutrality carries no implications about aetiology or treatment. Worse still is the emphasis in many texts, and in the titles of some of them, on classroom control. Fontana (1985) suggests using the phrase in the sense of controlling an aircraft rather than a string of donkeys or a cage of lions. Another way of looking at it is to see virtue in increasing a teacher's power in the classroom: power is here understood as energy, a force from which pupils as well as teachers benefit. Davies (1984) claims that pupil deviance results when they are in danger of losing struggles in the classroom; giving the teacher more control may involve giving the pupil more power: absolute power and absolute powerlessness corrupt absolutely.

Control of oneself and a feeling of empowerment are important in social relationships: defensiveness distorts perception, isolates individuals and destroys relationships.

References

Balson M (1982) *Understanding classroom behaviour* ACER

Bastide R (1972) *The sociology of mental disorder* London: Routledge & Kegan Paul

Becker HS (1963) *The outsiders* New York: Free Press

Beynon J (1985) *Initial encounters in the secondary school* Lewes: Falmer

Blishen E (1980) *A nest of teachers* London/Lewes: Hamish Hamilton

Cheesman PL & Watts PE (1985) *Positive behaviour management* London: Croom Helm

Chisholm B, Kearney D, Knight G, Little H, Morris S & Tweddle D (1984) *Preventive approaches to disruption* London: Macmillan

Cronk KA (1987) *Teacher-pupil conflict in secondary schools* Lewes: Falmer

Curtis SJ (1963) *History of education in Great Britain* Foxton: Cambridge University Tutorial Press

Davies L (1984) *Pupil power: deviance and gender in school* Lewes: Falmer

Davies JVG & Maliphant R (1974) 'Refractory behaviour in school and avoidance learning' *Journal of Child Psychology, Psychiatry* 15: 23–30

Delamont S (1976) *Interaction in the classroom* London: Methuen

Denscombe M (1985) *Classroom control: a sociological perspective* London: George Allen & Unwin

DES (1989) *Discipline in schools: report of the committee of inquiry chaired by Lord Elton* London: HMSO

Docking JW (1980) *Control and discipline in schools* London: Harper & Row

Dreikurs R (1957) *Psychology in the classroom* London: Staples Press

Dyke S (1987) 'Psycho-analytic insight in the classroom: asset or liability?' *Journal of Educational Therapy* 1 (4): 43–64

Fontana D (1985) *Classroom control* London: Methuen

Furlong VJ (1985) *The deviant pupil* Milton Keynes: Open University Press

Galloway D, Ball T, Blomfield D & Seyd R (1982) *Schools and disruptive pupils* London: Longman

Galvin P, Mercer S & Costa P (1990) *Building a better-behaved school: a development manual for primary schools* London: Longman

Gathorne-Hardy J (1977) *The public school phenomenon* London: Hodder & Stoughton

Goffman E (1968) *Asylums* Harmondsworth: Penguin

Hammersley M & Woods P (1984) *Classrooms and staffrooms* Milton Keynes: Open University Press

Hanko G (1985) *Special needs in ordinary classrooms* Oxford: Basil Blackwell

Hewett FM & Blake PR (1973) 'Teaching the emotionally disturbed' in RMW Travers (ed) *Second handbook on research in teaching* Chicago: Rand-McNally

Holman PG & Coghill NF (1987) *Disruptive behaviour in school* Bromley: Chartwell-Bratt

Jackson P (1968) *Life in classrooms* New York: Holt, Rinehart & Winston

Kohl H (1970) *The open classroom* London: Methuen

Laslett R (1977) *Educating maladjusted children* London: Staples Press

Laslett R & Smith C (1984 and 1992) *Effective classroom management* London: Croom Helm

Lawrence J, Steed D & Young P (1977) *Disruptive behaviour in a secondary school* London: University of London

Lawrence J, Steed D & Young P (1984) 'European voices on disruptive behaviour in schools: definitions, concerns and types of behaviour' *British Journal of Educational Studies* 32 (1)

Porter R (1990) *Myths of the English* Cambridge: Polity Press

Pring R (1976) *Knowledge and schooling* London: Open Books

Shostack JF (1983) *Maladjusted schooling* Lewes: Falmer

Shostack JF (1986) *Schooling the violent imagination* Lewes: Falmer

Storr A (1968) *Human aggression* Harmondsworth: Penguin

Spooner B (1988) *Lay stone on stone* Leeds: The Gerbil Press

Stott DH (1982) *Helping the maladjusted child* Milton Keynes: Open University Press

Topping KJ (1983) *Education systems for disruptive adolescents* London: Croom Helm

Tyldesley J (1994) *Daughters of Isis: women of ancient Egypt* London: Viking

Wills D (1945) *The Barns experiment* London: Allen & Unwin

Wills D (1967) *The Hawkspur experiment* Harmondsworth: Penguin

Wittrock MC (ed) (1986) *Third handbook of research on teaching* New York: Macmillan

Woods P (ed) (1980) *Teacher strategies* London: Croom Helm

15. Approaches to Disruption: A Review of the Literature

Judy Bradley

[Editor's note. The paragraph numbering in this extract is from Appendix III of the 1987 FEU publication: *Behaviour and motivation: disruption in further education*.]

Towards a conceptual framework

12) Research on the problem of disruption has been undertaken from a variety of different perspectives. In general, however, they may be broadly divided into two main schools of thought. Some investigators (predominantly psychologists) have tended to look for psychological explanations relating to the individual and the family and to devise treatment strategies designed to reconcile the 'disruptive pupil' to the existing demands of the institution. Others (predominantly sociologists) have focused instead on features relating to the social and organisational context in which disruption takes place. Thus disruption is seen as a warning signal of tensions within the educational system, and the possibility is acknowledged that disruptive behaviour may express a legitimate criticism of aspects of school or college organisation and teacher practices.

13) This is not to suggest that all researchers have adhered rigidly to one or other of these approaches. Sociologists have carried out detailed studies of what goes on in classrooms, while psychologists have begun to examine relationships and interactions. A growing use of phenomenological analyses has gradually shifted the overall focus of attention from the disruptive individual to disruption as a complex interrelationship of a variety of factors.

14) Disruption is not a unitary phenomenon with a single cause. Its study has, then, been undertaken at a range of different levels. The types of explanation advanced – and hence the strategies recommended for dealing with disruption – depend on whether the focus of attention is on the individual 'disruptive' student, the behaviour itself, the classroom, the institution, or the wider context in which it takes place (see Frude & Gault, 1984). We shall now consider each of these in turn.

The individual

15) The traditional approach to the problem of disruption concentrated on looking at causes in the personality and background characteristics of the individual 'disruptive pupil'. While studies of this kind have gone out of favour in recent years, they have produced evidence with some degree of consistency on the relationship between disruptive behaviour and variables such as age, aggressiveness, neurological problems, low academic attainment, low academic self-image, and home backgrounds characterised by low or erratic discipline (Farrington, 1978; Galloway *et al.* 1982). It must, however, be noted that there is no typical profile of a disruptive child or adolescent. While this 'medical model' of disruption cannot be rejected out of hand, it

is now recognised that the study of the individual should form just one part of a broader strategy that also takes account of the context in which disruptive incidents take place.

The incident

16) Data for the analysis of disruptive incidents has been gathered in a number of different ways: systematic observation of classroom interactions (Clarke *et al.* 1981; Parry-Jones & Gay, 1980); accounts as reported by the teacher (Comber & Whitfield, 1979; Lawrence *et al.* 1983); accounts from both teachers and pupils (Galloway *et al.* 1982). Several points of consensus have emerged from studies adopting these various methods. In particular, it is agreed that many major incidents derive from an event that is initially trivial and that, overall, disruptive incidents are based on a logical sequence involving a series of behaviour patterns that can be identified. This sequence is described by Pik (1981) as being composed of the building-up, the trigger event, the escalation and the finale. It can be initiated either by the teacher or the pupil, or both.

17) Information from studies of this kind increases our understanding of disruption as based on interaction rather than on the characteristics of individuals. It may also have important implications for teacher training in relation to classroom management techniques. If the teacher is able to identify potential trouble spots, to clarify the options open at any one time and to consider the consequences of following up each option, he or she should be better equipped to defuse the incident at an early stage. Only when teachers recognise the importance of their responses to pupil acts – and Parry-Jones & Gay (1980) suggest that teachers do not generally see these as a causative factor – will they be encouraged to acquire the skills necessary for preventing escalation.

The classroom

18) The relationships between teachers and their pupils vary enormously. Some teachers will relate positively to the majority of their pupils; others to relatively few. In a similar way pupils will get on with most of their teachers, though there are undoubtedly some teachers who are more generally disliked. The reasons are complex. They may have to do with individual personalities, teaching styles, attitudes or reputations. Certainly we cannot dispute the existence of 'grapevines' among both teachers and pupils that can establish reputations of pupils as 'likely troublemakers' and of teachers as 'aggressive' or 'unfair' (see Delamont, 1976; Hargreaves *et al.* 1975). Just as the self-fulfilling prophecy effect has been recognised in relation to academic achievement, so the expectation of confrontation is likely to influence the probability that disruption will actually occur. Whole classes may similarly acquire reputations for 'good' or 'bad' behaviour. Pupils within them will be aware of the particular reputation their class has and will come to identify themselves with it. This phenomenon may be of particular relevance to what is currently happening within the colleges. Students following YTS and other 'new FE' provision already appear to be gaining a reputation for disruptive behaviour.

19) Relationships between pupils have been the subject of a very great number of research studies dating from the 1930s to the present day. In comparison, the

literature on teacher-pupil relationships is scant. An increased attention to this area may well be useful in helping us to understand the antecedents of disruption and in building up a more general picture of the factors bearing on the problem. Galloway *et al.* (1982) call for 'more information on the development of prolonged tension between teachers and a small minority of pupils'. The research techniques for gathering such information have already been well tried and tested in other social contexts and could be adapted for use in educational institutions.

20) Many young people report that a principal reason for going on to college is the fact that they will be 'treated as adults'. This would suggest that they expect to see a change in the kind of relationship they have so far experienced with teachers. Exactly what they do expect an 'adult' relationship to be and how far their expectations are fulfilled are questions that still remain to be answered. If in the event there is a mismatch between their expectations of the teacher-pupil relationship and that held by their lecturers, the evidence from school-based studies would indicate that disruption could be a possible response.

The institution

21) Numerous research studies have established that considerable differences exist between schools in the level of disruption experienced and in their rates of suspension and referral to outside agencies. In an attempt to explain this they have examined aspects of school ethos and organisation associated with different patterns (Bird *et al.* 1980; Galloway *et al.* 1982; Gath *et al.* 1977; Grunsell, 1980; Power *et al.* 1967). Low rates of disruption would appear to be associated with schools characterised by such disparate factors as: small size, lower institutional control, close parent-school relationships, democratic organisation of teachers, less rigorous enforcement of certain key rules, higher co-option of pupils into positions of formal responsibility, a high rate of recognition for positive achievements, well-cared-for buildings, a feeling on the part of pupils that they can approach staff for help with a personal problem, and a willingness on the part of teachers to reach a compromise on good behaviour in order to accommodate the school as an institution to pupils who do not share its dominant values (Bird *et al.* 1980; Clegg & Megson, 1973; HMI, 1977; Reynolds, 1975, 1976; Reynolds & Sullivan, 1981; Rutter *et al.* 1979).

22) A number of studies have focused more specifically on the mismatch between curriculum content and young people's needs and expectations of what the school should be offering. The available evidence indicates that many older pupils, particularly those of lower ability, may experience a general disenchantment with subjects which they feel contribute little of relevance to their future lives. In the FE context, students may feel that a pre-vocational curriculum is not sufficiently relevant to the incipient vocational aspirations they may have. Even where the curriculum has a specific vocational focus, students may well perceive a mismatch between their studies and the job opportunities currently available.

23) Pupils may have an adverse experience of the curriculum if they find it irrelevant or too academically demanding or if it leaves them with a sense of failure (Evans, 1981; Galloway *et al.* 1982; Ramasutt & Upton, 1983). They may disrupt lessons

either to distract attention from their difficulties or to alleviate their boredom and frustration (Willis, 1977; Woods, 1979). Bird *et al.* (1981) have described such pupil strategies as an 'inarticulate critique of schooling'; while Tattum (1982) highlights the role of certain pupils who, by their actions and disruptive outbursts, draw attention to features of school life which their peers also find frustrating, undermining or unfair.

24) School organisation, streaming, teacher behaviour, formal rule enforcement and even routine pastoral care have been seen as magnifying the problem of disruption. Various solutions have been proposed, such as a more democratic model of the classroom, curriculum reform to give a more adequate reflection of students' needs and interests, democratisation of staff decision making and a move towards community schooling (Schostak, 1983). Above all, it is suggested that educational institutions need to adopt a policy of flexibility both in terms of the opportunities offered and in the use that is made of resources to meet a range of educational demands. An institution's ability to do this may be a critical factor in preventing the conditions leading to disruption.

The wider society

25) Other studies have looked for explanations of disruption as an outcome of certain educational policies or in terms of structural factors in society as a whole.

26) Thus streaming, banding, setting and comprehensivisation have variously been seen as contributory factors. Particular attention has focused here on the school as an agency of social selection and on the mismatch between school (middle class) values and the values held by working class pupils. The pioneering studies of Hargreaves (1967) and Lacey (1970) showed how pupils already predisposed to reject school values may be encouraged in their formation of a countercultural response by the organisation of the school.

27) The raising of the school-leaving age has similarly been seen as creating problems by compelling young adults to remain in an institution in which the primary response to them is as children. While these young people may have adult status and exhibit adult behaviour outside the school environment, they are called upon to change this behaviour when in the classroom. Smoking, swearing, refusing to pay attention are examples of the sorts of behaviour that are frequently cited to demonstrate the mismatch of expectations that pupils see as existing between school and out-of-school life. A similar mismatch may exist between the rules of the college and those of the workplace. We have already noted the widespread change in attitudes to teacher authority and the role this has played in creating a context for disruption. Redefining perceptions of the new relationships entailed in this change is a complex process.

28) In recent years the prospect of unemployment on leaving school or college has added another dimension making students dubious of the value of education and training. The promise of secure and satisfying employment in return for effort can no longer be held out to many students as a realistic reason for compliance with the rules of the organisation.

A multidimensional approach

29) The distinction that is made by researchers between disruptive behaviour and disruptive individuals is a useful one. Explanations based solely on individuals can encourage teachers and schools to believe that they have little or no part to play. By contrast, the current multidimensional approach to the study of disruption suggests not only that research can usefully proceed along a number of avenues, but also that modifications to institutional organisation and teacher behaviour can produce significant beneficial effects.

References

Bird C *et al.* (1980) *Disaffected pupils* Brunel University, Educational Studies Unit

Clarke DD *et al.* (1981) 'Disruptive incidents in secondary school classrooms: a sequence analysis approach' *Oxford Review of Education* 7 (2): 111–117

Clegg A & Megson B (1973) *Children in distress* Maidenhead: Penguin Educational

Comber LC & Whitfield RC (1979) *Action on indiscipline: a practical guide for teachers* NAS/UWT in association with the Department of Educational Enquiry, University of Aston

Delamont S (1976) *Interaction in the classroom* London: Methuen

Evans M (1981) *Disruptive pupils* London: Schools Council

Farrington D (1978) 'The family background of aggressive youths' in LA Hersov & M Berger (eds) *Aggression and anti-social behaviour in childhood and adolescence* Oxford: Pergamon

Frude N & Gault H (1984) *Disruptive behaviour in schools* Chichester: John Wiley

Galloway DM *et al.* (1982) *Schools and disruptive pupils* York: Longman

Gath D *et al.* (1977) *Child guidance and delinquency in a London Borough* Oxford: Oxford University Press

Grunsell R (1980) *Beyond control? Schools and suspension* London: Writers and Readers

Hargreaves DH (1967) *Social relations in a secondary school* London: Routledge & Kegan Paul

Hargreaves DH *et al.* (1975) *Deviance in classrooms* London: Routledge & Kegan Paul

HMI (1977) *Ten good schools: a secondary school enquiry* London: HMSO

Lacey C (1970) *Hightown grammar* Manchester: Manchester University Press

Lawrence J *et al.* (1983) 'Monitoring teachers' reports of incidents of disruptive behaviour in two secondary schools: multi-disciplinary research and intervention' *Educational Studies* 9 (2): 81–91

Parry-Jones W & Gay BM (1980) 'The anatomy of disruption: a preliminary consideration of interaction sequences within disruptive incidents' *Oxford Review of Education* 6: 213-220

Pik R (1981) 'Confrontation situations and teacher support systems' in B Gillham (ed) *Problem behaviour in the secondary school: a systems approach* London: Croom Helm

Power MJ *et al.* (1967) 'Delinquent Schools?' *New Society* 19, 264: 542–3

Ramasutt A & Upton G (1983) 'The attainments of maladjusted children' *Remedial Education* 18 (1): 41–44

Reynolds D (1975) 'When teachers and pupils refuse a truce: the secondary school and the creation of delinquency' in G Mungham & G Pearson (eds) *Working class youth culture* London: Routledge & Kegan Paul

Reynolds D & Sullivan M (1981) 'The effects of school: a radical faith restated' in B Gillham (ed) *Problem behaviour in the secondary school: a systems approach* London: Croom Helm

Rutter M, Maughan B, Mortimore P & Ouston J (1979) *Fifteen thousand hours: secondary schools and their effects on children* London: Open Books

Schostak JF (1983) *Maladjusted schooling* London: Falmer Press

Tattum D (1982) *Disruptive pupils in schools and units* Chichester: John Wiley

White R (1980) *Absent without cause* London: Routledge & Kegan Paul

Willis PE (1977) *Learning to labour* London: Saxon House

Woods P (1979) *The divided school* London: Routledge & Kegan Paul

16. Four Rules of Classroom Management

Colin Smith & Robert Laslett

Is there some special personal magic which enables some teachers to quieten excitement merely by arriving at the scene, quell misbehaviour with a glance, make classrooms bustle with activity and hum with cheerful industry? Perhaps at this highest level of perfection there may indeed be some extra ingredient of individual charisma but studies of teacher behaviour (Rutter *et al.* 1979; Wragg, 1984) have noted specific skills which are demonstrated by effective teachers. These skills can be learned and applied by newcomers to the profession.

As McManus (1989) sensibly points out 'teaching is more than the sum of its parts' but it is possible from research, observation and autobiographical anecdote to discern 'four rules' of classroom management applied by successful teachers which like the 'four rules' in arithmetic, once assimilated, can be applied in many different situations.

Rule one: get them in

This rule emphasises the point that a lesson which makes a brisk start will avoid the difficulties which can arise if pupils are not promptly engaged in useful activity. If teachers are pre-occupied with setting up displays, distributing materials or searching for equipment then there are ample opportunities for idling, chatter and other unproductive activities. The activities are of no great disruptive impact in themselves, but they often build up to a cumulative disorder, which leads in turn to further distraction in the form of exhortation, reprimand or even disciplinary action by the teacher which extends the delay in beginning the lesson. The process of 'getting them in' can be seen to involve three phases: greeting, seating and starting.

Greeting

Simply by being there before the class arrives the teacher establishes the role of host receiving the class and he is quietly able to underline his authority by deciding when pupils are invited to enter the room. There is also the vital practical advantage of being able to check that the room is tidy, that materials are available, displays arranged, and necessary instructions or examples are written on the board. This will all help to provide the mental composure essential to relaxed assurance. In larger schools, this tactic may not be easy, though professional commitment appears to be a more significant factor than distance between teaching areas in ensuring a prompt start to lessons (Rutter *et al.* 1979).

Seating

Although arrangements will vary according to the type of lesson, age of pupils and nature of activity, it is important that initially teachers decide where children should sit. Like entrance to the room, this is another aspect of the natural establishment of responsibility. Teachers may choose to encourage children to sit with friends to promote co-operation or they may deliberately and arbitrarily disperse such centres of potential distraction: but they establish that placement and movement in the classroom are matters which they control. A seating plan showing who sits where quickly enables teachers to learn and use individual names, so although later regrouping will be desirable, it is very useful for at least the first few lessons if a fixed pattern is set and maintained.

Starting

Starting a lesson smoothly and promptly depends not only on managing the physical entrance and disposition of the student body but also the mental tuning-in of the student mind. One teacher interviewed as part of the Teacher Education Project study of first encounters between teachers and new groups of pupils, expertly and neatly sums up how to start a lesson:

> *Right at the start of the lesson there is something for them to do: games, workcards, anything, because they rarely arrive at the same time. I try to create an atmosphere in which they start science as soon as they come through the door.*

(Wragg, 1984)

Whatever the subject or topic each lesson should start with some activity which occupies every child quietly, whilst teachers deal with registration, latecomers, lost or malfunctioning equipment. The type of activity will depend on the age and ability of the child and the nature of the lesson, but it must be something within each child's capacity to accomplish without additional help. It should reinforce previously acquired skills, recap earlier work or set the scene for new learning. This warming-up period might only last four or five minutes, perhaps a few sums or a short paragraph to be read with two or three questions to be answered will be sufficient to set the tone and establish a calm and positive atmosphere before moving on to the main content of the lesson.

Rule two: get them out

Though most disciplinary problems arise from a poor start to a lesson, the next most vulnerable time providing many opportunities for trouble making is the end of a teaching session. For this reason 'get them out' is cited as the second rule of classroom management. Carefully planning the end of each lesson is a crucial part of the way in which experienced teachers successfully handle transition from one activity to another. As Gray & Richer (1988) put it, 'structure at the end of a lesson is all too easily lost in a sigh of relief that it is nearly over'. The lasting effect of an interesting learning experience can be wasted and pleasantly developing relationships between teacher and class can be spoilt if a productive session dissolves into a noisy, chaotic and stressful finale. So teachers need to consider the two phases of concluding a lesson and dismissing a class.

Concluding

An orderly procedure for stopping work should include consolidation and reinforcement of learning and this is difficult to achieve if children are still busy writing or engaged in collecting books and gathering materials together. It is helpful to give an early warning that it will be time to stop in 'two minutes precisely' or whatever is a suitable time to avoid stopping pupils in mid-sentence. It is vital that all work must cease in good time for material to be collected, books put away and still give opportunity for some revision and recapitulation. This could take the form of a brief question and answer session which will enable the teacher to check on how successfully objectives have been attained or identify points which require further attention. Additionally or sometimes alternatively this time should be used for a summary reminding the class of what has been covered during the lesson and how this links in to previous learning or prepares the way for the next activity.

Gray & Richer (1988) point out how valuable it is to use this time to give positive feedback to pupils, praising good work and reassuring those who have had difficulties that next time things will be different. It is an opportunity to refresh, restate and reinforce the theme of the lesson. It can also be a good idea to reserve some time for a game, quiz or story so that the conclusion of the lesson becomes a reward for earlier effort, particularly for those who may find the main subject content a bit of a struggle. Ending on a light and positive note in this way should leave even the least competent pupils feeling that though it will never be a favoured activity, even a difficult subject offers them some possibility of pleasure and enjoyment.

Dismissing

Decisions about the precise method for dismissing a class will vary according to the age of the pupils. As Gray & Richer (1988) suggest, 'Arms folded, sitting up straight!' or similar ritualised instructions may be appropriate for controlling young children, but they are more likely to provoke confrontation with older pupils. Yet some sequence or pattern which facilitates the movement of bodies from inside to outside the classroom with minimum contact with furniture, equipment or each other does need to be established. Otherwise the teacher will finish up wasting valuable preparation time clearing debris from the floor, readjusting desks and tables or remonstrating with pupils who ought already to be somewhere else...

Some simple system of traffic regulation has to be established in early meetings with a class. Eventually, self-discipline based on awareness of the teacher's reasonable expectations of polite behaviour may suffice to ensure an orderly departure, but initially some standard routine for dismissal ... is likely to be necessary. The sequence should be clearing up and collecting books and material, checking up on learning and giving feedback, enjoying a game or other relaxing end to the session, setting up the group for its next move ... and finally supervising departure, if necessary standing at the door to continue supervision of progress down the corridor.

Rule three: get on with it

In this context 'it' refers to the main part of the lesson, the nature of its content and the manner of its presentation. Pupils' feelings of self-esteem and sense of competence in a particular subject area will depend to a considerable extent on the teacher's ability to 'get on with it'.

Content

Difficulties in learning and consequent problems with behaviour often happen because the content of a lesson is not matched to the ability of the pupils to whom it is delivered. Because persistent failure can easily result in disgruntled disaffection, careful scrutiny of the curriculum by subject departments and by individual teachers is needed to ensure that it is appropriate. Methods and materials should also be closely examined to see that learning experiences are suitable and study tasks are attainable for pupils with a range and diversity of aptitudes and abilities. Raban & Postlethwaite (1988) offer some useful advice on how this can be done by finding out what pupils already know, starting a little further back to build on what is understood, planning small steps towards each teaching goal and being prepared to adjust these plans if progress is not being made.

Within an individual lesson, variety and pace are needed to maintain momentum. Activities planned for the beginning and conclusion of the session will go some way to achieving these aims, but it is also important to provide variety in the main body of the lesson particularly in double periods. Breaking topics up into smaller units, switching between quiet individual study and arranging some active, co-operative learning in pairs or groups will go some way to combating the inexorable law that the alertness of the brain is inversely proportionate to the numbness of the posterior!

Though difficult to attain, the ambition to see that every child has something finished and something marked in every lesson will help maintain the pace of teaching. Such immediate feedback and reinforcement is especially important for pupils with learning difficulties, whose previous failures leave them needing frequent reassurance that they are on the right track. These children will also benefit from teachers taking particular care to deliver instructions clearly and precisely since 'if children know what we want them to do, they will usually do it' (Lovitt, 1977).

The momentum or flow of classroom activity is vital to discipline because interruptions lead to distraction and loss of interest for pupils and teachers. Although a general briskness sets the normally appropriate tone, there are also occasions when teaching less and allowing more time for practice or discussion are necessary.

Finding the correct balance is not always easy, too much of the same thing becomes tedious, too many changes become confusing, but most lessons should involve some listening, some looking, some thinking, some talking, some reading and some writing.

Manner

Positive relationships develop from the manner in which people communicate with each other. For teachers, this means thinking about how they address and question children and how they convey expectations about behaviour. The atmosphere in a classroom is like any 'weather system' subject to change and the effective teacher is skilled at spotting and dispersing a minor disturbance before it builds up into a major depression. As in meteorology, successful forecasting requires alertness to early warning signals and these are most readily picked up by teachers who display what Kounin (1970) and Brophy & Evertson (1976) have described respectively as 'withitness' and 'smoothness'.

'Withitness' is the somewhat dated term which describes the timeless virtue of being able to provide work at a suitable level and administer a system in which pupils know what to do, where to get help if needed and what to do next when they have finished an assignment. For example, where there are difficulties in reading or comprehension, help can be provided through topic guidelines, summaries and key word charts giving explanations and spellings.

'Smoothness' refers to the ease with which pupils move from one activity to another. Transitions can be handled more easily and problems avoided by ensuring that supplementary activities are readily available to usefully occupy anyone who has completed their original assignment. This enables the teacher to ensure that all the class will be ready to change together from one activity or location to another. The smooth flow of classroom life is also helped by teachers avoiding too many disciplinary interruptions. The more that punishments are dealt out, the more nagging that goes on, the more negative comments that are made, the more tension will increase and the more the class will be distracted from the work in hand.

The manner in which a teacher addresses a class reflects an attitude and conveys a message not only through what is said but also through how it is said. Before speaking to the class it is essential that attention is gained by getting pupils to stop work and listen carefully. It follows that any information to be delivered in this way should be vital enough to merit the inevitable interruption to the lesson. Facial expression and tone of voice are as important to any communication as making sure that it is being heard. A persistent frown or intimidating scowl is likely to convey anxiety as much as displeasure and an angry shout can awkwardly modulate into a shriek more suggestive of hysteria than confident control.

The old adage 'quiet teacher, quiet class' offers good advice but should be followed with some caution as the comment 'inaudible teacher, insufferable class' may equally be true. A clear and sufficient volume is required to satisfy an assumption, that in any class there is likely to be at least one child with some hearing loss, but speech should be delivered as Fontana (1986) advises in 'a voice which children find it pleasant to listen to, and a voice which the teacher can use all day without undue strain.'

The importance of teachers using their eyes to communicate is emphasised by what might be described as a 'lighthouse technique' for addressing the class recommended by Marland (1975). Each sentence is spoken to an individual child with established eye contact. At the end of a sentence or as a new idea is introduced or as the theme changes the teacher's gaze is shifted and eye contact established with another pupil in another part of the room to whom the next comment is expressed. A third pupil is chosen as the focus for the next comment and so on. In this way the teacher's eye sweeps the room like the beam from a lighthouse and the teacher's brain picks up a 'feel' for what is going on in different areas of the room. Thus is the impression of 'eyes in the back of my head' fostered particularly if teachers noticing some minor misbehaviour in one part of the room, wait until they have turned to address someone elsewhere before naming the wrongdoers and requiring them to cease their transgression.

Another aspect of the manner of teaching is the point and purpose of the teacher's use of questions. Are they seen as tricks and traps set to catch the unwary and inattentive? If so, they become a likely source of negative interaction serving to keep attention focused, but at a cost of potential embarrassment and humiliation for the less able pupil. A more positive orientation is for teachers to see questioning as a means of checking whether material is understood and to treat an incorrect answer as the teacher's fault for inadequate explanation and an occasion for further expansion and illustration instead of reprimand. Of course, this may not always be true, but it offers a perspective in which questions are a source of feedback rather than friction with answers responded to with praise if possible, with tact if not.

Rule four: get on with them

Teachers develop good personal relationships with their pupils by fostering mutual trust and respect. To do this effectively teachers need to be aware of each child as an individual and be sensitive to the mood of the class as a whole. This means knowing who's who and keeping track of what's going on.

Who's who?

Awareness of individual differences begins with the mundane but essential task of learning names and putting them accurately to faces. Once a child's name is known, discipline is immediately easier because wrongdoers will realise that they can be identified and because requests or rebukes can be personalised. Direct instructions to 'be quiet please Quentin', or 'sit up straight Cydonia' are much more likely to be heeded than vaguely addressed summonses to 'that boy at the back' or 'the girl over there'. However, recognition has a much more positive aspect too since it conveys the teacher's interest and reflects a willingness to spend time and effort in learning names.

Keeping the same seating plan, at least for the first few meetings with a group enables the teacher to use names correctly albeit at first by discreet reference to the plan. An active strategy should then be employed to revisualise the plan, to scan the room mentally recalling names whilst pupils are working and to always address questions and comments by name. Attempting to fill in a blank copy of the plan when the pupils are not present can be very revealing about a teacher's own perception of individual characters. Whilst the bright, the backward and the baleful may come readily to mind it is often less easy to remember pupils who are less demanding of attention, though they may need it just as much.

Other useful tactics in fixing names and faces are adding a brief written comment using the pupil's name each time work is marked and taking every opportunity to chat informally to children outside class in playground, corridor and dining room so that some additional background information is added to the teacher's mental picture. At first most information will be social, perhaps which football team or pop group is supported, but together with the academic information gleaned from observation in class a fuller rounder picture of each individual will emerge. For such tactics to be successful it is essential that they are based on a natural and genuine personal interest not merely an assumed and intrusive nosiness.

What's going on?

Few classes or groups of pupils within a class are likely to be so purposefully malevolent as to set out on a planned campaign of disruption. However, individually minor irritations can develop collectively into more serious sources of friction. As suggested by the analogy with weather forecasting mentioned earlier, alertness to early warning signs can enable accurate prediction of developing storms but unlike meteorologists teachers can do something about it. Acquiring this sensitivity to the class atmosphere depends on a combination of mobility and marking.

Mobility involves the avoidance of teachers becoming 'desk-bound' by queues of children waiting for attention or by over-reliance on a lecturing style of teaching. Moving around the room, quietly marking work in progress, offering advice and guidance keeps attention on the task in hand. It is a natural contact between teacher and pupil which provides immediate feedback and means that if attention has wandered the teacher's response can be to offer help with an assumed difficulty rather than reprimand about misbehaviour.

When working at one pupil's desk or with a group around a table, a brief glance around the rest of the room will identify any potential trouble spots. Often merely moving to an area where shuffling feet or an increasing volume of noise may indicate the beginnings of disruption can refocus attention but if not, then a mild rebuke, quietly spoken to an individual can be more effective and certainly less distracting than a loud public admonition.

Through this active involvement at child level, allied to the aforementioned 'lighthouse' technique when addressing the class as a whole, the teacher becomes more responsive to the prevailing mood of the group and better able to judge the times for emphasis on serious brisk endeavour or for more relaxed and light-hearted amusement.

Framework for analysis

Following the four rules outlined above will not in itself provide a panacea for trouble-free teaching, but it does suggest a framework for analysing aspects of lesson planning and management which contribute to a productive partnership in learning between teachers and pupils. By attending to the different phases of their lesson and reflecting on personal relationships with pupils, teachers can begin to identify areas where a changed approach might be needed. Two important areas in which further analysis will be helpful are classroom organisation and reducing sources of friction.

References

Brophy JE & Evertson CM (1976) *Learning from teaching: a developmental perspective* Boston: Allyn & Bacon

Fontana D (1986) *Classroom control* London: Methuen

Gray J & Richer J (1988) *Classroom responses to disruptive behaviour* Basingstoke: Macmillan Education

Kounin JS (1970) *Discipline and group management in classrooms* New York: Holt, Rinehart & Winston

Lovitt TC (1977) *In spite of my resistance I've learnt from children* Columbus, Ohio: Merrill

Marland M (1975) *The craft of the classroom: a survival guide* London: Heinemann

McManus M (1989) *Troublesome behaviour in the classroom: a survival guide* London: Routledge

Raban B & Postlethwaite K (1988) *Classroom responses to learning difficulties* Basingstoke: Macmillan Education

Rutter M, Maughan B, Mortimore P & Ouston J (1979) *Fifteen thousand hours: secondary schools and their effects on children* London: Open Books

Wragg EC (1984) *Classroom teaching skills* London: Croom Helm

17.   Mismatch and Disruption

Merillie Huxley

[Editor's note. The paragraph numbering in this extract is from Chapter 3 of the 1987 FEU publication: *Behaviour and motivation: disruption in further education*.]

42)   In this paper the concept of 'mismatch' is explored as an analytical tool for examining the complex and sensitive issue of 'disruption'.

43)   Though disruption has always been a dimension of both school and college life, indications from the field suggest that there is an increasing expression of concern. It is intimated, for example, that the extent of disruption is on the increase, a possible reason being the changed employment situation resulting in a larger proportion of young people deferring entry into employment by undertaking pre-vocational education and training.   The literature review by Judy Bradley [see pp143–148 above] suggests that disruption, rather than being a new issue, may simply be one that has begun to be talked about in a more constructive way.

44)   Other papers say that concern about disruption may be related to some extent to what is often described as the 'new FE'. This has brought a number of changes... Some of these relate to a new clientele, new content, changed timetable, team-teaching and new modes of delivery...   What happens in classrooms is no longer exclusively the responsibility of teachers.   The indications are that teachers and others work collectively on curriculum issues and there is an increasing expectation that they will discuss and share their problems. When disruption does arise, to assist the process of discussion, 'mismatch' is offered as one way of examining the multidimensional issue.

45)   The expectations of teachers, learners and institutions often do not coincide. An examination of the extent to which disruption is the consequence of a mismatch between various aspects of the FE system may provide a means of exploring a potentially broader range of issues. This may avoid disruption or, at least, assist in the search for reasons, responses and remedies to the problem.

46)   The response to the FEU call for evidence ... indicates that a few people are requesting guidance to help them in exploring the nature of disruption. Difficulties in approaching the issue may stem from the fact that disruption is often associated with failure and that lack of disruption has been associated with a popular image of good teaching.

47) Mismatch can be used, therefore, to address the degree to which there is a match between the expectations of teachers, learners and institutions and the aims of curriculum programmes within FE.

48) Gathered from a review of responses to the issues of disruption from the field, the following offer some examples of mismatch in certain aspects of the FE system:

i) the aims and content of FE programmes and career aspirations, work and job opportunities

ii) teachers' expectations and students' expectations and actual ability and motivation

iii) students' potential and actual achievement

iv) the young person's desire to perform adult roles and the opportunities to do so

v) the teaching mode and the preferred learning mode

vi) the rules of the college environment and those of the outside world

vii) the authority of the teacher and the desired autonomy of the learner

viii) the constraints of provision and the needs of the learner

ix) adolescent values and the teaching of social and moral competence.

49) There are, of course, other examples. The above are not in any particular order and they are not necessarily discrete. Mismatch is not solely associated with adolescence. Perhaps surprisingly, some of the material referred to in the response to the call for evidence concerns adults on graduate and professional training courses...

51) What then is the potential of 'mismatch'? First, use of the concept as an analytical tool attempts to shift the focus away from blaming the student for disruption. Common sense conceptions of disruption usually lead to blaming students and associating disruption with rule breaking, discipline and punishment. The behaviour of young people who cause disruption may only be the tip of the iceberg. Fundamental issues usually underlie it. By avoiding blaming students or teachers for disruption, it is possible to avoid looking at a cure peculiar to that particular teacher or student. Mismatch may prevent looking for reasons within that individual. Rather, using the concept of mismatch provides an opportunity for an analysis of the process of disruption, whereby the disruptive act is but a snapshot in that process and a starting-point for discussion.

52) The emphasis in many school-based responses to disruption is on a deficit model of the student, thereby offering compensatory or remedial education in order to reconcile the disruptive student to the existing demands of the institution. In this compensatory model the *institution* is left untouched, and the *student's* needs are considered in the light of the 'norms' of the institution.

53) Using mismatch, a broader range of issues can be addressed. The situation is helped by explaining disruption and its consequences as a dimension of the *whole curriculum process*... The opportunity is generated to examine the aspects of the system which may contribute to mismatch of expectation, e.g. poor motivation and low achievement.

54) For example, teachers themselves may precipitate disruption as they experience the mismatch between their traditional and new role within FE. Their role is now more complex: as managers of the learning process; tutors; co-ordinators and members of a course team. Their role is less curtained off and more open to comment.

55) Secondly, an analysis via mismatch holds within it the possibility of an argument for improved match whereby disruption will be prevented. A preventative model would consider the expectations and needs of, for example, teachers, managers and learners, of various aspects of the FE system, in relation to the curriculum process. Using the FEU model of curriculum development ..., these aspects would comprise needs analysis, curriculum design, implementation, review and evaluation.

56) Where disruption does exist, the second approach may have potential to lead to an agenda for staff and organisational development. A possible approach to the process is given below:

1) occurrence of disruptive incident
2) questioning of the practices in terms of mismatch of expectations
3) admission of mismatch
4) mismatches provide an agenda for action to improve match
5) staff development to support change.

57) An advantage of this process is that it does not label failure as disruption or vice versa. Rather, it provides an analysis which identifies, via a mismatch of expectations, a failure to meet needs. The implication of this is the inclusion of a range of 'others'. Staff development initiatives to support this process should put in place the systems to improve 'match'... Some of the elements of this are:

• self-help team;
• mechanisms for supporting, maintaining and reviewing staff development strategies;
• a 'whole college' approach;
• consultancy for self-help approach.

58) Thirdly, the use of the analytical tool of mismatch provides a less threatening approach to the issue. Because teacher appraisal is not usually an ongoing endeavour, dealing with disruption is often undertaken in a climate of anger, frustration and crisis. Though this situation will remain, analysing the incident using mismatch should ensure an agenda for consideration by teachers, learners and the institution to provide modifications to improve match.

59) Finally, mismatch does not always, of course, lead to disruption. Resolving mismatch of this kind is what most of us do daily.

60) Similarly, the vast majority of young people pass through the education system coping with a whole range of mismatch. It is probable that people tolerate a great deal before becoming disruptive. In an article 'Attention Please' (TES 16.5.86), Brian Cox (ex Workers' Educational Association tutor) said, 'Students are surprisingly passive to poor teaching. They must be woken up to what they are missing'. Some would consider that putting up with mismatch is a good thing. It would be ridiculous to argue that acting disruptively improves the situation; however, if disruption is taken seriously and acknowledged and understood as a method of communication, there is the possibility of starting a dialogue.

61) There is positive advantage in institutions taking disruption seriously, since this may lead to a discussion about mismatch.

62) Colleges make a difference to achievement and behaviour. By addressing the issue directly, and by accepting the possibility of using the concept of mismatch of expectations, the institution can be led towards the consideration of wider issues likely to influence its effectiveness and efficiency. These issues are likely to include: the devising of new strategies; review and reallocation of resources; and rethinking processes of teaching and the management of learning. This may contribute to an improvement in the match of expectations of various aspects of the FE system.

Part Six – Responding to Disruption

The extracts in Part Six recognise that no matter how consistently teachers apply the preventative principles outlined in Part Five, most will experience disruption at some time or other. The key theme of all of this last selection of readings is the need to prepare for and respond to disruption rather than simply react to it.

Bill Rogers analyses the language used in typical dialogues between teachers and students in secondary schools. He presents examples of potentially disruptive encounters and indicates how the balance of appropriate content, timing, tone and emotional context can effectively deal with them. The key to good discipline is skilful planning within a recognition of fundamental human values, though we might note, in relation to what we have read in Part Three – *Managing Difference*, that not all our students or colleagues live within the Judaeo-Christian heritage of which he writes.

Mick McManus, in his third and final contribution, lists students' expectations of their teachers (keeping order and making demands on them, for example) and shows how they 'explore the boundaries' of behaviour by 'testing' their teachers early in the school year to find out how far their expectations will be realised.

Many of the extracts in this Reader have been written from perspectives which, by and large, embrace cognitive and humanist principles of learning. In the next reading Bill McPhillimy proposes a strategy which additionally draws on behaviourist psychology, and which he calls a 'behavioural, reflective, relationship approach' to classroom control.

In his contribution, Clark Lambert concentrates on the personality characteristics of trainees who might be troublesome to the instructor. He identifies six types of potentially disruptive participants in training events:

1. the important person ('I'm too busy, but I'm here')
2. the superior one ('I know better than you')
3. the authority figure ('I'm in charge here')
4. the dependent student ('I need your help')
5. the complainer ('Everything is wrong, as usual')
6. the chatterbox (The constant talker).

Lambert gives examples of each of these and offers pragmatic advice to trainers confronted by such individuals.

Carole Mitchell and her colleagues carried out research into the management of disruptive behaviour in eight FE colleges in various parts of the country on behalf the Further Education Development Agency.

Our last two readings are from their report and offer a model for a 'whole-college' approach to disruption. The three-tier model (the *strategy* level – involving governors and senior managers; the *systems* level – involving middle managers, departments, sections and units; and the *delivery* level – involving teaching staff and students) indicates a shared responsibility between all levels in the college, and forms a conceptual framework for examples of procedures and codes developed in identified colleges, as well as providing a self-assessment schedule for activities at each level.

The lengthy extract in section 22 also gives an opportunity for revisiting a number of the themes and issues introduced and discussed in earlier readings. The final contribution takes us back to the very practical business of recording and documenting college disciplinary support procedures.

18.   The Language of Discipline

Bill Rogers

Teachers daily have to address a wide range of student misbehaviour from calling out and butting in, not having equipment, a student noisily late to class as well as the students who argue and defy a teacher's discipline. It is a taxing feature of a demanding profession helping students to own their behaviour, be responsible, respect the rights of others. Teachers are in dialogue with students many times during the course of a school day from the brief non-verbal reminder or correction through to assertive comment and one-to-one counselling. Through supportive dialogue teachers are enabling those aims.

A key feature of this text is its focus on language as a primary tool in creating a workable relationship between teacher and students. Most discipline is a balance of what we say (content), when we say it (timing) and how we say it (tone) and the emotional context (our emotions and those of the students). Of course, language, without a serviceable working relationship, would be mere technique. This book is concerned with how in practice to balance building a positive relationship with the need to discipline. The emphasis throughout is on skills one can learn to enhance a discipline style based on respect and dignity without sacrificing appropriate assertion and leadership.

As you work through the text you'll come across many teacher (T) and student (S) dialogues. Attention is drawn to the effect of what we say and how we say it as teachers especially the discipline context. As you read these dialogues imagine yourself in the room, twenty-five odd eyes and ears listening, watching. Try saying the teacher dialogues in different tones – fun tone, hostile tone, sarcastic tone, aggressive tone, sycophantic-indecisive tone (pleading) – and work on a confident, firm, pleasant, assertive tone. Students pick up largely on how we say something as well as what we say.

Because discipline often occurs in an emotionally affected setting, our discipline language is more effective when it is planned rather than left to chance. This is the theme of this book; a conscious language repertoire planned ahead of time so that we can deal more effectively, and economically, with 'the thousand natural shocks that flesh is heir to' (Shakespeare, *Hamlet)*.

What do I do when . . . ?

I take demonstration classes (masochism, heroism, stupidity?) – one of my colleagues calls it the 'world's cheapest enema'. Taking classes while other teachers watch, though, has taught me a lot about teaching, management, students, myself... My colleagues and I use such 'lessons' as part of a peer-coaching programme.

A year 10 class: I walk into the room as thirty-two 14 and 15 year olds file in noisily. Two teachers are already ensconced at the back waiting to observe the lesson. I've been warned about a few customers: Ben, Neil and Mark; and watch Vanessa. That helps me no end!

Ben takes the back left seat with a coterie of friends, grinning, with 'What's this then?' and 'Who's he anyway?' looks. Vanessa is leaning back in heavy chair lean mode and having a 'two bob each way' chat with her friend while checking me out. There is the ritual settling noise. I notice as I 'start' a couple of mouths chewing. Normal. It's establishment phase. Natural testing time. They need to sort out (for themselves) what this teacher is like. I wait for them to settle, scanning the room.

'Morning, I'll be taking this class today. My name's Mr Rogers. I don't know you all; a quick whip around with the names . . .' As I get feedback on the names I see a small rubber ball parabolically aimed at, and hitting, the chalkboard. It bounces off on to the floor near my feet. What do I do? I see Vanessa leaning back talking to Lisa. What do I do? The gum-chewers? Craig has his foot (his large Reebok foot) on the desk and is seat leaning.

Neil calls out, clicking his fingers. What do I do? He later says, 'Can I go to the toilet?' (during instruction time). Do I let him go? Is he 'playing to the gallery'? I suspect so. Several of the students are after 'street credibility' – a pecking order of 'belonging'. Whatever I do I need to be aware of the social dynamics as well as what I'm teaching; to be aware of the discipline I give, and avoid silly win/lose power struggles. 'What do I do, say, and when?' and 'What happens if what I do doesn't work?' are valid questions. I have to juggle my own emotions with my discipline and their reactions.

What if I *say*, for example, 'Right!! Who threw that, come on, who threw it?! Was it you, yes, you down the back, Ben isn't it?' 'Me?!' (he is likely to feign).

Let's say I walk up to Ben (I *think* it was he who threw the ball – aiming for the bin) with shoulders tense, chin out, fists clenched, the racing thought 'I'll maim that little acronym'. I telegraph via my body language that he's a threat. If I then say, 'Right, it was you, wasn't it – why did you do that?! Eh?!' He might reply, 'Wasn't me?!', (Here he'll look around at his coterie for support – the Greek chorus says 'yeah!' – 'Shut up you – I wasn't talking to you!') C'mon, you, yes you Ben isn't it? Pick it up!' 'Told yer I didn't throw it, what you picking on me for?!'

This approach is based on win/lose, high status and is often doomed to failure as each 'side' vies for emotional and verbal supremacy. It arises from strong cognitive demands (and beliefs) that children *must* respect their teachers and *must* do as they're told and that teacher *must* . . . whatever.

'You, get that gum in the bin!' If the teacher walks over, especially during up-front, instructional time, on a 'small beer' issue like this and acts and speaks confrontationally, is it any wonder the 'secondary' behaviour of the students is a 'lie'? 'Wasn't chewing,' 'Don't lie to me get it in the bin!' 'I was just chewing me tongue – get real!' 'Don't you-speak-to-me-in-that-tone-of-voice!' The teacher's reaction is immediate. All this, over chewing gum. He notices two students whispering, chatting:

> T   *You, yes you, Vanessa and Lisa, don't talk while I'm teaching!*
>
> Ss   *We were only talking about the work!* [This is said with a pouting, curled lip, arms folded with a 'hurt' sigh to finish off the 'effect'. These students are seeking to gain some public attention – 'Notice me!']
>
> T   [Walks up close] *Don't con me. You were not talking about the work at all – do you think I'm stupid or what?!* [Here they grin] *And wipe that smirk off your face.*
>
> Ss   *Anyway, watchya picking on us for? Ben 'n' Daniel were talking before, didn't say nothing to them. No they're boys!* [here Lisa tosses her head]

By this time the teacher is getting close to terminal frustration mode. Anything can happen. He believes he has to control all these incidents *directly*, but each time he speaks, and the way he speaks, is feeding a self-defeating cycle.

Attempting to control

There are a number of characteristic teacher behaviours that flow from teachers believing that it is in their direct power to control, by fiat:

- The tendency to take on all the responsibility for the child's behaviour.
- The verb 'to make' is applied to their method of 'control'. 'I'll make him do as he's told.' A belief that 'I can force him to obey me!'
- They minimise 'choice' or appropriate negotiation.
- They get locked into self-defeating power struggles.
- They will, on occasion, use hostility, sarcasm, 'bolshie' tactics. They will not allow appropriate 'face-saving' for the student and will resort to 'public' embarrassment if necessary in order to win and control the situation. If there is one thing students hate it is being directly put down in front of their peers.

Of course, these teachers, in 'safe' schools, may still get results through obedience based on a fear-compliance authoritarian approach. They also get rebellion, resentment, alienation, and defiance from their students.

In a day and age when students believe they are our social equal this method is increasingly failing to work. But even if it does, is such an approach right? (A value question.)

There are also teachers who discipline in this way because they get so frustrated by students answering back and having the last word. Because emotion, beliefs and behaviour are so intertwined, reactive discipline styles go on being repeated and become self-justifying.

Non-assertion

Conversely there are teachers who have unclear expectations, uncertain, unclear and poorly enforced rules. Such teachers have difficulty asserting their rights as teachers. Their voice tone and body language may convey that they are threatened by student behaviour. They *look* passive, anxious, uncertain of where they are going in behaviour-management transactions. In a conflict they often allow children to dominate by discussion of secondary issues (Rogers, 1991; 1992a; 1992b).

T   *Daniel, come on please. Put the chewing gum into the bin.* [His voice implies, 'I don't expect you to do this, but I really hope you will and I don't want you to dislike me but it is a rule . . .']

S   *C'mon Sir, get real, s'only a bit of gum. I'm still doing my work!* [Hurt tone as if to say 'you're most unfair to address a minor issue like this!']

T   *But Daniel it's the rule* [rising inflection, hands outstretched, wrinkled brow], *please put it in the bin.*

S   [Student butts in] *But other teachers here let us chew gum, don't they?* [Here Daniel appeals to the supportive chorus of his peers close by – 'Yeah!' says Rob folding his arms in closed body language. It's a 'social-justice' issue now involving other students.]

T   *Oh, c'mon Rob, which teachers let you eat chewing gum in class?* [So it goes on – the side issues begin to take over, what ought to be the teacher's reminder of a fair school rule.]

Back to Ben and co.

OK. What in fact did I do? I picked up the ball *while* I was talking to the class *as if* it was no big deal, dropped it in the bin and carried on instructional time. After all, I wasn't certain Ben had thrown it.

I could have used many approaches depending on:

• my beliefs and attitudes about the nature of power and control,

• how threatened I felt,

• what my skill repertoire in discipline was,

• how well I felt on the day, how relaxed,

• my understanding of group dynamics,

• how well I had planned my discipline (the key theme of this book).

I used humour, a powerful defuser: 'Poor shot [wink] I'll discuss basketball tactics after class', then resumed the lesson flow.

What about Craig with his foot up? What if I walk up and make a scene? 'Do you put your feet on the furniture at home!' 'Yeah, was only resting it [smirk]!' He may well put his feet up at home.

I got a better response by just using directional language:

> T *Craig* [brief eye contact – without moving too close when teaching 'up-front'] *feet down, thanks, and facing this way.*

The tone is relaxed, expectant and moving on with the lesson flow *as if* he'll do it. If he doesn't I'll repeat and redirect but not argue.

Same with the two girls talking during instructional time.

> T *Vanessa and Lisa* [establish eye contact] *facing this way and listening, thank you.* [Firm, pleasant, with an 'as if' tone.]
>
> Ss *We're only talking about the work!*
>
> T [Tactically, ignore their silly voice tone and refuse to get drawn into the 'secondary' issues. Redirect to the primary issue.] *Maybe you were but I want you to face the front and listen, thanks.*

It is important, then, to resume the flow of the lesson. This demonstrates control, not of the two girls, but of the lesson, allowing Lisa and Vanessa take-up time and enabling them not to lose face. When we *overdwell* (Kounin, 1971) on secondary issues we break the 'flow' of the lesson.

Planning for effective discipline

The point is I cannot effectively discipline if I don't have a plan. This plan has to take into account four major aspects of discipline:

1) preventative
2) corrective
3) consequential
4) supportive.

Effective discipline balances these four essential areas.

1) Preventative

The preventative aspect of discipline is particularly important in the 'establishment' phase of the year. This covers aspects of the classroom management such as lesson planning, both the units of work and individual lessons; catering for mixed abilities; thinking about the seating and aesthetics in the room (air flow from windows, movement flow around the room, carpet helps noise level, fixing any broken furniture quickly, lighting); communicating routines (for work, monitors, partner-voices in work-time, how to get teacher attention appropriately, toilet procedures, packing up); and planning a language of discipline prior to the need to use it. It's difficult to know what to say *when* we're under emotional pressure. A plan can help. We know (as research confirms: Elton, 1989; Rogers, 1992a) that teachers rate calling out, talking out of turn, argumentative (and the 'last word' syndrome) students, seat-wandering and task avoidance as their major disruptions. While these are not serious it's the frequency of the behaviour that is so frustrating.

Effective management, and discipline, is a matter not merely of personality or good fortune but of skill:

> *The most talented 'natural' teachers may need little training or advice because they learn so quickly from experience. At the other extreme, there are a few teachers for whom training and advice will not be properly effective because their personalities do not match the needs of the job. It is clear, however, that the majority of teachers can become more effective classroom managers as a result of the right kinds of training, experience and support.*

(The Elton Report, p69)

Preventative management includes an awareness of group dynamics and some of the 'games' students play... It is also essential to make the classroom 'rules' or 'agreements' clear in the establishment phase of your time with the group. Fair, clear and 'owned' rules help protect the rights of all and give a basis for corrective discipline where necessary.

2) Corrective

However well we plan for a lesson, there will be minor disruptions such as calling out, chit-chat, off-task behaviours. In 'difficult' schools there will be regular bouts of clowning, teacher-baiting, task avoidance and task refusal.

An effective principle of discipline is to begin at the least intrusive level and only move to the most intrusive as the situation, context and circumstance necessitate. For example David has sneaked his Walkman cassette recorder into class.

T   *Right!* [Teacher walks over, heavy footed, hand outstretched.] *Give it to me! Come on, hand it over!*

S   *Come on, I didn't have it on!*

T   *I don't care, hand it over.*

S   *No way, I'm not doing anything wrong; anyway I can put away . . .*

This most intrusive stance *invites* a power struggle and with some students offers them, on a plate, the win/lose game they may be looking for.

A least intrusive stance sees the teacher walk quietly over, establish eye contact (smiles are even appropriate), after all it's not a major crime! and say in a firm but calm voice:

> T *David, nice Walkman.* [This *prefaces* the discipline direction you're about to give, it creates a relational context.] *You know the school rule.* [Rule reminder] *Put the Walkman in your bag or on my desk, thank you.* [This gives a directional 'choice'.]
>
> S *Oh, come on, Miss Snaggs in art lets us have them on!* [A sulky pout appears.]
>
> T [Instead of arguing, 'I don't care if every teacher in the school lets you have it, WHAT DID I SAY?!!' – the teacher redirects.] *Maybe she does but the rule is clear. In your bag or on my desk, thanks.* [At this point the teacher walks away from David as if he'll do it, allowing take-up time and some 'face-saving'.]

If David refuses to put his Walkman away in class (most students will comply) I can hardly just make him. If I go to snatch it and a counter-grab plus verbal heat is exchanged, what's the point? Win/lose confrontations only service power exchanges. I can walk away leaving David to own his 'choice', to put it in his bag or on my desk, or he can face a deferred consequence. All my ranting or pleading (in front of the class audience) won't change his attitude.

'Dave, if you continue to keep it on your desk, I'll have to follow it up later – after class.' The 'tribal tom-toms' of the group will soon know that the deferred consequence was carried out by the teacher.

By using the least intrusive measures (directional choices, casual and direct questions, reminders, encouragement, distraction and diversion, privately understood signals, redirections) teachers can keep transactional heat down and increase the likelihood of behaviour ownership in the student.

This is not merely words either. The teacher's tone is pleasant but assertive, the eye contact is established, but the ball is in the 'student's court'. If he refuses this reminder/'choice' the teacher can come back with a consequence statement (see later). Each intervention by the teacher is reminding without arguing that the student is required to own his (or her) own behaviour and respect others' rights in that room. It is the reasonable consistency of a teacher's daily corrective style that will communicate fairness, assertion and care: the language of discipline...

3) Consequential

If students refuse to own their behaviour they will be faced with 'choosing' the consequences. Students need to be treated as if they can 'choose' the consequences of their behaviour. To do that they need to know the fair rules, and the positive rights behind those rules. They also need encouragement and positive reinforcement when they work by the fair rules. If students choose to resist the rules they need to face the reasonable consequences.

4) Supportive

Finally, supportive discipline completes the cycle. When any consequence has been carried through it is important to re-establish a working relationship between teacher and student, to repair emotional breaches. With repeatedly disruptive student behaviour the teacher (with collegial support) will need to work on a longer term plan (beyond consequences) to repair and rebuild dysfunctional patterns of behaviour.

Leadership, not merely control

Traditionally the word discipline has concentrated on punishment and control, often couched in combative metaphors. Schools have a history of corporal (physical) punishment, canes, straps, ear-pulling, hair-pulling, shoving, finger-poking-in-shoulder, public embarrassment – even humiliation. In the mid-1980s, in most democratic countries, the cane and corporal punishment were abolished. Nowadays the emphasis is on self-discipline rather than teacher control alone.

I prefer to use the concept of *discipline leadership* rather than 'control'. *How* can we lead, guide, direct, encourage, remind, teach and (sometimes) assert and confront students to:

- 'own' their own behaviour, accept responsibility for, and accept accountability for their behaviour?
- respect the fundamental rights of others to be safe, feel safe, learn and be treated with respect?
- embrace fundamental values of honesty, a fair-go, the dignity of the person?
- co-operate in a group (classroom and wider school community)?
- believe in themselves?
- value themselves (self-esteem)?
- gain the best they can from their schooling experience?

The *way* we daily guide, lead, teach is in effect part of the discipline process that seeks to reach these goals. Ambitious!

Rather than merely control the student we are asking: how can I set up the classroom (and the school) environment, how can I manage and discipline, so that the goals outlined above can be realised in any meaningful way? Discipline, then, under this definition is what I say and do on a *characteristic* basis, that enables the student/s to embrace those goals.

Having a discipline plan

To do this in any effective way we need to recognise the need for a plan. The major emphasis of this book is that if discipline is going to be effective it needs to be planned. The goals mentioned above will rarely be met by accident; fortuitously. Like most things in teaching *effective* discipline needs planning.

Few teachers go into class without a lesson plan (of some sort), yet I've worked with and met significant numbers of teachers who will daily walk into classroom settings where calling out, butting in, seat-wandering, procrastination, argumentative students, task avoidance ... are occurring – without a discipline plan.

A discipline plan embraces the four aspects of management mentioned earlier: preventative, corrective, consequential and supportive.

Central to this discipline, management and teaching process are fundamental values we hold about dignity, human worth, the way we treat individuals in our society (the Judaeo-Christian heritage on which these *values* are built). *Human rights* are fundamental expectations arising from those values. *Rules* are social constraints designed, within the group, to bring some protection of those rights and indicate responsibilities and duties with respect to those rights. *Consequences* are the way the group brings accountability to bear upon those individuals who affect, or abuse, others' rights.

Bringing natural justice to bear on these elements is never easy. In the Western tradition the balance of freedom and responsibilities is addressed by a framework of rights, responsibilities, rules and consequences, and (hopefully) the willingness to engage in restitution and reconciliation.

References

Elton Report (1989) *Discipline in schools, report of the committee of inquiry* London: HMSO

Kounin J (1971) *Discipline and group management in classrooms* New York: Holt, Rinehart & Winston

Rogers B (1991) 'Dealing with procrastination' *Topic 2* Issue 6 NFER

Rogers B (1992a) 'Peer support: peers supporting peers' *Topic 1* Issue 7 NFER

Rogers B (1992b) *Supporting teachers in the workplace* Milton, Queensland: Jacaranda Press (now published in the UK by Pitman as *Managing teacher stress*)

19.   Testing Teachers and Discovering Rules

Mick McManus

From time to time pupils, like any other workers, seek a little light relief from the inescapable tedium and tension of daily life: they like to 'have a laugh' and they prefer their teachers to have a sense of humour too... (The particularly difficult motives of pupils who may be in an extreme state of distress and confusion will be discussed separately.) Motives may be in conflict. For example, a pupil may wish to develop and display a personal identity as a bright pupil, pleasing to adults. He or she may also wish to retain an acceptable status in a classroom group where over-zealous, compliant pupils are rejected as 'swots and creeps'. Apparently incomprehensible behaviour may thus be witnessed from time to time. A successful and academically ambitious pupil may be caught in a piece of extravagant misbehaviour by which he or she intends to demonstrate to classmates an enjoyment of, and affinity with, their irreverence for schooling. For example, a bright primary school girl put a drawing pin on her teacher's chair, explaining that she feared that other pupils thought of her as a 'goody-goody', which of course she was. For an example of this in a prestigious grammar school, see Lacey's (1970) discussion of Sherman, a top pupil who balanced his achievements with mischief.

How pupils perform under each of these headings will depend upon their beliefs, expectations and attitudes. Their accumulated experience of dealings with adults, and in particular their parents or guardians, will to a large extent set the context for their first encounters with teachers. For some pupils, classroom disruption is no more than a temporary strategy adopted to break the tedium of a boring lesson or to punish an incompetent or humiliating teacher. Their misbehaviour is transient, of no wider or deeper significance, readily abandoned and easily controlled. Other pupils perceive the classroom as an extension of a harsh, unjust, unpredictable and unforgiving world: a world of stress, poverty, indifference or cruelty that most of us are fortunate enough never to have encountered. For such pupils, school offers a relatively safe environment for the exploration of their distrust, apprehensions, anger and insecurity. Their class-room disruption and disaffection may appear even in the most exciting and well-conducted lessons. It is difficult to bear and apparently impossible to eradicate whatever the level of care and encouragement given. Its significance and source of energy are largely from without the classroom.

This is not to say that such behaviour is a straightforward, determined effect of domestic environment: this behaviour is part of an active strategy. It is not determined in a mechanistic sense, and it is this that allows the teacher some purchase upon it. Pupils of all ages want to know what rules are in operation in any given situation. The less specific and convincing the teacher, the more the pupils will explore the boundaries of what they suspect to be permissible... It is not enough to state rules and expectations verbally: tone of voice, expression and demeanour are among the non-verbal types of communication by which pupils assess whether teacher means it and whether he or she has the determination and ability to control their wayward experiments. Pupils, like adults, form expectations of others in the light of their appearance and perhaps their reputation. They may be pleased to discover that they were correct in their prediction or disappointed and troublesome if the teacher turns out to be unexpectedly permissive or unaccountably strict. A pupil interviewed in a unit for disruptive teenagers blamed his present placement on the fact that he had not had 'big enough teachers'. The boy was of small build and physically unprepossessing, so we may assume he was speaking metaphorically.

Teacher testing is particularly prevalent at the start of the school year. And equally prevalent at the same time are teachers' attempts to make rules and expectations clear and to make them stick. For a long time this particular teacher activity remained invisible to university researchers and writers, partly because higher education takes a longer summer break than schools do and partly because teachers are reluctant to be observed 'licking the pupils into shape'. This has had unfortunate consequences for the training of teachers.

One of the studies reported by Wragg (1984) is of a trainee science teacher who had observed the regular class teacher conducting orderly lessons while lounging on the desk, making quips and flirting with the girls. The student attempted a similarly relaxed performance when his turn came, only to find it received with outraged indiscipline. The student had not observed, and had not been informed about, the extensive rule setting that this relaxed teacher had engaged in earlier in the term. The majority of secondary school science teachers choose rules and safety procedures for the first lesson of the year. The implicit message is here congruent with the explicit one: the teacher decides what is allowed and what is not; the pupil is expected to comply.

To recognise these skirmishes as merely teacher tests is usually all that is necessary to prevent them escalating into hostility. Teachers who perceive them as personal attacks on their authority and competence, or who explicitly identify them as stupidity, risk prolonging and aggravating the behaviour. From one point of view, pupils are not so much challenging the teacher's authority as trying to discover its form and extent in each particular case: they rebel in order to find out to what rules they must conform. McDermott claims that some low-ability pupils used misbehaviour in order to 'draw the teacher back to their group so that reading instruction could continue' (Wittrock, 1986: 420). Forms of misbehaviour which are often taken as tests of the teacher's authority may also have a beneficial function. For example, Delamont & Galton (1986) note that for some pupils fighting is an essential part of sorting out peer-group relationships. It may be that in more liberal schools pupils' increased area of discretion requires more of these sorting activities. 'Rough-housing' may help to produce an orderly school. Whether this is so or not, there is no doubt that to accept these testing encounters as part of the ordinary routine is to cut away their power to offend: pupils find not an opponent but an understanding and indestructible adult with whom they are content.

Teacher testing takes many forms. A powerful negotiating counter on the pupils' side is the level of noise in the classroom – a matter over which they have considerable control. The closed classrooms so prevalent in primary schools, and to a greater extent in secondary schools, are an organisational feature largely responsible for creating the noise weapon. Noise is one of the few features of classrooms that can be detected from without: above a minimal level it betokens indiscipline and disorder. As Nash (1973) noted, keeping pupils quiet is part of the teacher's job. It is no help to cite evidence that pupil talk is essential to learning in a wide range of subjects, including science, where practical activity might be thought a suitable substitute for talk (for example, Barnes *et al.* 1969 and Driver, 1983). The significance of noise in classrooms is extensively treated in Denscombe (1985) and in his chapter of the book edited by Woods (1980b).

Not all pupils need to be actively engaged in testing behaviour, and many members of a class may gain much valuable information from the active service of a few. Ball (1981) noted that the fate of those explorative pupils who elected to test the boundaries influenced the behaviour of others in the class. A noisy dispute between two pupils may be serving as a test. Teachers who seek to pacify and mediate in such public arguments may unintentionally and implicitly display their ignorance of pupils' more subtle forms of warfare. The appropriate tactic is to silence the parties briskly, perhaps with an offer to settle the dispute for them in their own time after the lesson. Teachers who did not lose their tempers, did not ignore the tests and did not show confusion were more effective in establishing control (Ball, 1981).

Verbal disputes may take a stylised and alarming form as in 'sounding or woofing' imported from American youth culture, though Doyle says it is not widespread (Wittrock, 1986: 418). Beynon (1985) observed this type of misbehiour and noted that a smiling 'victim' indicated that a teacher-testing tactic was in progress. Verbal tests include requests for readily available information or the offer of counterfeit or absurd answers. Non-verbal tests often take the form of outdoor clothing and hats if the encounter takes place indoors. Other strategies include an over-literal response to instructions, a walk that is too fast or too slow, an inappropriately relaxed or stiff posture and extravagant yawns and displays of tiredness. Werthman (1963) provides an interesting early description of some of these tactics employed by American teenagers. The wise teacher will expect to be tested by pupils in early encounters and he or she will therefore be neither disappointed nor dismayed. It is important not to identify testing behaviour wrongly: it is not so trivial that it can be ignored but it is not so serious that it merits excessively vigorous suppression. Pupil mythology contains stories of teachers who were easily baited and driven into rages in which they sometimes injured themselves. The best tactic is to appear unsurprised and to react in a calm, clear and unconfused manner. Early encounters between secondary school teachers and their classes have been illuminatively researched by Beynon (1985). The topic is also treated by Ball in his chapter of the book edited by Woods (1980a). Pupils expect teachers to keep order and to make curricular demands upon them. They expect teachers to be worthy of their attention and respect and to be able to withstand their probing and provocation.

References

Ball SJ (1981) *Beachside comprehensive* Cambridge: Cambridge University Press

Barnes D, Britton J & Rosen H (1969) *Language, the learner and the school* Harmondsworth: Penguin

Beynon J (1985) *Initial encounters in the secondary school* Lewes: Falmer

Delamont S & Galton M (1986) *Inside the secondary classroom* London: Routledge & Kegan Paul

Denscombe M (1985) *Classroom control: a sociological perspective* London: George Allen & Unwin

Driver R (1983) *The pupil as scientist* Milton Keynes: Open University Press

Lacey C (1970) *Hightown grammar* Manchester: Manchester University Press

Nash R (1973) *Classrooms observed* London: Routledge & Kegan Paul

Werthman C (1963) 'Delinquents in schools' in BR Cosin (ed) *School and society* Milton Keynes: Open University Press

Wittrock MC (ed) (1986) *Third handbook of research on teaching* New York: American Education Research Association/Macmillan

Woods P (ed) (1980a) *Pupil strategies* London: Croom Helm

Woods P (ed) (1980b) *Teacher strategies* London: Croom Helm

Wragg EC (1984) *Classroom teaching skills* London: Croom Helm

20. A Behavioural, Reflective, Relationship (BRR) Approach

Bill McPhillimy

... In this chapter, I shall outline an approach which I think is likely to be successful for most teachers. It is a combination of elements of two approaches rooted in two different kinds of psychology often held to be incompatible: behaviourist and cognitive psychology. A brief account of the nature of the different approaches to classroom control that stem from these different viewpoints is therefore necessary before I go on to suggest how they can be profitably combined.

First, the behavioural approach. Traditional behavioural psychology embodies three basic ideas, as follows:

I) Psychology should deal with observable behaviour, that is what people do and say, and not with things that cannot be observed and measured, such as thoughts, feelings and purposes.

II) Behaviour is learned, that is, it is a product of experiences the person has had, and it is possible for a person to stop behaving in certain ways, and to begin to behave in different ways, as a result of further experiences.

III) Changes in behaviour are governed primarily by the consequences of our actions. We tend to repeat behaviour which leads to consequences we desire, and not to repeat behaviour which leads to consequences which are undesired by us or unpleasant to us.

The teacher who applies these principles to classroom control will concentrate on pupils' behaviour, that is, what they do and say in the classroom, rather than spend time and effort thinking about their feelings or their reasons for misbehaving. Her general strategy will be as follows:

I) decide what is wanted in terms of pupil behaviour;

II) apply behavioural techniques to increase desired behaviour;

III) apply behavioural techniques to lessen undesired behaviour.

The main behavioural techniques available to teachers are reward, extinction and punishment. If a behaviour is followed by a reward, it is more likely to occur again. Behaviourists prefer the term 'reinforcer' to reward, principally because things that would normally never be thought of as rewards can have the effect of 'reinforcing' a behaviour, that is, making it more likely to recur. For instance, a teacher's reprimands to a pupil for silly behaviour in the classroom can have the effect of increasing the occurrence of such behaviour, in that the teacher's attention to him is acting as a reinforcer. He is seeking attention, and any attention is better than none to him, but neither teacher nor pupil would think of the reprimands as rewards.

However, for our present purposes, the everyday term reward, rather than reinforcer, will be used. To a behaviourist, reward should be the main strategy for changing classroom behaviour. Rather than focus on misbehaviour, the teacher should identify desirable behaviour ('catch them being good', rather than bad), and encourage this by means of rewards of different kinds, applied systematically on either a group or an individual basis.

Misbehaviour, to the behaviourist, can be dealt with in different ways. First, if good behaviour which is incompatible with certain bad behaviour is established by reward, the bad behaviour, logically, cannot take place. For instance, if 'going straight to your place' after breaks is fully established, the communal area misbehaviour which previously occurred at this time will not now occur. Second, extinction of behaviour can be utilised. Extinction is the process whereby a behaviour that is no longer rewarded will occur less and less frequently, before finally disappearing. Applying this technique requires the teacher to identify the rewards that are keeping the misbehaviour going and eliminating them. This is not easy to do in the classroom, for reasons that will be discussed later. The third main behavioural way of dealing with misbehaviour is by punishment, that is, by arranging for something unpleasant to or undesired by the misbehaving pupil to happen to him after the misbehaviour. This makes the recurrence of the misbehaviour less likely. Behaviourist writers on classroom control tend to advocate a minor role (or no role at all) for punishment, regarding it as a very negative strategy. They much prefer reward, which guides pupils to good behaviour, to punishment, which merely stops misbehaviour. The term 'negative reinforcement' is sometimes used for punishment, but this is not strictly accurate. Reinforcement always increases the likelihood of behaviour, whereas punishment decreases it. Negative reinforcement, correctly, is the kind of 'reward' that is involved when something unpleasant is stopped or removed after the occurrence of desired behaviour. This has the effect of increasing the likelihood of the desired behaviour occurring again. For instance, making a pupil who is reluctant to work sit by himself is a punishment; letting him rejoin his group when he starts working properly is negative reinforcement.

A final point about the behavioural approach is that the teacher is expected to be systematic in her approach. Behaviour is observable and therefore measurable. It is not satisfactory, for example, simply to reward certain behaviours in ways that seem appropriate and to hope that control will improve. The thoroughgoing behavioural teacher will identify the target behaviour precisely, and, by observation and counting, obtain a 'baseline' or initial level of occurrence for it. Then the behavioural technique will be applied and further observation and measurement carried out to detect any change.

To sum up, the behavioural approach is a matter of discouraging undesired behaviour, and, especially, encouraging desired behaviour, in a systematic way. The steps involved are: (i) identifying a target behaviour to be changed; (ii) obtaining, by observation, a measure of the frequency with which it occurs, thus establishing a baseline; (iii) applying an appropriate behavioural technique (usually a reward of some kind) to effect the change; and (iv) measuring the change in the incidence of the target behaviour.

The second of the main approaches mentioned earlier is the cognitive approach. This approach comes from a psychological viewpoint quite different from, indeed opposed to, the behavioural one. From this viewpoint, the idea of disregarding pupils' thoughts, feelings, motives, etc, and concentrating simply on their behaviour is regarded as folly, for it is thoughts, feelings and motives that are held to be the essence of the person. Behaviourism is therefore seen as so narrow as to be of little use in understanding people and what they do. In particular, in thinking about and trying to cope with the problems of class control, a teacher would be encouraged, from a cognitive viewpoint, to try to see the classroom situation from the pupils' point of view. The cognitive psychologist sees the pupil as a person trying to make sense of the world around himself, and trying to deal with it in ways that contribute to his survival, well-being and development. If he sees what the teacher has created around him as relevant to his concerns and likely to help him to develop in ways he likes and thinks are important, then he is likely to co-operate in the work of the class. But if he sees what is going on as worrying, or boring, or irrelevant to his concerns and how he wants to develop, then he is unlikely to co-operate. It is therefore clear that 'making the work interesting' to pupils is seen as crucial in this approach, and the teacher who is having difficulties would be advised to consider what it is about what she is teaching, or how she is teaching it, that is responsible for her failure to connect with the pupils. In trying to answer this question, she would be urged to try to see things from the pupils' point of view, bearing in mind their age, interests, home background, general ability, existing skills and knowledge etc., and to make appropriate changes in what and how she is teaching.

Another central aspect of the cognitive approach is the importance it attaches to the influence on a pupil's behaviour of his self-concept, that is his view of himself as a person, and, in particular, of his academic self-concept, that is, how he sees himself as a pupil and learner. From the cognitive viewpoint, this aspect of the self-concept is very important in determining how a pupil behaves when he is engaged, or is supposed to be engaged, in school work. If he has a positive academic self-concept, he regards himself as a person likely to be able to undertake the task set for him and to succeed reasonably well. He is therefore likely to tackle the task in a realistic and positive way, in other words, he will make a genuine effort to cope with it, feeling that such an effort is likely to be worthwhile because his attempt is likely to be fruitful. With such an attitude and behaviour, he is unlikely to engage in misbehaviour. However, many pupils have negative academic self-concepts. Their expectations are of difficulty and failure, and engaging in a set task with such expectations will produce feelings of anxiety and unhappiness. Such pupils are likely to try to avoid such feelings, naturally enough. This can be done in different ways. A pupil might directly refuse to undertake the task; he might find excuses not to attempt it; he might merely pretend to engage in it; he might engage in it, but set himself a very low target (for example, attempting only the first few and easiest maths examples in an exercise). All of these are likely to be seen by the teacher as 'not trying', with consequent potential for conflict. No one likes failure and difficulty (how many adults persist with a sport or leisure activity for which they show little talent?), but teachers, who have all been relatively successful academically, often find it difficult to appreciate just how dispiriting it is for pupils to have to persist day in and day out in activities where they feel doomed to failure. 'Not trying' is therefore often a means to avoid failing, rather than defiance of the teacher's wishes.

Another way in which the pupil with a poor academic self-concept can avoid coming to grips with his work is by making his feelings about himself open to others – 'I can't do it, I'm too stupid, there's no point in me trying'. This can also be exasperating to the teacher, but less so than defiance, avoidance or minimal engagement, and can often induce in the teacher some admiration for the pupil for being 'honest', as well as sympathy for his difficulties. Perhaps most worrying from a control point of view, however, is the low self-concept pupil who not only shields himself from failure by refusing to engage in set work, but who, instead of blaming himself for this, blames the teacher, the school or adult society in general. The most common way of doing this is to decide that the work is boring and irrelevant, that the teacher is boring, incompetent and unfair, and that school and education in general are a waste of time. It makes matters worse if there is an element of truth in such views, even if the pupil's main reason for forming them is his own fear of failure. If a pupil, or a number of pupils feel like this, then misbehaviour is very likely to occur, in a form that will be extremely difficult to cope with.

What are the implications for class control of this analysis from a self-concept viewpoint? These are, in principle, fairly clear, if difficult to put into practice. The teacher's aim should be to improve the pupil's self-concept, both generally as a person, and, in particular, as a learner. To help enhance his general self-concept, the teacher has to get across the message that she genuinely values him as a person; that he is acceptable and worthwhile as a member of the class; that she likes his company and wants to help him. This can only be achieved through friendly interaction with pupils, and by taking a genuine interest in their ideas, opinions and work. As far as the pupil's academic self-concept is concerned, the main way towards improvement is to structure his work carefully so that he begins to experience success and to feel competent, albeit at a low level at first. If this can be achieved, he should become progressively more willing to engage in the work. If a large group or whole class of pupils has much the same needs, this gradation of work is likely to meet with some success, but if only one or two pupils are involved, their desire not to be obviously 'behind' their peers can make them very unwilling to engage in work within their capabilities.

The above brief accounts of the behavioural and cognitive approaches should have made it clear why they are often held to be incompatible, and in their extreme forms they probably are. However, I believe that elements from each can be combined to produce an approach which is more in tune with teachers' everyday perceptions of pupils and classrooms, and therefore more likely to be acceptable and successful in practice, than either approach by itself.

The first step in formulating such a combined approach is to identify the elements of each of the two constituent approaches which seem useful and compatible with one another, and those which seem incompatible, unnecessary or unproductive. This can be done by comparing and contrasting the two approaches under three headings: first, the significance of misbehaviour in each (in two senses of significance, i.e.

importance and meaning); second, the kind of relationships between teacher and pupil in each; and third, the techniques for improving control suggested by each.

1) The significance of misbehaviour

In the behavioural approach, behaviour and misbehaviour are all-important. Whatever is in the hearts and minds of pupils, it is what they do and say that constitutes order or disorder, and which has to be encouraged or discouraged. From a cognitive viewpoint, behaviour is seen more as an indicator of whether such things as motives and self-concepts are in a healthy state. Misbehaviour in itself is therefore mainly a symptom of a problem, rather than the problem itself. If the underlying problems are dealt with then the symptom is likely to disappear. Which is the right side to be on here? ... I strongly believe that misbehaviour must not be left to 'sort itself out' while underlying problems of one sort or another are addressed. If this is done, work and learning will be subject to long-term disruption, which simply cannot be allowed in the classroom. Having said this, however, the notion of behaviour as the be-all and end-all, and consequent exclusion from consideration of such matters as motives and pupils' perceptions of events, seem equally wrong. In trying to stop misbehaviour and encourage good behaviour, the reasons why pupils engage in one or the other are often of importance, and it is surely far too narrow to restrict the consideration of possible reasons for their behaviour to the past consequences of pupils' actions, as the extreme behavioural approach does. To sum up, the 'combined' or compromise view I take here is that, from a control point of view, behaviour and misbehaviour are very important in themselves, and misbehaviour has to be directly and speedily addressed. However, in coping with misbehaviour, and encouraging good behaviour, pupils' motives, as well as other reasons for their behaviour, are of importance and must be taken into consideration.

2) The relationship between teacher and pupil

The roles of teacher and pupil and the teacher's attitude to the pupil are quite different in each approach. In the extreme behavioural approach, the teacher's role is a detached, mechanical, even manipulative one. The teacher simply defines the behaviour she wants, and arranges the consequences of the pupil's actions so that desired behaviour becomes more likely and undesired behaviour less likely. The teacher takes on a role not unlike that of a scientist with the pupils as the subjects in her experiments, as she observes behaviour, establishes baselines, measures changes, and so on. In the cognitive approach, on the other hand, the quality of the human relationship between teacher and pupils is all-important. Great stress is laid upon the teacher trying to see things from the pupils' point of view (that is, to empathise with them in the way that a counsellor does), and upon trying to improve pupils' self-concepts by means of a genuinely warm and positive attitude to them.

When contrasted like this, both of these models of teacher-pupil relationships seem somewhat inappropriate to real-life teaching. The behaviourist teacher does not seem like a normal human being interacting with other human beings in anything like a natural way, but like a scientist with her subjects, as suggested previously, or a puppet-master. The cognitive teacher, on the other hand, seems impossibly virtuous, warm, positive, caring and understanding about all of her pupils, no matter how horridly they might behave towards her, and extremely non-directive. As a model, the cognitive approach seems, perhaps, more appropriate for a counsellor than a classroom teacher. A compromise between the two extremes is necessary... A little detachment is probably a good thing for a teacher. The behavioural teacher above is too detached, the cognitive one probably too involved. Genuine interest and human warmth towards pupils are highly desirable in a teacher, but, from a control point of view, it is also clearly necessary for the teacher to be 'in charge', and not just an adult friend, helper, or counsellor.

3) Techniques for improving control

The behaviourist approach offers very clear guidance on techniques, which are relatively easy, at least in principle, to apply. Concentrating on desired behaviour and encouraging it with rewards, while discouraging undesired behaviour where necessary by means of punishments of different sorts, is an attractively simple and direct strategy. The main techniques suggested by the cognitive approach, namely making the work interesting to pupils and endeavouring to improve pupils' self-concepts, are more general, more difficult to apply, much less clear-cut and seem likely to take a much longer time to have an impact on pupils' behaviour than rewards and punishments. However, both techniques seem worthwhile from a control point of view, as well as desirable from a general educational viewpoint. A compromise between the two approaches with regard to techniques does not necessarily involve a choice between the behavioural and cognitive ones. In my view the techniques are compatible. The more direct behavioural ones and the less direct cognitive ones can be applied by the same teacher with the same class; for instance, rewards of certain kinds can be used to build self-esteem. A compromise approach to control can involve both sets of techniques.

Before going on to list the elements of the two approaches that can be combined, it is necessary to invent a name for this compromise approach. The term 'behavioural, reflective, relationship approach', although clumsy, seems appropriate. It is behavioural because it acknowledges the importance of behaviour and misbehaviour and addresses them directly; it is reflective because, rather than addressing the problems of control in a mechanical, impersonal way, it stresses the need to reflect upon the thoughts, feelings, desires, needs and motives of pupils; and it is a relationship strategy because it requires the teacher to enter into genuine human relationships with pupils. The elements from the behavioural and cognitive approaches that comprise this BRR approach (an unfortunate acronym for an approach that requires a warm relationship) can now be listed.

---

1)   From the behavioural approach

i) The teacher is in charge of, and responsible for, pupils' behaviour.

ii) Behaviour is important in itself, and not just as a symptom of underlying problems.

Continued...

---

iii) Misbehaviour must be stopped as quickly as possible.

iv) There should be an emphasis on the positive, i.e. encouraging good behaviour.

v) Techniques directly aimed at changing behaviour, such as rewards and punishments, should be used.

2)   From the cognitive approach

i) Pupils' purposes or motives in behaving well and badly are often important and must be taken into account.

ii) The teacher must try to see things from the pupils' point of view, as well as her own.

iii) The teacher must try to create warm, positive, genuine relationships with pupils.

iv) Pupils' general and academic self-concepts have an important influence on their behaviour.

v) The teacher must try to bring about positive changes in the self-concepts of misbehaving pupils.

vi) Pupils will behave better if they are engaged in work they find interesting.

These principles seem to me to be useful and compatible and to form a sound basis for a balanced, directive yet humane approach to classroom control. Some aspects of the behavioural and cognitive approaches have been omitted: from the behavioural approach, the mechanical, impersonal way of regarding pupils' behaviour, the unwillingness to take pupils' purposes and feelings into account, and the 'teacher as experimenting scientist' role; from the cognitive approach, the tendency to relegate misbehaviour to the status of a symptom. 'Making the work interesting' as a means of achieving control has been relegated to the end of the list in view of what I have said earlier about it. While I regard it as a highly desirable educational aim, and as an aid to class control, I have already made clear, I hope, why I feel it should not be given anything like the primacy that the cognitive approach attaches to it...

The main points of this chapter

• However successful a teacher is at being the kind of person and creating the kind of classroom atmosphere likely to produce good control, misbehaviour will always occur and a well worked-out general strategy to deal with it is necessary.

• An approach likely to be successful for most teachers can be formulated by combining elements of behaviourist and cognitive psychology.

• Traditional behaviourist psychology embodies the notions that observable behaviour should be the focus of concern, that behaviour is learned from experience and can be changed, and that behaviour is governed by its consequences.

• The three main behavioural techniques which can be used by teachers are reward, which makes behaviour more likely to recur, and punishment and extinction (absence of reward) which make behaviour less likely to recur.

- The behaviourist approach requires systematic identification and quantification of behaviour as well as the application of techniques to effect change.
- Cognitive psychology focuses on processes internal to the person, such as thoughts, beliefs and motives.
- Taking a cognitive approach to control involves the teacher in trying to see classroom situations from pupils' points of view and making sure that pupils see what they are asked to do as relevant to their concerns and in their interests.
- The cognitive view also stresses the importance of helping pupils to develop positive self-concepts or views of themselves as persons and learners.
- With a positive academic self-concept a pupil will see himself as likely to succeed with his work and make genuine efforts, whereas with a negative self-concept he is likely to expect failure and may try to avoid engaging in his work.
- The behavioural and cognitive approaches differ in the significance they attach to misbehaviour, the kind of relationships between teacher and pupil they imply and the control techniques they involve. In their extreme forms, the behavioural and cognitive approaches seem incompatible, but a selection of principles and techniques from both of them can be combined into a compromise approach.
- This approach can be called the behavioural, reflective, relationship approach because it addresses behaviour directly, it stresses the need for the teacher to reflect upon pupils' thoughts, feelings and motives, and it requires genuine human relationships between teacher and pupils.

21.   Handling Class Disruptions

Clark Lambert

... Whether intentional, inadvertent, or even unintentional, disruptions are a common occurrence in the classroom. Left unchecked, they will surely decrease the learning rate for *all* participants.

It's been my experience that most participants who cause a class interruption do so unintentionally and certainly without realising the problem that they are creating. Proper handling of this problem rests on two basic sub-strategies:

1) Never embarrass or 'put down' the problem participant in front of the class.
2) Handle the situation early, before it becomes a serious matter.

Although it's sometimes tempting to react strongly to the individual causing the problem, don't do it. Your annoyance may certainly be justified, and expressing it may afford you a short moment of satisfaction, but doing so will create a still greater problem. The majority of the other participants will usually empathise with the embarrassment of the individual you just 'put down', resulting in a downward spiral of class motivation. After all, participants expect the instructor, the true authority figure in the room, to use his or her power wisely – and certainly with discretion.

It's crucial for the instructor to understand that minor disruptions, if not handled early, stand a good chance of becoming major ones. Accordingly, the guideline here is to move *quickly* toward problem resolution but do so with liberal doses of *discretion*.

Even with the most careful planning, the planned flow of the learning is occasionally disrupted. Under the best of circumstances, this can prove taxing to the instructor. Usually, one or more minor interruptions can be tolerated by the instructor – and to some extent, by the participants themselves. If ignored, however, a minor annoyance can turn into a major disruptive factor. In other words, if a real problem begins to develop within the meeting room, simply ignoring the disruption will not automatically cause it to go away within a given time. Furthermore, if undetected, a small problem slowly and insidiously can grow; by the time it is recognised it may be out of control.

To complicate matters further, the disruptive behaviour of one or more people can quickly become infectious. Other participants tend to 'catch' the same kind of unsettled feelings. If this is allowed to occur, the class is in real danger of disintegrating into a fiasco – whether vividly apparent or, even worse, submerged in participant apathy. Unless the instructor takes quick action to squelch any prolonged disruption, the result usually is quite predictable – an unsatisfactory learning level.

Let's now list some general types of disruptive personalities by category, together with suggested ways to inhibit them. Experienced instructors generally agree that there is never an automatic set of rules for handling a disruptive situation. Put another way, do not fall into the trap of thinking, 'If this occurs, I will immediately counter with that'. Simply taking a moment to think instead of acting on impulse can go a long way in handling most problems that occur.

Although it's very difficult to categorise aspects of human behaviour, the following groupings of *potential* problem personalities represent the six types of difficult participants that an instructor might encounter.

Type 1	'I'm too busy, but I'm here.'	(Importance)
Type 2	'I know better than you.'	(Superiority)
Type 3	'I'm in charge here.'	(Authority)
Type 4	'I need your help.'	(Dependency)
Type 5	'Everything is wrong, as usual.'	(Complainer)
Type 6	'The constant talker.'	(Chatterbox)

Let's examine each type, reviewing their specific characteristics, then discuss some helpful strategies to employ when confronted by them. Keep in mind, however, that some of these types are heavily interrelated to others.

Type 1   'I'm too busy, but I'm here'

Sub-Type: *See how important I am*

Characteristics: Whatever the hour, this person is generally late for class or, at best, the last one to arrive. He or she usually enters the room in a harried, frenzied manner, making certain that all other participants realise the 'sacrifice' this person is making by attending. At the same time, this person will usually throw a mild glance of annoyance at the instructor to make certain that the message has clearly gotten across. In some instances this same individual will either be called out of the room on an 'urgent' telephone call or will simply spend time in class writing down a huge variety of notes for apparent follow-up after the session has been concluded. On occasion, he or she will have to leave the meeting early and an apology will be made to the instructor. A favourite strategy here is, upon leaving the room (usually halfway out the door), to call out loudly to another participant to call him immediately at the conclusion of the meeting.

Counterstrategy: 'I'm too busy, but I'm here' individuals seek constant reinforcement of their importance, coupled with liberal doses of positive ego strokes to feed their sense of self-worth. A workable strategy (as they arrive late) is to involve them immediately in a task that requires an important follow-up on their part.

Example: 'Hi John, glad you could make the class. Really pleased that you could attend, since we're about to discuss the matter of (name a subject), and I know that you have an expertise in this area. As a matter of fact, I'd like you to stay for a minute after we break to make certain that we've captured all of your thoughts on this. It will really help what we are trying to accomplish here.'

Type 2   'I know better than you'
Sub-Type: Superiority syndrome

Characteristics: In most situations, these people will devote their main energy and attention to challenging the instructor in one way or another. Whatever is said or done, these individuals will either contradict it or (at best) enter 'clarifying' comment to what has just been said. While this rather cruel game can be played by those at any level of management, it can be accomplished most easily when the 'I know better than you' person is of a higher rank than the person conducting the class. A very favourite strategy for making their presence strongly felt is to manoeuvre themselves into a position to give a final summary of what has transpired, then add their own opinions, which will rarely be the same as the instructor's. Cleverly done, this summary will almost appear to have come as an afterthought, but it will be presented with an air of authority.

Counterstrategy: A definite aid in this sort of situation is to first recognise the fact that these individuals strongly seek recognition and are continually building up their power base. While this *may* be a defence for their own strong feelings of insecurity, it is very important to them to always be noticed through their discreet interruptions, which give them a chance to impress others with their self-perceived importance. An effective strategy here would be twofold: first, call on them early in the class before they have had a chance to pick the 'perfect moment'. Second, immediately after they have expressed their opinion, tactfully mention that while it was a good point, there may be several alternate opinions on the subject, and quickly ask the other participants for their viewpoints. In many cases this strategy defuses the 'I know better than you' type and may discourage their disruptive tactics.

Example: 'Well, Lynn, that was an interesting point of view and certainly deserves some additional thought. As a matter of fact, I'm sure that several people here can contribute even further on this subject. John, how about it? What are your thoughts on this?' (Note: Involving Types 1 and 2 here is an excellent strategy!)

Type 3   'I'm in charge here'
Sub-Type: Authority figure

Characteristics: While closely allied with 'I know better than you' types, Type 3 personalities concentrate their main energy on letting everyone know how important they are to the unit, group, or organisation. This strategy naturally leads into the fact that they are responsible for the assembled group and should be accorded a special status. While they may occasionally challenge the instructor (if it suits their purpose), their primary objective during the class is both to heighten and to reinforce the fact that they hold a position of authority. As a result, each response made during the class is usually done in such a way as to convey a domineering viewpoint – in either a subtle or an obvious manner. Naturally, the situation can prove to be rather disconcerting (to say the least) to the instructor, since nothing worthwhile can be accomplished with even a faint hint of intimidation in the room – and the person conveying it may even be the instructor's boss!

Counterstrategy: With this type, great care must be exercised at all times! Even though the instructor must walk a fine line here, objectives for a truly participative class can be reached. The technique is, first, to give the respect due the 'I'm in charge here' types, since they have reached a high position of authority. Basically, this is common courtesy. Then, immediately following this deference, ask a carefully worded question that will encourage these persons to talk freely, based on their high status. In other words, you can turn their elevated rank (a definite disadvantage to have in the meeting) into an advantage by reason of their experience and background. Granted, people of a much higher rank than most of the other participants should generally not be in the classroom, where a non-threatening, free-flowing environment is mandatory. As we all know, however, this situation cannot be avoided from time to time, and this suggestion offers one way to deal with it.

Example: 'As you can see Milt, we're faced with a really difficult situation here. The group has already come up with some worthwhile suggestions, but we could use the benefit of your own experience in matters like this. What are your thoughts, Milt? How would you handle it? Can you share some insights with us?'

Type 4   'I need your help'

Sub-Type: Highly dependent

Characteristics: In contrast to the first three types described, the 'I need your help' classification is a classic study in direct contrast. These types can be readily identified by their lack of self-confidence and strong dependency on others. They are generally plagued by feelings of insecurity and usually dread the thought of expressing an independent opinion and perhaps looking foolish in front of their peers. Left alone in a class, they will not participate; if forced to, they will always agree with the majority opinion and never disagree with a point of view expressed by another participant. But these individuals usually do have some very good ideas; they must be gently drawn out by the instructor and always in a non-threatening manner. (Caution: Pay special attention to this type during role plays and small-group exercises, which can be highly threatening to them.)

Counterstrategy: Type 4 people can become productive participants through a series of non-threatening questions that aid in building self-confidence, thereby paving the way for greater involvement. The instructor needs a high degree of skill to accomplish this, for the questioning must be done both discreetly and through carefully worded probes. Begin with a question they can easily respond to, one that has been designed to build their confidence levels. A bit later in the meeting, at an opportune time, pose a second question that is slightly more difficult. Once this second probe has been answered, the instructor is well on the way to having these individuals become productive members of the class. Again, however, extreme caution must be taken during this procedure to avoid having shy participants perceive themselves as being threatened in *any way*.

Example (first in a series of probes): 'Looks like we have a consensus on the decision to reduce departmental absences starting next week. It seems to be the most feasible course of action for us to follow at this time. Before we make it official, however, I want to make certain that we are in full agreement on this as a team. Let's see. There are still a few people we haven't heard from yet. How do you feel about this, Julie?'

Type 5   'Everything is wrong, as usual'

Sub-Type: Complainer

Characteristics: Nothing associated with the class is ever acceptable to Type 5 people. Furthermore, they appear to take a special delight in *pointing out* what they feel is *unacceptable*. Complaints can run the gamut of possibilities – the class started a bit late, the coffee is too weak (or strong or hot or cold), the lighting, heating, seating, or air conditioning is not right, even the agenda is not to their liking. However they express their displeasure (verbally, non-verbally, or a combination of both), they appear to have a definite need to voice their displeasure about various facets of the class, the instructor, and whatever else that they can think of!

Counterstrategy: The key strategy here is to take the initiative *before it is taken from you!* In other words, respond to each 'problem' as soon as it is voiced. Avoiding or deferring your response will only serve to strengthen the apparent unhappiness being generated. Conversely, by answering each complaint right away, the 'everything is wrong, as usual' types will shortly become discouraged from further complaints. As with the handling of all problem types, a very liberal degree of tact, patience, and diplomacy must be used by the instructor. It's not easy to do so, but it's very necessary!

Example: 'I agree with you, Laura – it is a bit warm in the room. We knew about the problem in the air-conditioning system before the class started. The maintenance department has already been notified, and we hope to have it fixed within the next few minutes. Thanks for bringing it to my attention. We're all a bit uncomfortable.'

Type 6   'The constant talker'

Sub-Type: Chatterbox

Characteristics: These individuals are perhaps the most disruptive of all, since they talk incessantly throughout the session. They appear to delight in carrying on side conversations with participants on either side of them, disrupting the flow of information for all concerned. On occasion, they even attempt to talk with a person across the table, completely ignoring what is being said by the instructor. Any way viewed, they present a serious situation for the instructor, and one that must be handled promptly.

Counterstrategy: The quickest way to terminate this type of disturbance is to draw the constant talkers back into the mainstream of the class. Without making it too obvious, thereby running the risk of being perceived as 'heavy-handed' by the group, the instructor should periodically solicit the opinions of these individuals about what has just been said. Use of this strategy over several minutes will usually discourage the constant talkers from further interruptions. Finally, it is also an effective strategy to call on the people engaged in conversation with the 'constant talkers.' It is a subtle technique and generally works very well – but use it with caution.

Example: 'That's really an interesting comment, Jack. I'm sure, however, that everyone may not completely agree with you. Let's see how the others feel about this. Uh . . . Joe, what are your specific thoughts on this?'

When you reflect on the difficult people you encounter during a typical class, you soon realise that it is hard to fit these people into neat categories. Rather than exhibiting a single difficult characteristic, some individuals exude combinations of several problem clusters, making the situation even more difficult for the person conducting the class.

While there are never automatic rules for handling *every* type of problem situation, it's well to recall the two fundamental guidelines that were discussed earlier in the chapter. As you will recall, they are:

1) Never embarrass a troublemaker.
2) Always handle the problem early.

We can now add two more basic rules:

1) Always use tact and diplomacy – even if it hurts!
2) Never show annoyance or lose your temper.

Use of these four basic guidelines will not completely guarantee a trouble-free class, but they will go a long way in helping you accomplish your objectives smoothly. These four guidelines, coupled with a liberal sprinkling of common sense, become a combination that is hard to beat. After all, although the instructor is the one who has to react and deal with the problem, it is the participant causing the disruption who really has the problem.

22. A Model for Developing a Whole-College Approach

Carole Mitchell, Douglas Pride, L Howard & B Pride

Effective practice in managing disruptive behaviour depends upon action at the three levels of strategy, systems and delivery, and the interactive relationship between them. Using a cone divided into three to show the different levels of activity and decision-making in a college expresses this relationship well (Figure 1).

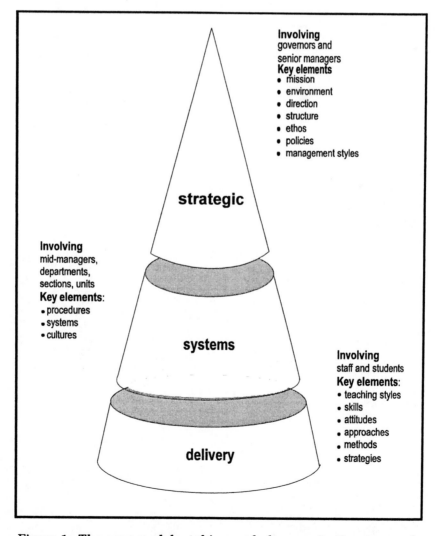

Involving governors and senior managers
Key elements
- mission
- environment
- direction
- structure
- ethos
- policies
- management styles

strategic

Involving mid-managers, departments, sections, units
Key elements:
- procedures
- systems
- cultures

systems

Involving staff and students
Key elements:
- teaching styles
- skills
- attitudes
- approaches
- methods
- strategies

delivery

Figure 1: The cone model – taking a whole-organisation approach to managing disruptive behaviour

To achieve a whole-college approach to managing disruptive behaviour, these three organisational levels must interact. Colleges can use this model to:

- understand issues and needs across the whole college,
- plan an eventual whole-college response,
- communicate issues and progress to staff at all levels in the college...

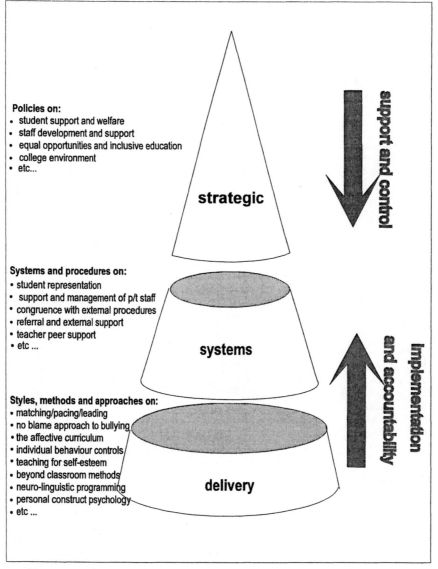

Figure 2: Examples of elements at each level of the cone model

Figure 2 gives a further breakdown of the elements at each level and indicates the importance of top-down support and control and bottom-up implementation and accountability.

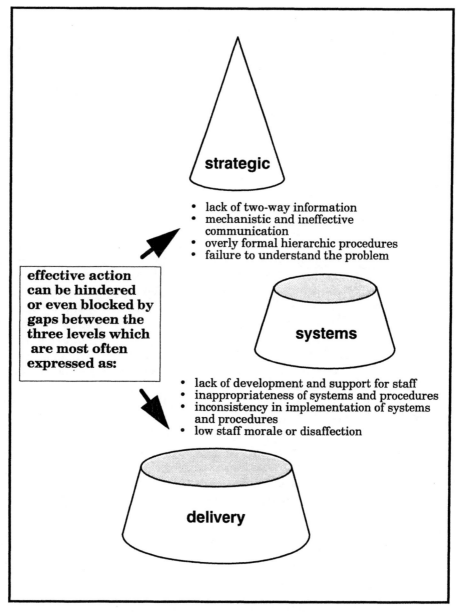

strategic

- lack of two-way information
- mechanistic and ineffective communication
- overly formal hierarchic procedures
- failure to understand the problem

effective action can be hindered or even blocked by gaps between the three levels which are most often expressed as:

systems

- lack of development and support for staff
- inappropriateness of systems and procedures
- inconsistency in implementation of systems and procedures
- low staff morale or disaffection

delivery

Figure 3: Fragmented college

Figure 3 illustrates how the college can become fragmented through ineffective interaction between the three levels.

The model provides powerful imagery for staff development sessions, and it is persuasive for grassroots staff because it emphasises that there can be no 'us' and 'them' in addressing disruption. It shows how effective action can be hindered or blocked between the strategic level, the systems level and the delivery level...

Delivery methods: theory and techniques

Many of the methods listed in the delivery level of the cone model have arisen from key areas of research by specialists in the field. The underpinning theory of the main techniques are briefly outlined below. To become more familiar with these techniques, further reading is recommended... These methods are organised in four categories:

1) learning/teaching/classroom-based methods

2) behavioural methods

3) cognitive/behavioural methods

4) counselling and therapeutic groupwork methods.

1) Learning/teaching/classroom-based methods

As Walklin (1990) indicates, in a sector which relies upon voluntary attendance, it is inappropriate for FE tutors to be seen as strict, controlling and domineering. They need to be seen as helpful, patient, unbiased and fair. However, there does need to be mutual recognition of responsibilities between institution, teacher and student. The college can work to produce a facilitative adult learning culture; the teaching staff can plan, prepare and deliver learning events to meet the negotiated goals and individual needs of students; and the learners can participate in the learning process using self-control and with due regard for others. In developing a whole-organisation approach to preventing disruptive behaviour, a college will benefit from reviewing its teaching and learning practice and staff development (see Mitchell, 1995/1997a). For example, carry out an audit of learning and teaching strategies to ensure that there is sufficient variety in the learning experience (Mitchell, 1997b).

There are a number of well-researched and applied techniques which can be used throughout the FE institution in a variety of settings from boardroom to classroom. Adopting these strategies across a college can help to produce an adult learning culture in which all participants behave in a responsible manner.

Students want discipline, and so they require tutors to exercise it. In a recent survey by Dewsbury College, teachers produced the following list as attributes of 'the ideal teacher':

- explains points clearly and at the appropriate level,
- conveys enthusiasm and interest for the subject,
- pays attention to revision and exam techniques,
- makes lessons interesting,
- has high expectations for students' work,
- teaches for understanding rather than rote learning,
- is confident,
- is constructive and helpful.

It is interesting to note that the teachers made no reference to a disciplinary role, whereas students placed this at the top of their list. In their view the ideal teacher has the following attributes:

- keeps order by being firm but not intimidating,
- explains things clearly,
- treats all students fairly and equally,
- is friendly and humorous,
- gets to know students' names/treats them as humans,
- tries adventurous strategies/variety of techniques.

Rule-based method

One of the most useful strategies that teachers can use is to negotiate with the students ground rules of behaviour. Staff and students make their expectations explicit by stating openly what behaviours they regard as desirable and they expect and what behaviours are unacceptable. Those commonly shared between staff and students will be particularly powerful.

The ground rules can be displayed in the classroom/s in a chart form as in Table 1, to remind both teachers and students of what is required.

Unacceptable to staff	Unacceptable to students	Unacceptable to both
Expectations of staff	Expectations of students	Expectations of both

Table 1: Ground rules of behaviour

Bill Rogers (1990) sees discipline as a complex concept and process which addresses:

- the socialisation process
- personal development and maturation
- moral development
- emotional security
- internal state control.

He advocates a positive approach to discipline based on four elements (see Figure 4, over).

The goals of his approach are to:

- develop self-discipline and self-control,
- enhance self-esteem,
- encourage accountability for behaviour,
- develop respect for others' rights,
- develop interdependence,
- promote social values,
- enable rational and fair conflict resolution.

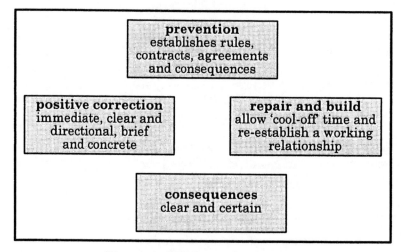

Figure 4: Bill Rogers' approach

Authoritarian or abdicating styles of teaching are unsuitable – a confident approach is needed:

- the *authoritarian* professional *demands* social behaviour;
- the *abdicating* professional *hopes for* social behaviour;
- the *confident* professional *expects* social behaviour (and usually gets it!).

Rogers suggests the following code of practice for tutors:

- establish mutually agreed *rights, responsibilities* and *rules*;
- minimise *hostility* and *embarrassment*;
- maximise *choice;*
- develop and maintain *respect*;
- *follow up* and *follow through*;
- avoid *disappointment*;
- maintain a sense of *balance*;
- encourage *support* from and for your colleagues and friends;
- lower personal stress levels.

His approach is strongly supported in the work of Bill Gribble (1993) who summarises that a positive approach to discipline *isn't:*

- an excuse for inappropriate behaviour;
- regarding inappropriate behaviour as an innate factor;
- a way of labelling students;
- counselling, punishment or suspension.

Instead, he advocates that a positive approach *is:*

- a shift from an 'authoritarian' to a 'democratic' approach based upon positive learning experiences;
- an attempt to emphasise the values of:
    - equality
    - respect
    - self-discipline;
- a method of organising and planning for responses to inappropriate behaviour;
- a recognition that the college and classroom environments do influence behaviour;
- an unambiguous attempt to teach students to behave responsibly, co-operatively and with concern towards each other.

Focus on learning

Gribble (1993) emphasises the importance of effective classroom control through planning how to handle disruption, but also by doing the utmost to prevent it, by developing the following teaching strategies:

- *lesson planning* – having a clear theme, aims, targets, variety, good seating arrangements, appropriate materials;
- *keeping attention* – using eye contact and body language, responding to feedback and inattention;
- *pace* – engaging students through a prompt start, keeping them on task and allowing time to conclude;
- *motivation* – through questioning, encouraging opinions and valuing them, involving all students;
- *question and feedback (in larger groups)* – including all those who wish to contribute by asking short, factual questions and indicating turn-taking;
- *confidence* – asserting control through voice quality and body language;
- *reducing unwanted behaviour* – by not rewarding attention-seeking, avoiding emotional outbursts, rewarding students for getting on with their work;
- *clear instructions* – for whole groups and individuals using manners ('please'; 'thank you') and a polite but not apologetic delivery;
- *reprimands* – only when necessary, and kept clear and brief;
- *consequences* – a pre-negotiated or directed set of logical consequences which are planned responses to disruptive behaviour...

The case study in Table 2 below, which describes the action planning strategy adopted by Bury College to combat disruptive behaviour, depicts this approach.

Student quality managers (SQMs) at Bury College arranged a series of visits to the classrooms of subject tutors who had agreed to work on the project to observe five students exhibiting difficult behaviour. The SQMs observed the classes and then discussed their perceptions with the subject tutors, agreeing possible strategies that could be used to combat challenging behaviour. Subject tutors then planned and delivered lessons, ensuring that the techniques were used. The SQMs observed these lessons and discussed with the subject tutors the effectiveness of the techniques.

How personal action planning was used with one of the students is outlined below. In this case, interviews with the student were held in between the lessons observed.

The student concerned was enrolled on the GNVQ Intermediate Business course. His behaviour in class was not appropriate. When asked to undertake independent work or to work in a small group he refused to comply with instructions, staring into space for prolonged periods doing no work at all or disrupting other students by talking to them and directing their attention away from the task.

The personal action planning strategy used to support the student was based on joint problem solving (JPS). This technique is different from counselling in a number of respects:

- tutoring based on the JPS approach works from the premise that there is a 'problem' but that each party – the tutor and the student – shares that problem and has a personal stake in its resolution;

- when using the JPS approach it is possible to suggest options and solutions and to outline the perceived likely outcomes, if adopted;

- the tutor is allowed to reject ideas and give reasons for that rejection; most importantly, both parties have to agree an eventual outcome, even if that entails some compromise and re-negotiation.

The stages of the process are to:
- identify and agree the symptom;
- identify and agree the causes;
- identify and agree the options for moving forward;
- discuss the pros and cons of each option;
- decide:
  – agree and record the course of action to adopt, from the options available
  – agree the consequences of not following through
  – agree and record the next steps (who is to do what, by when)
  – agree a review date.

Continued...

As a result of adopting the JPS approach, the student identified the causes of his behaviour. He found it difficult to organise himself to study. As a result, his coursework files were not in order, his notes were difficult to follow and he had fallen behind in his coursework. When asked to work in class he felt overwhelmed and unequipped to carry out the tasks. His response was to 'turn off' or to disrupt other students. An action plan was devised with the student with the following goals agreed (see below).

Action plan

Short-term goals
- Put course work files in order and index them.
- Buy a filofax diary and record key dates and deadlines along with other useful information such as telephone numbers and addresses.
- Tidy study area at home.

Medium-term goals
- Maintain the diary.
- Get into the habit of making lists of things to do and of giving priority to important and urgent tasks.
- Develop filing systems for study area at home.

Long-term goals
- Gain an understanding of time management and apply that understanding.
- Set study targets for self and use study sessions productively to meet those targets.

Short-term goals were achieved and had a positive, motivating effect on the student's behaviour. The subject tutor and a close friend of the student commented on the improvement in his behaviour and performance. Disruptive behaviour has continued to be reduced and the medium-term goals have been achieved.

Table 2: Case Study – Adopting an action planning strategy to combat challenging behaviour in the classroom.

Well-planned, well-organised and assertive teaching is essential to preventing and managing disruptive behaviour. A good physical classroom environment can help. According to the project colleges, features include:

- adequate lighting and good ventilation
- adequate sound control
- harmonious colours
- comfortable and flexible seating

- a spacious room area
- adequate whiteboard space
- bulletin board space
- learning centres
- teacher accessibility
- audio-visual aids.

Attention must be paid to the teaching process, including:

- stating outcomes and goals,
- knowing the students,
- being aware of student achievement levels,
- communicating clearly, both verbally and non-verbally,
- organising and sequencing material,
- maintaining student involvement,
- differentiating work,
- maintaining a sense of humour,
- observing the class and providing feedback and motivation,
- being flexible,
- establishing rapport,
- listening for language patterns,
- eliciting and installing individual learning patterns,
- knowing the learning subject matter and content.

The learning process is of paramount importance: students need to learn and if their learning is impeded, their behaviour can quickly deteriorate. The learning process involves:

- building the learner's self-esteem,
- increasing student involvement, via planning, feedback and rapport,
- stimulating interest, motivation and desire to learn,
- providing appropriate materials,
- determining clear-cut goals,
- teaching the subject matter in a relevant way,
- developing security and trust,
- encouraging self-determination and choice,
- eliciting excitement and enjoyment in learning,
- generalising and applying learning,
- using teaching techniques that allow for differentiation,
- eliciting and installing learning patterns.

McGill & Beaty (1992) detail how action learning can be made accessible for management development and learning in further and higher education. The focus is on enabling individual learners to progress from taking responsibility for their own learning to receiving support and critical feedback. The emphasis is on learning from the actions taken with the aim of strengthening the individual learner. They provide excellent guidance on how to set up and manage action learning groups to maximise effective personal learning and development. They suggest that assertiveness training will facilitate the development of effective action learning sets. There are many benefits of learning in this way. The promotion of good social behaviour is just one of them.

Gibbs & Jenkins (1992) propose that teachers have a choice between offering a system which highly controls and structures the student experience and a system which develops and relies on the independence of the student as a learner (see Table 3 below).

Problem areas resulting from large classes	Characteristic methods adopted	
	Control strategies	*Independence strategies*
1) Courses lack clear aims and objectives	Use of objectives Highly structured course	Use of learning contract Problem-based learning
2) Students lack knowledge about their progress	Objective testing Programmed instruction and CAL	Development of student judgement Self-assessment
3) Students lack advice on how to improve	Assignment attached forms Automated tutorial feedback	Peer feedback and peer-assessment
4) Library resources cannot support wide reading	Use of set books Use of learning packages	Development of student research skills More varied assignments
5) Tutors are unable to support independent study	Structured projects Lab guides	Group work Learning teams
6) Students lack the opportunity for discussion	Structured lectures Structured seminars and workshops	Student-led seminars Team assignments
7) Tutors are unable to cope with the variety of students	Pre-test plus remedial material Self-paced study	Variety of support mechanisms Negotiated goals
8) Tutors are unable to motivate students	Frequent testing High failure rates	Learning contracts, problem-solving, group work

Table 3: Control and independence strategies

From the student's point of view, the larger classes that are becoming a feature of FE today can make them feel alienated, that they lack personal attention, and as a result cause insecurity. Action learning, within the independence strategy, can provide an individual focus within a group-based approach which can help to lessen these problems.

Action learning can activate and enhance the learning process, as depicted in Kolb's Learning Cycle (see Figure 5 below). This underpins the action learning method.

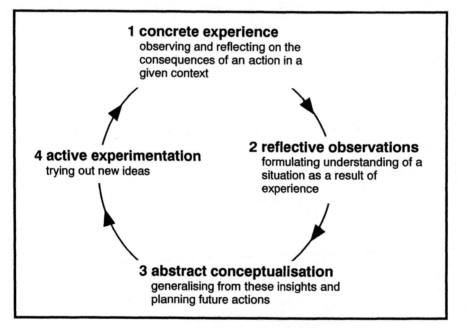

1 concrete experience
observing and reflecting on the consequences of an action in a given context

2 reflective observations
formulating understanding of a situation as a result of experience

3 abstract conceptualisation
generalising from these insights and planning future actions

4 active experimentation
trying out new ideas

Figure 5: Kolb's learning cycle

Self-esteem
Building learner self-esteem is central to the learning process. Learners sometimes find it difficult to express positive attributes about themselves – they can be helped through simple structured exercises, such as the one shown in Table 4. They could do this in pairs or groups to encourage them to complete it.

1	One thing I like about myself is
2	One thing others like about me is
3	One thing I do very well is
4	A recent problem I've handled very well is
5	I'm glad that I

Continued...

6	A compliment that has been paid to me recently is
7	An example of me caring for others is
8	People can count on me to
9	I think I have the guts to
10	If I had to say one good thing about myself I'd say

Table 4: Assessing your strengths

Co-operative learning
Co-operative learning promotes social development and increases teacher time for individual work. Many students arrive at FE with a 'failure' label and negative self-esteem which will impair their capacity to learn. Co-operative learning opportunities in FE can help them to build a positive self-concept.

Topping (1992) finds that students with learning difficulties and disabilities and pupils from ethnic minorities can benefit from co-operative learning in terms of improved social integration as well as attainment.

Much attention has been paid in management training programmes to the development of team work and group work, given that cohesive work groups may result in higher production, lower absenteeism and social satisfaction (Mullins, 1989).

Many employers look for effective teamwork skills in job applicants. As colleges are preparing students for employment and lifelong learning, they are justified in using co-operative learning strategies to improve behaviour and to prepare learners for work.

Colleges can use the research by McGill & Beaty (1992) on action learning as a basis to consider how co-operative activities can benefit the staff, students and the communities which they serve.

Peer support
Peer tutoring can also promote the development of learning. Most peer support schemes use students who are perceived as more experienced and capable to give help to students who are perceived as less able.

Peer support can be used to team up:
- students new to the college with a long-standing or Year 2 student – on the same course or from a panel of volunteers, on a self-selected or tutor-selected basis – to introduce them to the facilities, systems and ethos of the college;

- ESOL students with native English speakers;

- Year 2 students with Year 1 students for academic support on a one-to-one or group basis;

- students with emotional and behavioural difficulties with any one of a panel of students trained in counselling skills, who will refer them on to trained counsellors where necessary;

- able-bodied students with students with physical disabilities to provide physical support and companionship; this can be done on a small group basis and works well when the students with physical disabilities are able to help the able-bodied with academic work, or specific physical skills;

- full-time students with one or two part-time students, for friendship, induction to the college and help with organisational problems;

- young, unmotivated students with older students of the same sub-culture who have decided to knuckle down to work.

Peer support can also be useful to team up students with emotional and behavioural difficulties with students with learning difficulties and physical disabilities, to offer them support. A 'spin off' is that helpers often develop maturity and personal and academic skills. It is important that students are not given roles beyond their emotional maturity or ones which put them in positions where they can misuse their power.

2) Behavioural methods

Antecedents, behaviour, consequences (ABC)

As Dennis Child comments in his introduction to David Fontana's editorial on *Behaviourism and learning theory in education* (1984), behavioural approaches to teaching are seldom covered in teacher training courses because they are considered by many to be undignified. Yet Child finds that Fontana cites some useful practical techniques for teachers.

Within this text (Fontana, 1984), Wheldall & Merrett describe the ABC (antecedents, behaviour, consequences) model which shows how behaviour change can be achieved by manipulating either the antecedent conditions for behaviour or the consequences following behaviour, in line with the 'law of effect'. Wheldall & Merrett argue that if teaching is about changing behaviour through academic learning or from acquiring better social skills, then the teacher should be concerned with bringing these changes about. The ABC model helps teachers to observe and analyse behaviour objectively.

An example of the ABC method is provided by the National Star Centre (see Table 5 opposite).

Name
Age
Date of Behaviour Management Problem (BMP)
Antecedents (causes, early stages)   The behaviour is
and is triggered by
Behaviour (what the student actually does – intensity, frequency, duration)   The exact behaviour is
Consequences   Harm is caused to
by
The triggers can be avoided/reduced by
The behaviour can be controlled/modified by
The effect or results of the behaviour can be reduced by
Notes
Staff name
(National Star Centre)

Table 5: Using the ABC method

BATPACK

Some behavioural interventions have no long-term effect, especially with older children. While Wheldall & Merrett acknowledge this, they suggest that it may be due to lack of understanding about appropriate reinforcers (Fontana, 1984). So they designed the *Behavioural approach to teaching package* (BATPACK) to encourage teachers to reinforce desired behaviour by commenting on it positively and to eliminate undesirable behaviour by ignoring it.

The BATPACK emphasises the contingent use of praise and the reinforcement of desirable social behaviour as well as academic behaviour. It recommends the following teacher comments, which make up the REX model:

- Rule-related: 'Thanks for observing our rule about turning up on time for classes.'
- Example to others: 'That's a really helpful diagram – would you be good enough to explain it to the group?'
- Explicit statements of what is being praised: 'Thanks for clearing up the mess that had been left in the room.'

Teachers using the BATPACK state that they now give more positive feedback to students, although they do not significantly decrease their negative feedback. They find that the level of 'on task' behaviour from students increases.

The 'behavioural charter' (Table 6 below) sets out the key principles.

---

10 tactics for teachers

1) Arrange the classroom appropriately for task and students.

2) Make sure that the students know what they are supposed to be doing.

3) Negotiate with the students a few simple positive rules – beneficial to all.

4) Look out for good work and behaviour.

5) Try to praise quickly and consistently.

6) Remember to praise the behaviour/work rather than the student only.

7) Use a variety of social reinforcers.

8) Ignore inappropriate behaviour where possible.

9) Make sure that all the students know what behaviour is being praised.

10) Build 'treats' into your teaching as rewards for good work and behaviour.

Table 6: Behavioural charter

Fontana (1984) recognises that one of the most useful aspects of training in behavioural teaching techniques is that teachers recognise that behavioural problems are frequently initiated by themselves, and that one of the most effective ways to change behaviour in others is to change their own behaviour. He also acknowledges the importance of the social learning environment which is created by teachers and which, if constructed carefully, can bring about more efficient and effective learning.

Assertive discipline

During the 1990s, many schools have adopted the 'Assertive discipline' approach of Lee Canter (1989). Based on a marriage of assertiveness training and behaviourism, it advocates that teachers make their expectations clear and then follow through with established consequences. While Canter claims success for his technique, as well as many disciples, his methods may not be appropriate for creating an adult learning environment in which each individual's acceptance of responsibility for learning is the primary goal. It is more likely that such an environment will be produced by negotiating personal learning contracts and mutually-agreed group ground rules. Nevertheless, many FE tutors have to work with groups of unmotivated and uncommitted students, and in these circumstances it may be appropriate to use Canter's approach.

The following list of rules for teachers models the way in which the technique can be used:

DO:

- have a clear set of rules (no more than five) with an escalating scale of rewards and punishments;
- give a lot of praise and positive reinforcement and recognised rewards (prizes) for good behaviour as well as good work;
- involve students in deciding what behaviour is unacceptable and what sanctions should be given for breaking group rules;
- involve people related to the students such as tutors, employers, parents;
- start each day/session/week with a clean start.

DO NOT:

- be hostile to students;
- nag: 'How many times have I got to tell you...?' 'Why do you always...?'
- start with negative criticism – no student shall be told off before two students have been praised for doing things right;
- give negative strokes before at least one positive stroke (say 'hello', compliment, praise for something else).

Most teachers adopting this approach find they spend less time on disciplining students, which makes for a more pleasant atmosphere in the classroom.

How well the system works is likely to depend upon the:
- clarity of the rules – for example, 'treat objects with respect' is not clear since it depends upon a definition of respect which may not be commonly shared; 'students may not deface college buildings and furnishings' is clear;
- extent to which students accept the rules, which is likely to be influenced by how much they have been involved in making them;
- ability of the teachers to focus on the positives.

While schools using the system report that it works for most students, with older students there is often a hardcore who will rebel just for the sake of rebelling. Assertive discipline has been described as a method for 'crowd control', for improving relations with the majority of students. It is not designed for dealing with extreme cases of difficult behaviour.

Social skills training

The sector has recently acknowledged the need to become more inclusive in its practice. At the same time, it has also recognised that many college staff are ill-equipped to meet students' individual needs (see Tomlinson, 1996).

Some students with learning difficulties and disabilities have poor social skills or behavioural problems because they may have been subjected to environments where deviant behaviours are the norm. Alternatively, they may have low self-esteem because of being personally devalued. Given appropriate learning support, some students respond quickly to positive learning environments. Others with more entrenched problematic behaviours may require more specialised help. FE staff need the skills and confidence to handle these challenges. This can be developed through training which will probably emphasise the basic social skills training favoured by many psychologists in clinical and education settings.

There are various social skills training materials available. The *Social Skills Handbook* (Hutchings *et al.* 1991) could be used to train FE staff to promote appropriate behaviour. *Learning Support: a staff development resource pack* (FEU/Training Agency/SKILL, 1989) – contains some excellent training materials which can help staff to manage challenging behaviours. However, most of the principles advocated are essentially good basic teaching and learning strategies, including positive attitudes to learners, recognising the individual needs of learners, negotiating personal learning contracts, and providing learner-centred activities.

Many FE tutors, including trained teachers, may not have been formally trained in classroom management techniques or the management of learning. Some staff development in the behavioural techniques of, for example, Fontana, Wheldall & Merrett, and Bloom, and the neo-behaviourist conditions for learning set out by Gagné, can give teachers an insight into how to manage difficult behaviour. They will then be better prepared to consider how to create the conditions necessary to bring about effective learning and considerate behaviour.

3) Cognitive/behavioural methods

Since the 1960s, the importance of thoughts, actions and feelings in explaining human behaviour has been increasingly recognised. Cognitive behavioural approaches recognise that a core set of attitudes and beliefs give rise to thoughts, images and behaviour. Working at attitudes, values and beliefs is now part of several methods designed to change behaviour.

No blame approach to bullying

Little attention has yet been given to researching bullying in FE. However, colleges can learn much from the experiences of schools where bullying is now well recognised and documented. The DfE Circular 8/94 on *Pupil Behaviour and Discipline* states that:

Bullying may be distinguished from other unacceptable forms of aggression in that it involves dominance of one pupil by another, or a group of others, is premeditated and usually forms a pattern of behaviour rather than an isolated incident. Many pupils experience bullying at some point ... bullying or other forms of harassment can make pupils' lives unhappy, can hinder their academic progress and can sometimes push otherwise studious children into truancy. In extreme cases, it can lead pupils into taking their own lives. School staff must act – and importantly be seen to act – firmly against bullying...

The circular urges that bullying be addressed in school behaviour policies and associated rules of conduct, which should include explaining how pupils can bring their concerns to the attention of staff.

In a review of the substantial research in recent years, Lowenstein (1994) concludes that:

- there are three types of bullying – physical, verbal and psychological;
- the problem varies in nature from area to area;
- bullying is a predominantly male activity;
- females tend to adopt psychological and verbal forms of bullying while boys tend to use physical bullying;
- younger children are more prone to bullying than older children;
- both bullies and victims of bullying have personality deficits; for example, the tendency to be victimised correlates to negative self-appraisal and negative appraisal by others; the victims of bullies frequently become bullies themselves;
- bullies tend to display other forms of anti-social behaviour;
- certain personal characteristics, including clumsiness and learning difficulties, are related to victimisation...

Personal skills training is not the only approach taken to tackle bullying. Campaigns include getting young people to carry out surveys, make videos, put on plays for younger students and organise anti-bullying events. One of the most promising approaches emphasises the need to help the bullies as well as the victims because bullies are often victims themselves.

Maines & Robinson's paper (1994) – *The No Blame Approach to Bullying* – advocates that instead of being castigated the bullies should be asked for their own ideas about how the bullying could be stopped. This approach could work particularly well in FE colleges. Co-author George Robinson says that the approach has been successful in dealing with problems of bullying of special educational needs (SEN) students by students on other courses.

Bullying is not just a problem for students. In a recent survey by the National Association of Schoolmasters/Union of Women Teachers (NAS/UWT) of 3,500 members, seven out of 10 teachers claimed they had either been bullied themselves or had witnessed the bullying of others, mainly by school heads (Education, 1995). In its view, the best ways to deal with bullying is to agree a policy with management which defines what is acceptable behaviour at work. The types of bullying reported include the intimidatory use of discipline or competence procedures, staff being shouted at in front of colleagues or pupils and other threatening techniques including the setting of impossible deadlines, verbal and occasionally physical threats, removing agreed responsibilities without consultation and repeated written and spoken criticism. The National Association of Teachers in Further and Higher Education (NATFHE) has recently produced a paper, *Bullying at Work* which is part of its *Harassment at Work* pack (1996). This suggests that bullying is likely to flourish where aggressive management is the norm and that harder-edged management styles have developed within the FE sector post incorporation. A 'Whistleblowers Protection Bill' to safeguard the rights of employees who draw attention to the wrong-doings of their employers is proceeding through the Parliamentary stages. It is interesting to note that a 1994 research report from the National Foundation for Educational Research (NFER), commissioned by NATFHE, shows that lecturers' workloads have increased substantially in the last few years; 90% of lecturers are experiencing stress and most believe that managerial actions and attitudes are aggravating the situation.

Some colleges have developed codes of practice to deal with bullying, including it along with other forms of personal harassment and sexual and racial discrimination in policies on harassment.

The ideal system involves three strands:

- have a policy which defines clearly what behaviour is unacceptable and what to do when it occurs;
- make sure all staff and students understand the implications of the definitions of the behaviour, and what to do if they are bullied;
- provide personal and social skills support for victims and bullies.

Assertiveness training
One way to address challenging behaviour is to give all college users assertiveness training, including governors and support workers, and students. Figure 6 (opposite) outlines what is involved. Initiated in the United States to help raise the social competence of minority groups, these assertiveness techniques have proved useful in occupational training.

These techniques involve differentiating between passive, assertive and aggressive behaviours and acknowledging and analysing individual behaviours, usually in group-based activities. The main characteristics of these behaviours have been defined by Luton Sixth Form College as:

- *Assertive* – stating clearly what we would like to happen but without a demand that it should;
- *Aggressive* – making sure that we do get what we want, no matter what the other person feels;
- *Unassertive* – doing nothing and hoping, or trying to get what we want in a roundabout way.

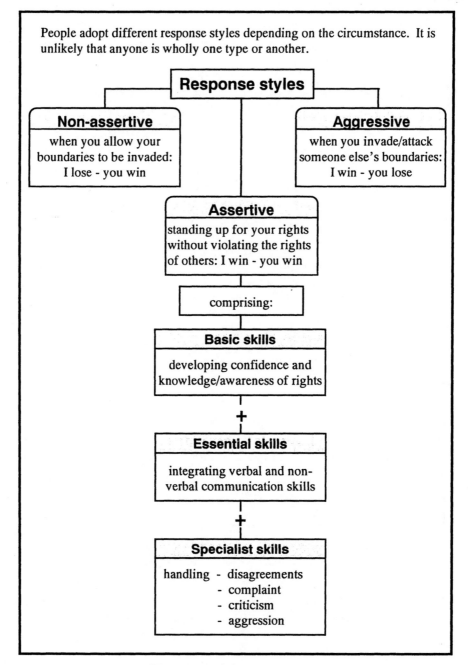

People adopt different response styles depending on the circumstance. It is unlikely that anyone is wholly one type or another.

Response styles

Non-assertive
when you allow your boundaries to be invaded: I lose - you win

Aggressive
when you invade/attack someone else's boundaries: I win - you lose

Assertive
standing up for your rights without violating the rights of others: I win - you win

comprising:

Basic skills
developing confidence and knowledge/awareness of rights

+

Essential skills
integrating verbal and non-verbal communication skills

+

Specialist skills
handling - disagreements
          - complaint
          - criticism
          - aggression

Figure 6: Styles of response

The training involves:
* exploring current patterns of behaviour;
* recognising the value of assertive behaviour;

- practising the skills of assertiveness;
- unlearning any existing aggressive or unassertive methods of behaviour;
- working through ideas and strategies for appropriate use of the new-found skills in various situations.

Suitable training materials include: the *Lifeskills Now* – open learning materials; *Assertiveness* – (a set of practical materials) (Lifeskills, 1991); *Assertiveness at Work*, which has become a classic workplace training manual (Back & Back, 1982); and the *Negotiating Assertively* (Richardson, 1991) and *Working with Assertiveness* (Fritchie, 1991) video training packs.

Most colleges are already offering assertiveness training within their adult education and health and social care programmes so probably have the trainers and materials already in place.

Assertiveness training is likely to build confidence and self-esteem and equip teachers with a democratic approach to teaching which is more likely to win co-operation from students (see Figure 7 below).

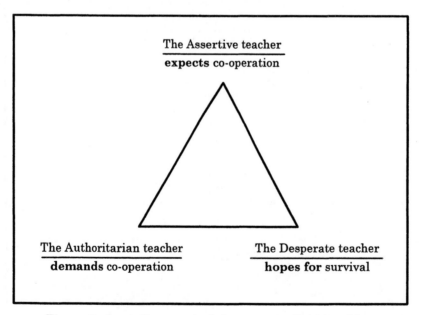

The Assertive teacher
expects co-operation

The Authoritarian teacher
demands co-operation

The Desperate teacher
hopes for survival

Figure 7: Assertiveness training approach to teaching

Neuro-linguistic programming
Neuro-linguistic programming (NLP), a relatively recent approach to understanding and influencing behaviour, looks below the surface behaviour to explore the underlying purposes and beliefs (see Figure 8 opposite).

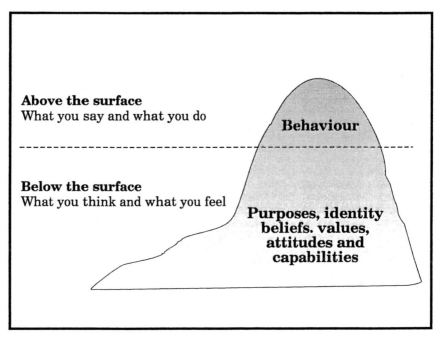

Figure 8: NLP approach

By examining the ways in which people perform with excellence, NLP identifies the conscious, sub-conscious and unconscious patterns which both create and prevent excellence in behavioural terms. The approach is based on modifying attitudes and beliefs and has led to powerful and subtle techniques for influencing behaviour (see Figure 9 overleaf, which is adapted from work on NLP).

However, NLP is not behaviourist in essence. It concentrates on the whole person at a number of levels: environment; behaviour; capability; beliefs, and identity. It focuses on attainable outcomes, on the accuracy of sensory perceptions and information, on behavioural flexibility and on the nature of relationships based upon mutual respect (O'Connor & Seymour, 1990; Lewis & Pucelik, 1990).

Transactional analysis
Transactional analysis (TA) can be readily adapted to provide excellent training on how to manage challenging behaviour, complementing the assertiveness training. Eric Berne, the American psychologist and behavioural scientist, developed the theory of Transactional Analysis whereby he proposes that our 'self-talk' and our communications with others are learned. They are based on our life experiences and influences, especially the examples given by our parents or guardians. Berne contends that it is these early childhood experiences that shape much of our behaviour in adult life.

'Transactions' are the mixture of messages and communications that are exchanged between people, and these transactions can be examined in a structured way through TA and then modified.

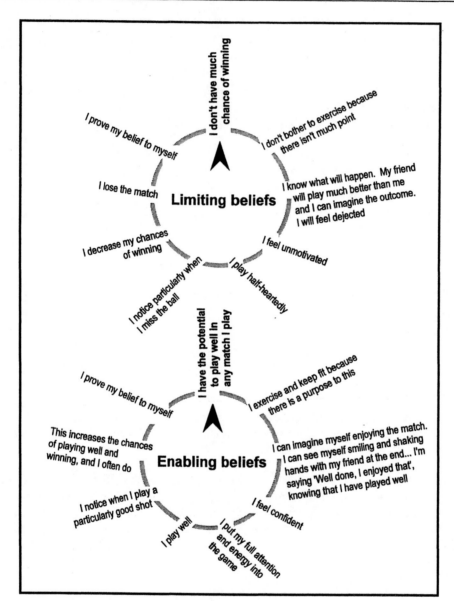

Figure 9: Limiting and enabling beliefs

The TA method is especially concerned with specific transactions that leave people feeling bad or exploited. It is a creative way of looking at social behaviour.

Berne (1968) observes that people transact overtly and covertly and he calls these dual transactions 'games'. Berne identifies three broad behaviour-response styles:

- Parent (P) Nurturing or dominating/controlling,
- Adult (A) Assertive,
- Child (C) Spontaneous.

He proposes that people conduct their 'transactions' or communications from one of these positions. Complementary transactions involve people behaving in similar ways (for example, adult to adult). Crossed transactions occur when non-complementary styles are adopted (for example, adult to child). Berne shows how people become 'locked' into certain styles of behaviour and responses, bringing about transactions which can be helpful or confrontational. Arguably the adult-to-adult transactions are most likely to succeed within FE.

Transactional analysis provides a useful way to analyse the behaviour of the whole institution and the individuals within it. Again, most colleges will have training expertise within counselling programmes. Materials such as *Egograms* (Dusay, 1980) and *Games People Play* (Berne, 1968) can be adapted to produce suitable training programmes. Video presentations on TA can also be adapted to provide training for staff and students...

Personal construct psychology
Personal construct psychology (PCP) is based on the ideas of psychologist George Kelly. He suggested that we should ask people why they do things if we want to understand them. The techniques involve exploring and communicating individual views.

Interventions promote alternative views of even the most entrenched situations. The PCP approach often proves useful in situations where traditional behavioural methods have failed. It is a means of reconstructing situations in ways which increase understanding between students, staff and the organisation. The techniques require some theoretical and practical understanding (Dalton & Dunnet, 1992).

4) Counselling and therapeutic groupwork methods

Behaviour which tutors find disruptive to the adult learning environment can sometimes be due to personal difficulties with which a college counselling service may be able to help. *Learner Support Services in FE* (FEU, 1993) found that 79% of colleges offer counselling and personal guidance; this figure must now be nearer to 100% following the introduction by the FEFC of the staged funding methodology. However, it is not clear the extent to which these services are used to help those with personal difficulties which may manifest themselves as behavioural problems. Colleges should clarify how their counselling services can help with such difficulties. They may wish to consider developing therapeutic interventions which can be particularly helpful in these circumstances.

Young people who are disturbed can be distinguished from those who are 'disturbing':

- By disturbed we usually refer to those whose emotional state is characterised by distress, lethargy, fear, apprehension, immaturity, isolation, unhappiness or inappropriate behaviour. Disturbed young people tend to affect themselves and those close to them rather than others generally. In the educational system those who are disturbed tend to be quiet and not to contribute, to have relationship difficulties, to drop out, to seek outside help or to break down.

- Disturbing young people have an effect upon others. They might be loud, aggressive or destructive. Disturbing behaviour may come from those who are disturbed or from those who are poorly socialised, have little self-control, have had inappropriate role models or who have become disaffected from the values that count in education. In the education system, behaviour which disturbs others tends to be trivial and wearing rather than violent. Often disturbed behaviour is not noticed by teachers or tutors while disaffected acting-out behaviour is.

Those in FE counselling services need to ask: 'Which students should we be concerned about and what type of identification and intervention procedures should we develop?'

There is little evidence as to the extent of emotional and behavioural difficulties in post-16 education. What is known is that when a counselling service is provided in colleges there is a strong demand for it from students with emotional difficulties as well as from staff concerned about students.

College counsellors will be able to advise staff on the extent to which they can help students with emotional and behavioural difficulties within the tutorial situation through individual and/or groupwork. It may be more appropriate for intervention in the fullest sense to be carried out by a trained specialist.

Beyond classroom methods
Although what was formerly known as 'the enrichment curriculum' has suffered severely because of funding cuts in recent years, many colleges still realise the importance of offering social and leisure activities to improve behaviour and reduce student stress levels. They offer a variety of games and activities, sports, teamwork, outward-bound opportunities, residential and extra-curricular clubs.

Several colleges have recognised the benefits of engaging youth workers not only to develop and run extra-curricular activities, but also to support tutors in personal and social education issues within the tutorial programme.

References

Back K & Back K (1982) *Assertiveness at work* McGraw-Hill
Berne E (1968) *Games people play* Penguin
Canter L (1989) 'Assertive discipline – more than names on the board and marbles in a jar' *Phi Delta Kappan* 71 (1) pp41–56
Dalton P & Dunnet G (1992) *A psychology of living* Chichester
DfE (1994) *Pupil behaviour and discipline* Circular 8/94 DfE
Dusay J (1980) *Egograms* Bantam
Education (1995) 'Victims of bullying seek redress' *Education* 1 (186) p3
FEU (1993) *Learner support services in FE* Further Education Unit
FEU/TA/Skill (1989) *Learning support: a staff development resource pack for those working with learners who have special needs* FEU/Training Agency/Skill
Fontana D (ed) (1984) *Behaviourism and learning theory in education* Scottish Education Press

Fritchie R (1991) *Working with assertiveness* Trigger Video Productions

Gibbs G & Jenkins A (eds) (1992) *Teaching large classes in HE* Kogan Page

Gribble B (1993) *Behaviour management for teachers* Bangor Monographs

Hutchings S, Comins J & Offiler J (1991) *The social skills handbook* Winslow Press

Lewis B & Pucelik F (1990) *Magic of NLP demystified: a pragmatic guide to communication and change* Metamorphous Press

Lifeskills (1991) *Lifeskills now; open learning workbooks* Lifeskill

Lowenstein LF (1994) 'The intensive treatment of bullies and the victims of bullying in a therapeutic community and school' *Education Today* 44 (4) pp62–68

Maines B & Robinson G (1994) 'The no blame approach to bullying' paper presented to the *BAAS* meeting 8.9.94 Lame Duck Publishing

McGill I & Beaty L (1992) *Action learning* Kogan Page

Mitchell C (1995) *Learning styles* FEU/FEDA

Mitchell C (1997a) *Educational psychologists in FE* FEDA

Mitchell C (1997b) *Transforming teaching* FEDA

Mullins L (1989) *Management and organisational behaviour* 2nd edn Pitman

O'Connor J & Seymour J (1990) *Introducing neuro-linguistic programming* Crucible

Richardson C (1991) *Negotiating assertively* Pavilion Publishing

Rogers B (1990) *You know the fair rule* Longman

Tomlinson J (1996) *Inclusive learning* FEFC

Topping K (1992) 'Co-operative learning and peer tutoring: an overview' *The Psychologist* 5 (4) pp151–157

Walklin L (1990) *Teaching and learning in further and adult education* Stanley Thornes

Wheldall K & Merrett F (1990) 'The behavioural approach to classroom management' in J Wragg (ed) *Talk sense to yourself: a program for children and adolescents* Longman

23. Procedures and Documentation

Carole Mitchell, Douglas Pride, L Howard & B Pride

[Editor's note. The following extract comprises three appendices from the same Mitchell *et al.* 1998 FEDA publication: *Ain't misbehavin'.*]

Appendix 12: Bury College's disciplinary support procedure

A) *Problem behaviour*

1) *Issue of concern notes*

1.1 When a problem arises with a student's work or behaviour which a Subject Tutor or member of the support staff wishes to be recorded formally and dealt with, then s/he must complete a concern note and send one copy to the appropriate Personal Tutor (full-time students) or Subject Tutor (part-time students), one copy to the appropriate Senior Tutor and retain the third copy as a personal copy.

1.2 The Personal Tutor must act upon any concern note received including:

In all cases:

- investigating fully;
- filing completed concern notes in the Student's personal file;
- recording discussion and action plan on the concern note reply sheet and circulating to appropriate staff;
- monitoring for recurrence of further transgressions.

In some cases:

- discussing with other tutors;
- referring to 'specialist', e.g. Counsellor;
- discussing with Senior Tutor and SQM;
- informing parents;
- informing employers, as appropriate.

1.3 If further problems arise, 1.1 above should be repeated – i.e. a second concern note should be sent to the appropriate tutor.

1.4 On receipt of a second concern note, the Tutor repeats 1.2 above in a further attempt to resolve the problem.

1.5 On receipt of a third concern note relating to the same issue, the Tutor is required to inform the appropriate Senior Tutor or Student Quality Manager, who in turn will initiate the procedure which leads to the composition of a formal Disciplinary Contract (see 2 below).

2) Issue of formal Disciplinary Contract

2.1 Disciplinary Contracts can be devised only by Senior Tutors, Student Quality Managers or members of the Senior Management Team.

2.2 Disciplinary Contracts will only be used to deal with serious and persistent concerns.

2.3 The Senior Tutor or SQM will arrange to see the student after the third concern note has been issued regarding work or behaviour (see 1.5 above).

2.4 Prior to the meeting, the Senior Tutor or SQM will consult as appropriate with the Personal Tutor, Programme Leader, Subject Tutors and support staff as part of the process of investigating the problem.

2.5 Parents and, where appropriate, employers will be informed and invited to discuss the matter.

2.6 A meeting between the student and the Senior Tutor or SQM will then take place. There may also be present parents and other members of Bury College staff, as appropriate. The purpose of the meeting is to negotiate the contents of a formal written contract, to include a review date and a leaving clause.

2.7 After negotiation, the formal written contract is drawn up by the Senior Tutor or SQM and signed by the student.

2.8 Copies of the signed contract are sent or given to the student, parent, Personal Tutor, Subject Tutors, Senior Tutor, Programme Leaders, Faculty Heads, and where appropriate support staff and employers.

3) Permanent exclusion from college as a result of failure to comply with the terms of a Disciplinary Contract

3.1 Failure to comply with the terms of a Disciplinary Contract should be drawn to the attention of the Personal Tutor by means of a concern note. The Personal Tutor should then notify the Senior Tutor or Student Quality Manager.

3.2 Once informed of failure to comply with the terms of a Disciplinary Contract, the Senior Tutor or SQM will inform the appropriate Faculty Head and Head of Curriculum and Quality, and organise a Disciplinary Hearing.

3.3 Parents and, where appropriate, employers will be informed of the Disciplinary Hearing and the circumstances leading to it and given an opportunity to attend.

3.4 A member of the Senior Management Team may be present at the Disciplinary Hearing.

3.5 Where it is established that a student has failed to comply with the terms of a Disciplinary Contract s/he is required to leave College.

4) Appeals procedure

4.1 If a student does not wish to leave college or is unhappy with the outcome of the Disciplinary Hearing, s/he and her or his parents can appeal to the appropriate Faculty Head, who can overrule or uphold the decision made by the Senior Tutor or SQM.

4.2 If the student is unwilling to accept the decision made by the Faculty Head, the case may be referred to the Principal, who can overrule or uphold the decision made by the Faculty Head.

4.3 If the student is unwilling to accept the decision made by the Principal s/he has the right of appeal to a Committee of three Governors. This Committee's decision will be final.

4.4 At any stage in this procedure, or where a student decides to accept advice to leave or is required to do so, appropriate counselling and advice will be available.

B: Gross misconduct

5.1 Gross misconduct or involvement by a student in a serious incident in College or in close vicinity to it should be brought to the attention of an SQM. This can be done by means of a concern note, but not necessarily so, if the seriousness of the incident necessitates urgent action.

5.2 In the case of gross misconduct, the SQM will arrange a Disciplinary Hearing at which either a formal Disciplinary Contract will be drawn up, as outlined in 2.4 to 2.8, or, in extremely serious circumstances, the student will be asked to leave College.

5.3 Any Disciplinary Hearing held in relation to an alleged act of gross misconduct will be held as promptly after the incident as is practicable, whilst affording adequate time for the incident to be fully investigated by the SQM, for staff and other relevant parties to be consulted, and for parents to be informed and given the opportunity to attend.

5.4 The College reserves the right to exclude a student from College from the time at which it is alleged an act of gross misconduct was committed until the time of the Disciplinary Hearing arranged to deal with the matter. Appeals against temporary exclusion pending a Disciplinary Hearing will be dealt with as outlined in Section 4, except that the Principal's decision is final. Paragraphs 4.1 to 4.2 therefore apply and describe the procedure, but not paragraph 4.3.

5.5 In establishing whether a student has been guilty of gross misconduct, other students and members of staff may be required to attend the Disciplinary Hearing.

5.6 Where a student is asked to leave College as a result of an act of gross misconduct, he or she has exactly the same rights of appeal as for students failing to comply with the terms of a Disciplinary Contract. Paragraphs 4.1 to 4.4 therefore apply and describe the appeals procedure in such a case.

C: Other sanctions permissible within the disciplinary procedure

6) Study contracts and contracted timetables

6.1 In responding to a concern note and attempting to address a behavioural problem drawn to his or her attention, a tutor can require a student to follow a contracted timetable and/or to agree to a study contract for an agreed period of time.

6.2 As an alternative to a Disciplinary Contract, for persistent problems relating to lateness or unacceptable absenteeism or failing to submit work, a Senior Tutor or SQM may, having examined the particular circumstances of the case, require a student to follow a contracted timetable or agree to a study contract. Failure to adhere to either of these would, however, lead to the student then being asked to sign a Disciplinary Contract.

7) Temporary exclusion

Where it is considered likely to contribute to 'cooling off' or as an appropriate sanction, a student can be temporarily excluded for a short while, in accordance with the College regulations. The appeals procedure against temporary exclusion is the same as that for permanent exclusion, except that the Principal's decision is final, so that 4.1 and 4.2 apply and describe the appeals procedure, but not paragraph 4.3.

Appendix 7: City and Islington College – code of conduct and procedures for dealing with conflict in the Learning Resource Areas

Code of Conduct:

- Always have your student ID card with you when you use the centre.
- You must show your student ID card to any member of staff who asks for it.
- Please respect the activities of other users, especially those who need to study in a quiet environment.
- Please do not eat or drink in the Learning Centre.
- Personal stereos must not be heard by other users of the learning centre.
- Mobile phones must be turned off before you enter.
- Abusive language or behaviour which contravenes the student disciplinary code will not be allowed in the Learning Centre.

Procedures for dealing with conflict:

- The Learning Resources/Learning Centre Code of Conduct will be reviewed every year and amendments made if necessary.
- Copies of the Code of Conduct will be made available to students when they enrol in the Learning Centre and during induction.
- Students without ID cards may not enter the Learning Centre/Resource Areas. If a student has gained access to the building without an ID but with their tutor's permission, they may attend classes, but may not use the Learning Centre/Resource Area facilities.
- The procedure as outlined below will be followed if a student is alleged to have committed a serious breach of the Learning Centre Code of Conduct or as outlined in the Student Disciplinary Procedures document:

  1) If a student contravenes the LC code of conduct, ask the student to modify their behaviour.
  2) If the student refuses or does not modify their behaviour after several warnings, ask them to leave the Learning Centre. At the same time, inform them that the incident will be reported to their tutor and the tutor's manager.
  3) You may wish to have another member of staff as a witness at this stage.
  4) If the student refuses to leave or show their ID card, call security and the manager on duty. If they are not available, call any co-ordinator available or director/assistant director.
  5) If a student has contravened the Disciplinary Code, formal proceedings must be undertaken. A formal written warning must be given to the student and, if appropriate, a written apology to the member of staff concerned.
  6) All incidents will be recorded in the Learning Resources Incident Book.
  7) For serious incidents, it is vital that the student receives a formal warning; without this, there is no record of repeated contravention of the Disciplinary Code.
  8) Make a statement as soon as possible after an incident so the events are fresh in your mind.
  9) Ask any witnesses to make a statement.

Appendix 13: City and Islington College – recording processes

---

Incident Report Form

1) Context in which the incident took place

Day: Date: Time:

Students present:

Staff present:

Others present:

Location:

2) What took place

Trigger:

Action/events:

Effects/consequences:

3) Comments

Students:

Others:

4) Staff comments and recommendations

Signed: Date:

Copy for: Key Worker [ ]   Personal Tutor [ ]   Student [ ]   Other [ ]

Student Complaints Form

1) You should refer to Students Complaints Procedures before filling in the form.

2) Have you attempted to resolve this matter informally through your tutor?

    [ ] Yes   [ ] No

Nature of complaint:

Signature of student:

Name of student:

Course:

College site:

Date:

Please hand this form to your Curriculum Area Manager (or Assistant Director at Sixth Form Centre).

Student at Risk Report

To: Tutor or Lead Tutor or Co-ordinator or Teacher

Student Name:

Subject:

Teacher:

Date:

Cause for concern:

Behaviour   Punctuality   Attendance   Time Management   Study Skills
Coursework   Other

Details:

Level of urgency required:

For immediate action   Before next tutorial   At the next tutorial

Action taken/explanation:

e.g. referral to workshop/referral to careers

by: Tutor [ ]   Co-ordinator [ ]Lead Tutor [ ]

Review date:

Student Statement

Name: Tutor Group:

Date of incident: Time:

Place:

Students present:

Staff present:

Others present:

What happened:

What caused these things to happen

Signed: Date: